A WOMAN'S GUIDE TO INVESTING

All information in this book is for informational and educational purposes only and is not intended as investment advice.

This material does not constitute a recommendation as to the suitability of any investment for any person or persons having circumstances similar to those portrayed.

An investment in a money market fund is neither insured nor guaranteed by the US government. While money market funds seek to maintain a stable net asset value of $1.00 per share, there can be no assurance that the funds will be able to do so.

Dollar cost averaging plans do not assure a profit or protect against losses in declining markets. Since such plans involve continuous investments regardless of price levels, investors should consider their financial ability to continue purchases through periods of low price levels.

Shares of mutual funds are not deposits or obligations of any bank, and are not insured by the FDIC or any other agency, and involve investment risks, including the possible loss of the principal amount invested.

Due to market volatility, performance may be subject to subsequent fluctuations, so that current performance may be more or less than results shown. Taxes may reduce your actual investment returns on any income or gains paid by a fund or any gains you may realize when you sell your shares.

Past performance does not predict the future performance of any investment or group of investments.

There are references to Ibbotson research throughout this book that refer to the following study: *Stocks, Bonds, Bills, and Inflation 2003 Yearbook.* Ibbotson Associates. Chicago (Annual updates work by Roger G. Ibbotson and Rex A. Sinquefield). Used with permission. All rights reserved. Large company stock performance based on the Standard & Poor's 500 Composite Index, an unmanaged index widely regarded as an indicator of domestic stock market performance. The S&P 500 does not take sales charges into consideration. Investors cannot purchase indices directly. Long-term corporate bond performance based on Salomon Brothers Long-Term High Grade Corporate Bond Index. Cash performance is based on a one-bill portfolio containing, at the beginning of each month, the bill having the shortest maturity not less than one month. Inflation is based on the Consumer Price Index. Average annual returns include dividend or interest reinvestment.

MassMutual Financial Group and Raymond Institute American Family Business Survey. Copyright ©2003 by George G. and Robin Raymond Family Business Institute and Massachusetts Mutual Life Insurance Company. All rights reserved. MassMutual Financial Group is the marketing designation (or fleet name) for Massachusetts Mutual Life Insurance Company (MassMutual) and its affiliates, including OppenheimerFunds, Inc.

Oppenheimer Funds Women & Investing survey, April 2002. Results are based on a study conducted between March 26, 2002, and April 9, 2002, among 401 men and 884 women. Of these women, 298 had household incomes over $100,000 per annum (total sample is 1,285 respondents).

LIGHTBULB PRESS
Project Team

Design Director Dave Wilder
Art Direction Mercedes Feliciano
Illustration Krista K. Glasser
Production Kara W. Hatch, Katharina Menner, Tina Sbrigato, Matthew Smith, Thomas F. Trojan

Lead Editor Tania Sanchez
Editorial Staff Joan Kim, Karen Halloran Meldrom, Mavis Morris

---

SPECIAL THANKS TO

OppenheimerFunds (www.oppenheimerfunds.com): John Blomfield, Jennifer L. Bosco, Bruce Dunbar, Cara Helms, Mitchell Lindauer, and Jennifer Stevens
MassMutual Financial Group (www.massmutual.com): Victoria Huff, Carol Johnson, John O'Connell, Susan Schechter, Lauren Stuart, and Susan Sweetser

---

PICTURE CREDITS

Alan Rosenberg, New York (pages 100, 101), Marilyn and Amanda Feliciano (page 19)

A WOMAN'S GUIDE TO INVESTING

VIRGINIA B. MORRIS
KENNETH M. MORRIS

LIGHTBULB
PRESS®

A WOMAN'S GUIDE TO INVESTING

THE NEW REALITY

6 Women and Investing

8 The Power of Investing

10 The Gender Issue

12 The Value of Advice

14 An Investment Spectrum

16 Some Details of Ownership

18 Investing on Your Own

20 Married, with Investments

22 Investing with a Partner

24 Investing with Children

INTRODUCTION TO INVESTING

26 Making Investments

28 Equity and Debt

30 Stocking Up on Stocks

32 Taking Stock

34 Bonds: The Basics

36 Bond Issues

38 Mutual Funds: Investing Together

40 Mutual Fund Marketplace

42 Specialized Funds

44 Buying Mutual Funds

46 Expanding Your Fund Portfolio

48 Fund Performance

50 Figuring Your Return

52 Searching for Yield

PRINCIPLES OF PLANNING

54 Financial Planning

56 Take a Closer Look

58 Managing Debt

60 Creating a Plan

62 Tailoring a Plan

64 Getting the Money Together

66 Choosing Growth or Income

68 Basics of Investing

70 Understanding Investment Risk

72 Managing Risk

74 Time and Risk

76 Keeping Ahead of Inflation

78 Building Your Portfolio

80 Allocating Your Assets

82 Diversification

84 Investing, Tax-Wise

86 Leaving a Legacy

CONTENTS

WORKING WITH ADVISORS

88 Financial Advice
90 Sources of Help
92 The Price of Advice
94 Set Your Standards
96 Conduct an Interview
98 Build a Partnership
100 Starting to Invest
102 Resolving Problems

INTRODUCTION TO INSURANCE

104 Insuring the Future
106 Types of Life Insurance
108 How Much Life Insurance?
110 Qualifying for Coverage
112 Ownership and Beneficiaries
114 Advanced Planning with Life Insurance
116 Disability Insurance
118 Long-Term Care Insurance

PLANNING FOR THE EXPECTED

120 Moving Ahead Toward Your Goals
122 To Buy or Not to Buy?
124 Qualifying for a Mortgage
126 Building Equity
128 Refinancing
130 The Cost of College
132 College Investing Primer
134 Education Investments
136 Strategies for Paying
138 Applying for Aid
140 Investing for Retirement
142 It Pays to Give at the Office
144 You're in the Driver's Seat
146 IRAs
148 More Tax-Deferred Alternatives
150 Deferred Annuities
152 Immediate Annuities

COPING WITH THE UNEXPECTED

154 Coping with the Unexpected
156 Out of Work?
158 Divorce: Financial Self-Defense
160 Financial Settlements
162 Widowhood
164 Marrying Again, Marrying Later
166 Taking Care of Others
168 Dealing with Fraud

GLOSSARY AND INDEX

170 Glossary
172 Index

Women and Investing

You've got the potential. You just need the know-how.

Today's woman doesn't need anyone to tell her that she has what it takes to invest. Women have long been earning and managing their own money to support themselves and others—often as the family's primary breadwinner. So it's not a question of whether you can invest. It's only that you may still need to know how to invest.

Unfortunately, the language of investing can turn off both novices and experienced investors with its technical jargon, ticker tape numbers, and news reports full of dry pronouncements about third quarter results and percentages. But you'll be glad to know that keeping track of the day-to-day jolts of the markets is less important to your investment success than understanding why you're investing and how investing works.

Smart, strategic, informed investing has the potential to help you accomplish the things you need and secure the future you want. Do you want to buy a home? Send your kids to college? Retire in comfort? Some women want to fund scholarships or make gifts to charity, and some dream of traveling around the world. The difference between a dream and a goal is the action you take. And the best time to start is now.

No matter what your own financial goals are, you have the potential to achieve them by creating a sound financial plan and an investment strategy to match.

YOUR INVESTMENT GOALS

Be prepared for financial independence

A WOMAN'S TOUCH

For the most part, women don't need different investment advice than men do. The basic principles of investing are the same, no matter what your gender or station in life. However, that's not to say that women and men view investments the same way and invest under the same conditions. For instance, on average women do more research before making a decision, and they trade less frequently than men do. As a result, women's portfolios actually tend to outperform men's.

Aside from differences in the ways they invest, women and men also face different circumstances. Women live longer—79.8 years, compared with 74.4 years for men, according to the National Center for Health Statistics. And the US Bureau of the Census reports that the average woman earns just 76% of what the average man makes. Those numbers are gradually changing for the better, however: Younger women tend to earn wages on par with what their male counterparts earn, and a growing number of married women are now earning more than their husbands.

The bottom line is that if you're earning money, you should be doing your best to make the most of it. Historically, the most effective way to make your money do more is by investing it.

MY INVESTMENT PLANS

ON YOUR OWN

Some women put off investing—and learning about investing—because they have husbands or partners who are willing to handle the family finances. Others put off investing because they're afraid of tying up money for the future that they could use for the present.

But stalling is a mistake. Whether you're supporting yourself or sharing finances with someone else, you should prepare to take care of your own financial needs. No matter what the future holds, you'll be better off if you learn now how to invest wisely as part of your bigger financial plan for life.

After all, the odds are that you'll have to take care of yourself eventually, whatever your situation is now. Many women marry late in life or never. Half of all marriages end in divorce, and of those that last, the wife usually outlives the husband. Establishing your financial independence makes sense.

So whether you're married, divorced, single, or partnered—whether you have kids, a job, a business, or an inheritance—whatever age you may be, it's important for you to learn the ins and outs of investing. The more you know now, the better prepared you'll be to shape your own future.

The Power of Investing

The more you know about investing, the more confident you'll be about making decisions.

None of the factors that defines you— your age, marital status, education, or occupation—limits what you can learn about investing or the uses to which you can put your investment knowledge.

The difference between women who make the most of investment opportuni- ties and those who don't isn't necessarily the amount they invest. Most of the time, it's how carefully they plan, how soon they start investing, the investment choices they make, and how consistently they stick with it.

PUTTING KNOWLEDGE TO WORK

Learning investing, like learning anything else, works best when you put your knowledge to work right from the start. It might help to compare learning about investing to learning how to handle a job or play a sport. You certainly weren't born with those skills, and chances are you had some help on your way to mastering them. But you did it. The same is true of learning about investing.

The knowledge you need to be an effective investor will come from a combination of the money management skills you already have, the information you can get in print and online, the experience of friends and colleagues, and the help of a financial advisor. The bottom line is that there are four basic things you need to know:

WHAT your financial goals are

WHICH investments are available

HOW they work

WHY specific ones may help you meet your goals

FOR FIRST TIME INVESTORS:

1 Identify a goal and one type of investment that may help you reach it—perhaps a mutual fund or stock.

2 Narrow your choice to a specific investment by talking to your financial advisor.

3 Invest promptly, reinvest any earnings, and add new money regularly.

4 Track how well your investment performs by reading the information you get in the mail, checking its price, and asking your advisor for regular updates.

5 After a year, evaluate how well your investment has performed in comparison with similar investments, with how well you expected it to do, and with what you had been earning on your money before you invested.

6 If the investment is meeting your objectives, keep building it systematically. If not, consider a different investment.

DIFFERENT PATHS

The best way to learn about investing depends a lot on your personality, your lifestyle, and your financial goals. That's true whether you pursue the information on your own or with the help of a financial advisor.

If you prefer to develop your investment skills independently, you might take an adult education course at a local school, ask your bank or legal advisor about investment seminars designed for women, or begin reading personal finance columns in the magazines and newspapers you subscribe to.

Whatever your initial approach, you'll probably find it makes sense to work with a professional advisor in developing your investment plan and putting the plan into action.

THE MORE YOU KNOW...

Research conducted by OppenheimerFunds, Inc., has confirmed that in the past women have tended to invest too conservatively and therefore less profitably than they might have. But women who are more confident about their investment knowledge regularly commit more of their income to investing and are more confident about making investment choices.

Some of that increased confidence is the product of greater commitment in the financial community to meeting women's needs. Some of it results from the experiences of women in the workforce, and some from a widespread sense that employer support for people who are retiring is being scaled back.

Part of your responsibility as an investor is to keep learning. New ways to invest emerge all the time, some of which may be appropriate for you. Tax laws change, which may mean rethinking what investments to make for your tax-deferred accounts. There's little question that staying on top of what's happening can be a major advantage as you make far-reaching financial decisions.

Investing may—and often does—mean the difference between realizing your goals and having to settle for less.

Investing rewards the people who make choices best suited to meeting their personal goals.

Successful investing is within everyone's grasp.

DJIA

SHOULD YOU KNOW WHERE THE MARKET IS TODAY?

If you can't quote the Dow Jones Industrial Average, the best-known stock market index, or aren't sure whether it's up or down, should you abandon any thought of investing? Of course not—any more than you'd abandon a trip you've planned to a special destination because you haven't tracked the average temperature there.

The DJIA and other stock and bond indexes do help you follow how certain markets are doing. But despite the attention the Dow gets, following its up and downs isn't what makes a successful investor. Knowing where your money is, why it's there, and how it's doing are far more important.

The Gender Issue

As a woman, you have a vested interest in being an informed and active investor.

Some things really have changed. More women invest than ever before. A growing number of women participate in employer sponsored retirement plans. Women who invest actively express confidence about their ability to make informed choices and manage their assets. And the majority of those women tend to invest more wisely than their male counterparts, in part because they are less inclined to take too much risk.

This investing evolution that has occurred since the early 1990s doesn't provide a complete picture, though. Many women still work in jobs where no retirement plan is offered. What's more, the majority of people in the US—women included—haven't saved enough to provide a comfortable retirement, based on information gathered by the Employee Benefit Research Institute (EBRI). But there are ways to continue to move toward resolving the fear that many women share of outliving their income.

INVESTING STYLES

Women investors, as a group, tend to be more conservative than men. In broad terms, that means they are less likely to buy investments they don't understand, act on tips from friends, or put primary emphasis on making a lot of money quickly. It also means that they buy and sell more deliberately than speculative investors, which may help make their portfolios more stable.

These characteristics have sometimes been criticized, or even presented as a derisive explanation for why women in general—though not all women—weren't accumulating more investment wealth. But in the economic downturn that followed the boom years of the 1990s, a more deliberate approach, with an emphasis on asset allocation and diversification, seemed increasingly the mark of a good investor.

There is a connection, though, between successful investing measured by increasing net worth and confident investing, according to an OppenheimerFunds, Inc., research study. The more assets a woman has, the more interested in investing she tends to be, the more she typically knows about investing, and the more assured she is in making investment decisions. What there's no way of knowing is which came first. Is the investment success the chicken, or is it the egg?

Earning Power

THE FACTS

Women now earn more than 76% of what men in comparable jobs earn, a statistic that leaves room for improvement but also represents progress toward income equality. In an encouraging sign, the income of younger, college-educated women is almost on par with that of their male colleagues. Women as a group earn more than $1 trillion each year. And more women than ever before own and run their own businesses, providing jobs and financial security to others—many of them women as well. However, women tend to move in and out of the workforce, which means they may accumulate fewer retirement credits.

THE SOLUTIONS

Increased earnings are important to long-term financial security, as is regular employment. Women who stop working full-time may want to continue part-time to stay in a retirement plan or preserve seniority. Another approach is to explore flexible hours or telecommuting, which may enable mothers with small children, or daughters with aging parents, to juggle their potentially conflicting responsibilities at work and home. A survey sponsored by MassMutual shows that a growing number of women run family businesses. Many of these firms are distinctive for their productivity, philanthropy, and employment of women.

WOMEN | Average salaries | MEN

$29,544

$38,961

Source: US Bureau of the Census, 2001

Managing Money

THE FACTS

Women head more than 50% of the households with high net worth, according to the US Census Bureau, and salaried wives earn at least 50% of their households' income. Those women are active investors. Women manage the day-to-day finances in 47% of married households and are responsible for purchasing most of the products and services the households buy. Unmarried women, who make up roughly 20% of the population, the 75% of married women who are eventually widowed, and the 50% who divorce are also active money managers.

THE SOLUTIONS

Increased earning power and more experience in money management both translate into greater participation in making investment decisions, both at home and as participants in employer sponsored retirement savings plans. One way that a woman who doesn't work outside the home can gain investment experience and begin to accumulate retirement savings in her own name is with a spousal individual retirement account (IRA). If her husband earns income, he can contribute up to the annual limit each year in her account, which she controls.

Source: Securities Industry Association and Investment Company Institute, 2002

Life Expectancy

THE FACTS

Because women have historically earned less and lived longer than men, it's not surprising that a disproportionate percentage of the elderly poor are women. While women make up 51% of the adult population, they constitute 62% of the people over 75 who live below the poverty line, according to the US Bureau of the Census. While the actual number of women in that situation has dropped over the years because of increased support from the federal government, retirement planning experts are concerned that that pattern may reverse itself as women who retire in the next 20 years may have less than one-third of what they need to live comfortably.

THE SOLUTIONS

As women invest more during their working lives and emphasize a diversified portfolio of investments that have the potential to grow in value, they have the opportunity to provide more of the income they'll need in retirement. Single women may be especially conscious of the need for long-term investments as they are likely to be dependent on their own resources. Married women should understand how their husbands' pensions are paid and the income to which they are entitled. Divorced women should know that they may have a right to Social Security benefits, and perhaps pension income, based on their former husbands' earnings.

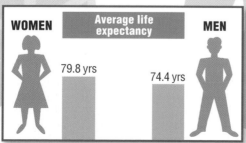

Source: National Center for Health Statistics, 2003

The Value of Advice

A trusted advisor can make the difference between timely action and time-wasting delay.

If you're like most people, you may be looking for someone who can explain your choices and help you make important financial decisions.

There are good reasons for getting professional investment advice, just as there are good reasons for consulting a doctor when you need medical care. Financial advisors can explain how different kinds of investments have performed in the past, since that's an indication—though not a promise—of how they may do in the future. Advisors can also describe different approaches to investing, from conservative to aggressive, to help you gauge what's best for you.

On a more personal level, an advisor can help you define your financial goals and estimate how much money you'll need to meet them. Together, you can create a financial plan and choose investments in an effort to make it work. When you've pinpointed the kind of financial advice you need, you can find someone with particular expertise.

ADVISORS YOU CAN CONSULT

- **Financial planners**
- **Registered representatives**
- **Stockbrokers**
- **Bank investment representatives**
- **Certified Public Accountants**

A GENDER BOND?

Should you be looking for a woman advisor? A majority of women investors—58%—in an OppenheimerFunds, Inc., survey says that gender isn't a factor when they decide which advisor to work with. Their primary concern is that it's someone who takes them seriously and treats them with respect.

PYRAMIDS AND OTHER SCAMS

How about an investment that promises to make you rich quick? If it involves a lot of money and little information, it's not an investment. It's a con-game.

Even though Charles Ponzi's infamous pyramid, promising a 40% return, collapsed in 1920, clever schemes surface all the time. Sadly, many of them are marketed to older people, especially women. There are plenty of tales of otherwise careful people who lose their shirts. The best defense is realistic expectations, healthy skepticism, and professional advice, from an expert you trust.

BUILDING A STRONG RELATIONSHIP

In the past few years, more investors—women and men—have been turning to financial advisors for help managing their assets. In a recent OppenheimerFunds, Inc., survey, 96% of the participants who use an advisor said that they came to rely more heavily on that advice following the market downturn, corporate scandals, and the events of September 11. And 98% believe that investors working with advisors fare better than those investing on their own.

Of those participants using an advisor, 94% agreed that diversification plays an essential role in achieving investment goals, while only 22% of investors without an advisor saw diversification as a key principle. And 92% of those working with an advisor expect to be comfortable in retirement, while only 36% of participants without an advisor do.

In addition, most investors reported that their advisors got in touch with them first when the markets weren't doing well, which may explain why 95% of those surveyed planned to continue their relationship with a current advisor.

EQUAL PARTNERSHIP

Eighty-five percent of the women and 83% of their financial advisors agree that they must be equal partners in making investment decisions. Both groups, however, agree that the advisor should be responsible for generating most of the investment ideas and explaining how they fit into the investment plan.

STRONG FINANCIAL PLAN

Ninety percent of the women surveyed said that having a structured financial plan in place is important. And by an overwhelming margin, financial advisors agree. Nearly all of the advisors surveyed—97% of them—believe it's important for an advisor to help a client develop a financial plan to meet her long-term goals.

CLEAR EXPLANATIONS

Women look to financial advisors for advice and recommendations, but they also expect to learn something. Ninety percent of women OppenheimerFunds, Inc., surveyed saw their advisors as teachers, compared with only 75% of men. By learning from advisors, women felt they could increase their financial knowledge and feel more confident about making investment decisions.

RESPECTFUL TREATMENT

In the past, women sometimes reported negative experiences such as being talked down to, ignored, or not taken as seriously as men investors. Many of those attitudes have disappeared as more women have invested and more investment professionals are women. But 54% of all women respondents to the 2002 survey said financial advisors still do not treat women with the same respect they show to men.

GOOD INTENTIONS

Long-time investors and people who are just beginning to invest may tend not to work with an advisor. Experienced investors with clearly defined goals and the time to do their own research often believe that they can do as well on their own—or simply enjoy the challenge investing provides.

Inexperienced investors, on the other hand, who would almost certainly benefit from professional advice are more likely to have other reasons, according to the OppenheimerFunds survey:

1 They'd like to work with an advisor, but don't know how to identify one.

2 They're concerned that they don't have enough money to be of interest to a financial advisor.

3 They know they should seek advice, but they haven't taken any action.

While there may be no easy solution to the third explanation, there are responses to the first and second.

Finding an advisor is not difficult, but you must be selective to ensure that the person you choose is experienced in guiding clients who have concerns and goals similar to yours. There's more about the process in Chapter Four.

While some advisors work exclusively with high net-worth clients, most advisors have a broad base of clients. Most successful investors begin small, and a trusted advisor who helps you move toward your goals is likely to have you as a client for life.

An Investment Spectrum

It's a mistake to think of investing as tying up your money.

You invest by putting the money you have to work, expecting it to grow in value, provide income, or both. Some investments keep your money safer. Other investments may move you toward your goals more quickly, but often expose you to a greater risk of losing money. Before you can choose among them, you need to understand the differences.

You'll also discover how spreading your investment principal among several different categories, or asset classes, can help limit your risk without significantly reducing your potential return.

◀ LESS LIQUID

COLLECTIBLES	REAL ESTATE	BONDS	STOCKS
Things you collect might be worth a great deal of money some day	Over time, real estate generally increases in value, sometimes dramatically	Most bonds offer regular income while you own them, and return your investment when they come due	Historically, stocks have provided better returns than other investments over time
Collecting is risky because buyers are hard—sometimes impossible—to find if you need to sell	You could have a hard time selling at the price you want, and property is not guaranteed to gain value	Bond prices vary, so you might have to sell for less than you paid if you need the cash before the investment period ends	Share prices may be volatile and do change regularly, so there's always a chance you could lose part or all of your investment

UNDERSTANDING LIQUIDITY

One comforting thing about money in the bank is that you know it's there when you need it. If you put $1,000 in your savings account, you can take $1,000 out. In contrast, if you use most of your money to buy a home, you have a place to live, but you may not have much cash. In a financial emergency, you can probably sell your home, but you may have to settle for less than you paid to buy it.

That's a simplified look at the difference between a liquid investment—your bank account—and a less liquid one—your home. The more liquid an investment is, the more easily you can sell it with little or no loss of value.

In fact, selling most investments, including stocks, bonds, and mutual funds, is as easy as giving instructions to your broker, financial advisor, or the issuing company. But these investments change value all the time. For example, if the stock market has lost value, the value of a stock you own may be down. If you sell at that point, you may have a loss.

On the other hand, liquid investments provide only very limited earnings, so a totally cash portfolio is likely to provide limited long-term financial security.

INVESTING YOUR CASH

What should you do if you have money in a checking or savings account and you want to invest, but would also like to be able to have cash to use in an emergency?

You could put some money in **cash equivalents**, such as money market mutual funds. They may pay more interest than savings accounts, and you can access the money easily by check or you can transfer it directly to your bank.

You could buy **US Treasury bills**, or **T-bills**. They usually pay more interest than savings accounts and can be sold easily, though you may find that you have to sell for less than you paid if you act before they mature. However, you buy T-bills for short terms—4, 13, or 26 weeks—so you can time them to come due when you need the money or wait until they mature. The minimum investment is $1,000, and you can buy any number of T-bills you want.

Or, you could purchase a number of **certificates of deposit (CDs)** with different maturities—say six months, one year, and three years. As each CD matures, you can use the cash if you need it or reinvest in a new CD with the same term.

MORE LIQUID ▶

MUTUAL FUNDS	CDs	MONEY MARKET FUNDS	CASH
Mutual funds offer built-in diversification, management expertise, and ease of investing	CDs are insured. You know what you'll earn and when the money will be available	These liquid mutual funds give you easy access to your money, and may pay interest income	It's readily accessible
Earnings and prices aren't guaranteed, so you might sell for less than you invested	Earnings probably won't beat inflation over the long haul, and you may owe a penalty for early withdrawal	The earnings won't stay ahead of inflation over the long haul, and most are not insured against loss	Cash doesn't grow, so as time passes, it loses value through inflation and may leave you short of money

SOLID INVESTMENTS

While some investments can be more difficult to sell quickly than others—including real estate—they still can be smart places to put your money. That's because their potential advantages more than offset the risks of tying up your capital. Land and buildings can increase significantly in value, and may provide you with a place to live or work. There can also be tax advantages to investing in real estate. You may be able to deduct property taxes and interest payments on mortgages and equity loans on your home. And investment real estate may have tax benefits too.

However, prices tend to move up or down depending on the economy, and on which geographic areas are growing. Those factors can make it hard to predict real estate's long-term performance as an investment.

WORKING THE SYSTEM

One reason all your investments don't have to be liquid is that you can often plan major purchases or postpone expected bills for a time when one of your investments is coming due. For example, you can plan to buy a new car with money from a maturing CD.

Some Details of Ownership

There's more to owning property than simply knowing where to sign your name.

You can own investments several different ways. If you buy a mutual fund, for instance, you can own it in your own name, jointly with one or more other people, or as a trustee for the benefit of someone else.

In each case, the way you own an investment determines your rights as an owner, including whether you can sell the property or give it to someone else. Your parents, for example, could give property to you and your siblings in equal shares, allowing each of you the right to sell your shares separately. Or they could require that you all agree before any part of it could be sold.

KINDS OF OWNERSHIP

Basically, there are four ways to own property, whether it's real estate (land and buildings), stocks, bonds, mutual funds, bank accounts, or almost anything else:

	SOLE OWNERSHIP	JOINT TENANTS WITH RIGHTS OF SURVIVORSHIP
Owners	One person owns the property and controls what happens to it	Two (or potentially more than two) people own the property equally
Right to sell	There are no limits on selling it, giving it away, or leaving it by will as long as you own the property outright	One person can sell his or her share, but usually only with the consent of the other owner(s) and only if the proceeds of the sale are shared equally with the other owner(s)
In a divorce	Property purchased during a marriage could be counted as marital property that's subject to division	If the owners are married, and they divorce, the property is marital property that may be subject to division
At death	Property can be left by will or put into a trust as the owner wishes	When one owner dies, that share becomes the property of the other owner(s). It can't be left by will to anyone else

YOU DON'T ALWAYS GET IT IN WRITING

When you buy certain property, like a car or real estate, you get a title, or certificate of ownership, that names you as the owner. It must be signed over to the new owner when you sell. In fact, the process of finalizing ownership is often referred to as **taking title**.

In the past, you also used to receive certificates when you bought stocks and bonds, which you had to safeguard and then sign and turn in when you wanted to sell. But when you buy securities today, ownership is recorded in book-entry form or held in the name of the brokerage firm. You can usually sell simply by giving instructions over the phone or online.

ACHING JOINTS

Joint ownership won't always protect you from having the rug pulled out from under you, financially speaking. When you have joint checking or savings accounts, or any account that doesn't require both signatures to transfer or withdraw money, either owner can take out every penny, perfectly legally.

FLEXIBLE OWNERSHIP

Ownership can be changed, often relatively simply. If you want to make your husband, your adult child, or some other person a joint owner of property that you now own alone, you can usually change the title with little hassle and rarely any charge. With a mutual fund account, for example, you write a letter 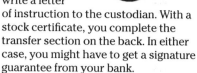 of instruction to the custodian. With a stock certificate, you complete the transfer section on the back. In either case, you might have to get a signature guarantee from your bank.

With joint ownership, you and the other owner(s) have to agree before a change can be made. But if you agree, you can make whatever changes you want.

However, you should avoid acting too hastily on any change in ownership, especially during a period of stress or at a major turning point in your life. For example, lawyers often advise newly married people to keep assets they had before marriage in their own names at least for a period of time. If you live in a **community property state**, in fact, you may decide to hold premarital property in sole ownership no matter how long you're married. Otherwise, you give up your right to own it exclusively in the future.

TENANTS BY THE ENTIRETY	TENANTS IN COMMON
This must be a married couple who own the property together	Two or more people own a share—generally an equal share—of the property
Neither can sell without the other's permission	Each owner can sell his or her share independently and keep the profit. The other owner(s) have no right to inherit (though they could), and they have no control over a co-owner's share
Spouses become tenants in common, and either has the right to sell his or her half without the consent of the other	Property purchased during a marriage could be counted as marital property that's subject to division
When one spouse dies, the other becomes the sole owner of the property. It can't be left by will to anyone but the spouse	Property can be left by will or put into a trust as the owner wishes

GETTING ADVICE

If you're married or involved in a long-term relationship, you should discuss ownership decisions with your lawyer and probably with your tax advisor.

Many married couples own all their investments, including their homes, jointly. There are good reasons for this, including the fact that it helps to establish financial equity between husband and wife and may prevent one partner—for whatever reason—from selling all the assets. But there are potential drawbacks to owning everything jointly, including protecting assets from federal estate taxes or claims from your or your husband's creditors.

Though you can't prepare for every eventuality, your lawyer might advise you to limit joint ownership if one of you might be vulnerable to lawsuits because of your profession or other activities. Trying to shift ownership in the face of a legal threat usually doesn't work.

WHEN TIME COUNTS

One caution: There are times when a transfer of ownership might be challenged in court, such as in cases when you're trying to protect certain assets or qualify for government assistance. In those cases, transfers must occur by a specific date—sometimes as long as three years or more earlier—to be valid.

Investing on Your Own

Being single isn't one category—it's many different ones.

As a woman, there's a 90% chance that you're managing your own financial affairs now or will be at some point in the future. Whether you find the idea exciting or frightening, the likelihood of making these decisions means you'll need to know as much as you can, not only about your day-to-day expenses but about investing. This knowledge will not only help you keep your head above water. It will also help make it possible to realize your personal financial goals.

INVESTING FOR ONE

There's no one right way for a single woman to invest. Single includes those who never marry, those who divorce, and those who are widowed. It also includes those who are heads of households, who live with partners, or who live alone. Your age will make a difference as well, since the period of time you have to invest for specific goals

SINGLE

If you are single and have no dependents, you may not be responsible for other people's welfare. If you don't have to worry about providing healthcare for your parents, paying for a college education, or making sure your husband or partner has enough to live on after you die, you can invest for the things you value for yourself.

At the same time, you are the only one responsible for your financial security. Most women who collect Social Security based on their own earnings collect less than men and less than widows. That makes it doubly important to invest through tax-deferred or tax-free retirement acounts, including employer sponsored plans and IRAs.

WOMEN WHO LIVE ALONE

Approximately 11% of women in the US live alone or with someone who isn't a family member. Some are unmarried, some are divorced, and others widowed. A small percentage of married women live apart from their husbands.

Source: US Bureau of the Census, 2002

will affect the investment strategies you use. For example, a woman in her 20s and a woman in her 60s might both be investing for retirement. The former is likely to look for investments that will grow in value, while the latter may be shifting to investments that produce income.

FINDING HELP

If you find that investment information that's generally available seems designed for a traditional couple, don't despair. You can get investment information that's tailored for you.

- Look for a financial advisor who has experience working with single women
- To find an investment discussion group or seminar that's designed for singles, check with your local library, civic center, or religious or educational institution
- Get information from your professional or union affiliation

- Find out about an existing investment club you can join or discuss forming one with your friends and colleagues
- Contact local or national women's groups for information and referrals. You can find the Older Women's League online at www.owl-national.org or call the national office at either 202-783-6686 or 800-825-3695.

FAMILY HEAD

If you're a single woman with children, you are responsible for their well-being as well as your own. In fact, you may have put your own long-term goals on hold to meet your children's needs.

No one can fault you for that. But you should also be looking for ways to invest for your future, even while your current investments are helping to pay for your children's education. You're likely to live a lot longer after they're on their own.

One good way to build your nest egg while meeting other expenses is by putting money into a retirement plan sponsored by your employer. These plans have the added benefit of reducing your current taxes and providing a source for loans should you need some cash in the short term.

NEWLY SINGLE

If you suddenly find yourself single and responsible for your own finances after many years of marriage, your primary concern may well be making the money you have last as long as you'll need it. And if you've never been involved in investment decisions, the responsibility may seem overwhelming.

But it doesn't have to be, because you can get the help you need to make wise decisions. Attorneys who specialize in elder law, for example, do much of their work for women. If you don't have a financial advisor, or are uncomfortable working with the one your husband used, ask your lawyer about finding someone to work with. Or you can ask for advice and professional referrals from your relatives or friends who have had similar experiences.

	15 TO 24	25 TO 44	45 TO 64	65 AND OLDER
NEVER MARRIED	96%	70%	22%	6%
MARRIED*	2%	7%	8%	4%
DIVORCED	0.4%	21%	49%	13%
WIDOWED	2%	2%	21%	77%

* Married women who live apart from their husbands.

EMERGENCY FUNDS

Financial emergencies happen in everybody's life, whether you're single or married. The real issue isn't whether, or even when, they will happen, but how they can be resolved.

One safety net that most financial experts recommend is an **emergency fund**, money set aside in an account you can tap easily—such as your savings or mutual fund money market account (though not your checking account), or in short-term investments like certificates of deposit (CDs) or US Treasury bills.

You'll find that different financial experts suggest different reserve amounts, with the most typical being the equivalent of three to six months salary. Experts differ dramatically, though, on how much a single woman should keep in reserve.

Some advisors, who recognize the consequences of keeping too much money in low-paying accounts, urge women to invest most of their emergency money in a balanced portfolio of stocks, bonds, and mutual funds. The argument is that you can always sell the investments if you must have the cash. It is possible that you might lose some money if you need to sell on short notice, but if you don't need to tap your savings, you'll potentially earn more in the long run.

Other advisors, who are concerned that women on their own may have more difficulty getting assistance from their families or a harder time finding a new job, think that women should keep more money in emergency funds than the amount they recommend for men.

While you'll have to make the final decision about the size of your reserve fund, you should resist the temptation to confuse being cautious with dragging your heels about putting your money to work.

Married, with Investments

Investing to meet your shared goals can forge a special bond between you and your husband.

Investing together may not strike you as especially romantic, but it can be a very satisfying part of marriage, something that you can do, and benefit from, together. If one of you has had some experience with investing, or is accustomed to working with a financial advisor, you'll be off to a head start. But it can also be fun to learn new skills together.

Sharing investment decisions may come about naturally if you handle the other parts of your financial life together. Or you may want to split up the responsibility, with one of you taking the lead on long-term investment decisions and the other on meeting short-term goals.

A MARRIAGE BONUS

Marriage has lots of benefits, financially speaking. Consider just a few:

Capital Accumulation

As a married couple investing together, you have some

Portfolio Diversification

It can be easier for a married couple to follow some of the basic principles of investing,

Estate Planning

Married couples should do estate planning to ensure that the surviving partner has lifetime

OUTSIDE INFLUENCES

If you and your husband have been postponing working together on investment decisions, other people's experiences can jar you into action—or encourage one of you to press for change.

For example, you may have a divorced friend who made decisions she later regretted because she was uncomfortable handling investments. Or you may have tried to help a relative cope not only with the grief of widowhood but the trauma of sudden financial responsibility.

Here's one schedule for getting started:

- Talk with your husband about the financial goals you share

- Discuss what you've done to help make them realities

- Make a list of your investment questions

- Find a financial advisor to help provide answers and plan future investments

- Review all your investment decisions together on a regular schedule

MINE, YOURS, OR OURS

Investing together doesn't mean you can't also invest separately, especially if you have some very different priorities. For example, you can decide how to invest money you put into retirement plans at work or into individual retirement accounts (IRAs).

Money or investments you inherit are also yours, as are investments you owned before you got married. You can continue to hold them separately, or share ownership with your husband. It's probably smart to discuss the alternatives—and their legal and tax consequences—with him, your family, and your lawyer.

advantages in accumulating the money you need and putting it to work for you.

While it may not be true that two can live as cheaply as one, you can certainly live more cheaply together than you could apart, leaving the balance for investment. If you both work outside the home, you may have more income to invest plus the added benefit of two tax-deferred retirement plans to which you can contribute. Remember, though, that IRAs and retirement savings plans are individual accounts, not joint ones.

such as **diversification**. The whole notion of diversification is owning various types of investments that perform differently as the economy changes. But the problem often is having enough money to do it.

If you have two incomes, you can buy a diverse mix of investments for each of your retirement and regular investment accounts. Or perhaps you'll decide to work together to diversify your overall investments. One of the advantages of planning your investments across the board is that you have a lot more flexibility in getting the diversification you want.

income, that their assets are distributed as they both wish, and that the smallest possible gift and estate taxes are due.

Married US citizens can give or leave each other assets valued at any amount without gift or estate tax. But assets left or given to other people, including your children or grand-children, may be taxed if the total value is higher than the amount that's exempt from tax.

By estimating your current estate value and what it has the potential to be, you can begin to make decisions that will accomplish your goals. It's essential to work with an experienced estate attorney and to stay alert to changes in the law.

WORKING WITH AN ADVISOR

If your investment partnership is going to be effective, you and your husband must both be comfortable working with your financial advisor. One of you may already have a working relationship that can be expanded to include a third person. If the three of you can consult as equals, it probably makes good sense to build on the existing association.

If either you or your husband is treated like a third wheel or feels ignored, however, it probably makes sense to look for a new advisor together. You both may be more comfortable asking questions or expressing opinions if you're starting with a clean slate.

You and your husband can make your partnership approach clear if you both participate in the conversation, both ask questions, and consult with each other, instead of having one of you seem to be making all the decisions.

Investing with a Partner

When the tie that binds you is not marriage, investing together can be a bit more complex.

Unmarried couples don't share the same ownership and property rights that married couples do. And that has a major impact on investment decisions that unmarried couples face.

For example, while married couples can transfer investment property to each other, or divide assets between them any way they like, unmarried couples can't without risking potentially serious tax consequences.

And while a wife would be automatically entitled to a share—rarely less than one-third and often more—of her husband's property should he die without a will, an unmarried partner would be entitled to nothing.

Without those legal protections, unmarried investment partners must plan carefully, right from the beginning, for equitable ways to own and distribute their property, not only in case of separation, but also when one of them dies.

Women involved in long-term partnerships often need to handle their investments differently than either single or married women.

The annual ceiling on tax-free gifts applies to property transfers between unmarried partners.

If your partner dies without a will, you may not have a legal right to property held in his or her name.

Older couples may choose not to marry to make it easier to leave their entire estates to children from earlier marriages.

SHARING THE WEALTH

JOINT OWNERSHIP

With the exception of the arrangement known as tenants by the entirety, unmarried partners can own investment assets any way they choose: solely, jointly with rights of survivorship, or as tenants in common.

Joint tenancy works the same way for unmarried as for married people. At the death of one owner, the property automatically goes to the survivor.

However, when a couple is unmarried, the total value of the property is legally considered part of the estate of the first to die unless you can prove otherwise. That could mean potential estate and inheritance taxes. While there's no federal estate tax due on assets that are passed to a spouse who is a US citizen, that marital exception doesn't apply when the assets go to an unmarried partner.

NAMING BENEFICIARIES

If you name your partner as beneficiary for your pension, retirement plan, or insurance policy, that person will collect the money the plan provides when you die.

Your partner won't have the same right a husband would to roll over any retirement payout into a tax-deferred IRA, but you will have provided that the money goes to the right person. An added advantage is that documents naming beneficiaries may be less likely to be contested than wills.

CREATING TRUSTS

Another way to pass investment assets to your partner outside your will is to create a **trust,** a legal document that transfers ownership to a trustee until it goes to the beneficiary either at your death or at any time you name. Of course, there are many other uses for trusts. Married couples use trusts for tax-saving reasons as well as naming

beneficiaries and controlling how the assets are spent. Many people who own property in more than one state or want to leave assets to minors prefer trusts as well.

You shouldn't attempt to create trusts without legal advice, though. They must be drawn up correctly to achieve the results you want.

IN TRUST FOR...

You can arrange to leave money directly to a specific person when you die, without the expense of establishing a formal trust agreement or including the bequest in your will. You can set up a Totten Trust, a bank account **in trust for** the person you want to have it. Or you may be able to set up transfer on death (TOD) registration for your mutual fund or brokerage accounts. At your death, the beneficiary you've named becomes the owner. But at any time before you die, you can change your mind about any aspect of the bequest, take the money out, or add assets to the account.

It's always best to get legal advice about any arrangements you make to dispose of your property. That's especially true if you're concerned that your family might contest bequests you make to your partner.

BUYING AN ANNUITY

Annuities, which are insurance contracts designed to provide retirement income, are another way to provide financial security for your unmarried partner.

Basically, you buy the annuity, either with a lump sum or over a period of years, naming your partner as beneficiary or co-beneficiary with yourself. At a date you select, the annuity begins to pay out the accumulated assets, providing an income for life or for a set period of years. Here, as with other assets that are transferred outside a will, there is less risk of legal challenge.

You and your partner may have more trouble arranging for a mortgage than a married couple with comparable income.

IF THE SHOE FITS

All the techniques described on these pages as ways of transferring investment assets to an unmarried partner work similarly if you use them on behalf of your husband, children, family, or friends. (Remember, though, you have to make special arrangements for children who are minors.)

Except for certain trust documents, most of these techniques are **revocable,** which means you maintain control of the assets while you are alive, and you can change the beneficiary. Yet all of them are designed to let you pass along assets with less time, trouble, and expense, and, if it's important to you, with less publicity than through a will.

Investing with Children

Money doesn't grow on trees—but it has the potential to grow when it's invested.

Investing for your children is important, especially if you want them to go to college or you plan to help them establish or expand a business. But investing with your children can give them another important kind of education. By showing them how to manage their money and invest for their future, you can help prepare them for a self-sufficient, responsible adulthood.

One of the best ways you can instill good financial discipline in your children is to set a good example. Remember that kids learn by seeing, so if you want them to budget and invest, do so yourself. If instead they see you making impulse purchases on credit and never saving a dime, it's unlikely that they'll take your other financial lessons to heart.

THE THREE-JAR ALLOWANCE

To learn how to manage money, a child needs some money to manage. Most childcare experts recommend that parents separate a child's allowance from his or her responsibilities, since paying for things like good grades and chores makes those jobs seem optional rather than required. Instead, you can use the allowance as a chance to show your child how to create a budget and stick with it.

One popular suggestion to illustrate the concept of budgeting is to give your child three clear glass jars that represent current expenses, short-term savings, and long-term savings. Separating cash into jars discourages children from cheating and makes it easy for them to watch savings grow.

To create the budget, you and your child first determine an amount to cover current necessary expenses—such as lunch money and school supplies. Some parents also encourage their children to donate 10%

of their allowance to charity each week. Next, talk about money for short-term saving goals. List things like toys, video games, and other big-ticket items your child might want. Finally, as part of the budget, make sure to earmark a regular sum to set aside for the future.

To give your child an incentive to put money in that third long-term savings jar, you can offer a matching contribution by putting in fifty cents or a dollar for every dollar your child contributes. And when your child is old enough, you can replace the second jar with a savings account and replace the third jar with an investment account.

You may also want to establish an auto-investing account in your child's name. The amount you specify—from as little as $50 a month—will be automatically debited from your checking or savings account and added to the account.

SPARK AN INTEREST IN INVESTING

You may want to use common stocks to introduce your children to investing. Stocks are easy to explain and can be fun, especially if you start with companies your children already know. Ask them to find companies that interest them—those that produce their favorite cereal, sports equipment, soft drink, or toy, for example. Once you buy shares, you and your children can track the company's performance and stock price in the news.

To make learning fun, you can also set up a mock online portfolio. Some online portfolio trackers simulate real trading with a cash account you can use to buy stocks and pay broker commissions.

You might also help them find websites designed especially for young investors. There's a list at www.jumpstart.org.

ONE AT A TIME
Some companies offer special educational materials for young investors, such as collectible share certificates. Check www.oneshare.com for a list.

COLLECTIBLES
Children are natural collectors. If your child collects baseball cards, collectible toys, or comic books, some of those items might appreciate in value as time goes by—and some will depreciate. You might explain investment as a way to grow money by buying things that may rise in value, just like a rare baseball card or coin.

SETTING UP THE ACCOUNT
One easy way to give your child ownership of stock is to "sell" your child some of your own shares. If you're planning on buying 100 shares of a company, for example, you could buy 101 and sell the extra share to your child at market price. You can keep track of which shares are your child's in a separate register at home and transfer those shares when your child is old enough to open his or her own brokerage account.

If that arrangement is too casual for you, you can open a separate account for your child's investments. You'll have to decide how to set up the account, either in your name or the child's.

There are three main ways to set up an investment account for a child:

1 **Guardian accounts**. You're the owner of the guardian account and manage it as you see fit. Earnings are taxed at your rate.

2 **Custodial accounts**. The child owns the account, and earnings are taxed at the child's rate. You control the account until the child reaches the age of majority—generally 18 or 21, depending on the state.

3 **IRA accounts**. If your child earns taxable income, you can open a regular or Roth IRA in the child's name. You control it until he or she reaches the age of majority.

Making Investments

Stocks, bonds, and cash are the substance of a diversified portfolio.

Most investors—from the newest to the most experienced—focus on three investment categories: stocks and stock mutual funds, bonds and bond mutual funds, and cash or cash equivalents, including money market mutual funds.

Each type of investment puts your money to work in a different way, but they have similarities that help make them attractive. They're easy to buy and sell. They're available at a wide range of prices. And they have the potential to provide the primary benefit of investing—the possibility for growth.

Mutual Funds

A mutual fund invests money that you and others put into the fund. With those resources, a fund can buy many different investments and provide more **diversification**, or variety, than you could achieve on your own for the amount you have to invest. Since each fund is professionally managed, you benefit from that investment expertise. What's more, each fund's prospectus describes the investments it makes, its goals and management style, as well as the level of risk that you're taking.

OTHER INVESTMENT OPPORTUNITIES

CDs
CDs are income investments that pay interest on a specific amount of money for a specific period of time.

REAL ESTATE
Real estate may increase in value and can provide tax advantages.

ANNUITIES
Annuities are tax-deferred savings plans designed to provide future income, at either a fixed or variable rate.

INVESTMENT VOCABULARY
Stocks and bonds are **securities**, a term that once referred to the documents companies and governments issued to represent ownership or obligation. Today most investment information, including records of ownership, is stored electronically. You don't get stock or bond certificates—but the name securities has stuck.

It's also helpful to know that investments are sometimes referred to as **products** or **vehicles**, since you're apt to hear those terms. A product or vehicle is usually an investment that gives you access to a number of securities in a single package. Often that package includes something of additional value, such as professional investment expertise in the case of mutual funds or the guarantee of lifetime income in the case of annuities.

BUILDING A PORTFOLIO

Your goal as an investor is to build a diversified **portfolio**, or collection of varied investments. Diversification means that rather than buying just one stock, you buy a number of stocks in different types of companies. At the same time, you put some of your **principal**, or investment capital, into a number of bonds or bond funds, and some in cash or cash equivalents.

The reason you diversify is that investment categories, also called **asset classes**, have their ups and downs. When stocks are strong, bonds may not be. The reverse is true as well. When bonds are strong, stocks are often weak. Sometimes, though not all the time, cash equivalents, such as certificates of deposit or US Treasury bills, do better than stocks or bonds.

Since there is no way to predict which category will be the best investment to own at any given time, you can be ahead of the game by having some money in all three categories, either directly or through mutual funds.

Stocks

Stocks are **equity** investments, or ownership shares in a business. When you and other investors buy shares, you actually buy part of the business. If it prospers, you may make money because you're paid a portion of the profits, because the value of the stock increases, or both. While you can't predict the future, stocks have historically been stronger long-term performers, but have also been more volatile than the other types of investments described here.

Bonds

Bonds are loans that investors make to corporations or governments. When they borrow, these bond issuers promise to pay back the full amount of the loan at a specific time, plus **interest**, or a percentage of the loan amount, for the use of your money. Investors buy bonds, also known as **fixed-income investments**, because they expect to receive their investment amount back, and because they like the idea of regular interest income.

ART AND COLLECTIBLES

Art and collectibles are investments whose value varies based on quality, availability, and fashion.

GOLD

Gold and other precious metals are investments of enduring worth, though their market prices vary as supply and demand changes.

FUTURES AND OPTIONS

Futures and options are speculative investments, which change in value as the investments they're derived from change in price.

RISK AND REWARD

With all investments, there's an expectation of reward—known as return—and an element of risk. And in general, the greater the chance for a substantial reward, the greater the risk of a loss. Though it's almost impossible to predict any investment's behavior accurately, a time-honored approach to achieving a better balance between risk and return is to own a number of investments in several asset classes.

In fact, the ideal investment portfolio for a typical investor is often described as a pyramid, with low-risk/low-reward investments providing the base and high-risk/high-reward opportunities at the apex.

Equity and Debt

When you make certain investments, you buy a piece of the company or get a promise of repayment.

Investing means using money to make money. That may happen when:

- You buy an investment that increases in value, pays you **dividends,** or does both

- You lend money, giving the borrower the right to use it for a specific period of time, and you collect **interest**, or a percentage of the loan amount, as payment

Of course, there's no guarantee that your investments will do as you expect. As an investor, you have to be prepared for downturns, especially in the short term, and have a strategy for dealing with losses.

Stocks are equity investments

You own a piece of the company.

APPEAL OF STOCKS

- May increase in value over time, faster than the rate of inflation

- May pay dividend income

- Historically have provided the best return on investment over the long term

RISKS OF STOCKS

- Volatility, or rapid change in value, especially in the short term

- Performance dependent on company management and overall economy

- Possibility of losing some or all of investment capital

Bonds are debt investments

You loan money, which is repaid with interest.

APPEAL OF BONDS

- Regular income from interest payments

- Return of principal, or investment amount, at end of specified term

- Usually less volatile than equities, so there's less risk of losing principal

RISKS OF BONDS

- Income and principal vulnerable to inflation and default

- Possibility of losing money if sold before end of investment term

- Investing when interest rates are low means being locked in to less income

EQUITY AND DEBT

If you buy certain investments, you have **equity**, or an ownership share. With stocks and mutual funds, for example, you get partial ownership, usually shares in the company or fund that issues them. What you get back as a return on your investment depends on how well the company or fund does and how many shares you own.

If you lend money, as you do when you buy a bond, you've made a **debt** investment. Although those two words seem to contradict each other, it's the most accurate way to describe exchanging your **principal**, or money, for the promise of getting it back, plus interest. Unless the borrower defaults, you can be fairly certain of what you'll earn (the interest) and when you'll get your principal back (the date the loan **matures**, or ends). Knowing how much interest you'll earn, and when you'll receive it, is one of the things that makes bonds appealing.

Mutual funds buy equity or debt investments, or both

You buy shares in a mutual fund, and the fund buys stocks, bonds, or other investments. If the fund earns interest or dividends on those investments, it pays your share of the earnings, after expenses, as distributions.

APPEAL OF STOCK FUNDS

- May increase in value over time and may provide income
- Invest in many securities, which reduces investment risk

RISKS OF STOCK FUNDS

- Performance depends on the return of underlying investments
- Even though investment is diversified, there is still market risk

APPEAL OF BOND FUNDS

- Provide more flexibility than buying actual bonds
- Provide regular income, which can be reinvested or used to supplement other income

RISKS OF BOND FUNDS

- Do not assure return of principal, or pay fixed rate of return
- Returns vulnerable to inflation
- Interest rate changes affect bond value

Stocking Up on Stocks

Stocks historically have had the strongest overall performance record, but they're not predictable.

Many people equate investing with buying stocks, and for good reason. Stocks have, over time, produced stronger returns and produced them more consistently than any other investment. Despite that record, some people still hesitate to put money into stocks, perhaps because they're concerned about possible losses.

Most experts agree, though, that buying stocks, either directly or through stock mutual funds, is essential to successful long-term investing. The more you learn about the long-term advantages of owning stocks—despite the risk that stock prices may fluctuate more than other types of investments—the more comfortable you may feel about allocating a larger percentage of your portfolio to them. What remains is identifying those stocks that are best suited to your overall plan.

PERFORMANCE

The best argument for buying stocks is that they have historically provided stronger returns than any other asset class. According to the research firm Ibbotson Associates, large company stocks have averaged an annual 10.2% return on investment, long-term corporate bonds, 5.9%, and cash, 3.8% between 1926 and 2002.* Records going back to 1800 confirm that stocks as a group have provided an average annual real return of about 7% for more than 200 years. Real return is the return minus the rate of inflation.

However, there are also risks in investing in stocks. Investors have faced a 30% chance of losing money invested in stocks in any single year since 1926*, and there have been several periods when stocks have lost value several years in a row, requiring an extended period of positive gains to get back to previous highs.

COST

When you buy an individual stock, you pay the price per share times the number of shares, plus commission and fees if they apply. The price changes all the time, reflecting the balance between supply and demand. If investors are mostly buying the stock, the price tends to go up, and if they are mostly selling, the price tends to fall.

You can buy through a traditional or online brokerage account, or, if the issuing company has a **dividend reinvestment plan (DRIP)** or a **direct stock purchase plan (DSP)**, you can buy directly from the company. It's generally inexpensive to buy through a DRIP or DSP, as you pay only a small fee on each transaction.

Brokerage firms charge either a commission each time you buy or sell or an annual management fee based on the value of your account. Although the commission varies from firm to firm, it tends to be lower when you trade online.

SELECTION

You have a wide selection of stocks, including those listed on US stock markets, those trading over the counter (OTC), and those sold in overseas markets. There are many ways to compare stocks. One of the most widely used is **market capitalization**, figured by multiplying the current price by the number of existing shares.

Mid-caps, or middle-sized companies, may have greater growth potential and may be lower in price than large-company stocks. But they generally provide less income, if any, and may pose more risk. Their market capitalization is usually between $2.3 billion and $10.9 billion.

Large companies, known as **large-caps**, are the most likely to pay dividends, have higher prices per share, and the most reserves to protect them against downturns in the market. The best-known are often referred to as **blue chips**. Their market capitalization is usually over $10.9 billion.

Small companies, or **small-cap** stocks, with a market capitalization of under $2.3 billion, may offer the greatest chance for big price increases and the highest risk of your losing money. There may also be considerably less information available about the performance of small-cap stocks, which makes them harder to evaluate.

BUYING WHAT YOU KNOW

One investment strategy is buying stock in companies whose products and services you know. If what a company provides appeals to you, or fills a need, you may conclude that other people will react in the same way. You can always ask your financial advisor for a profes-sional analysis of a stock's potential, and you can research its recent and long-term performance. Similarly, you may decide to buy stock in the company where you work, to share in its potential profits. But you'll want to be cautious about being too dependent for both income and investment return on one source.

near the low point. There have been several examples in recent years where well-known companies have made dramatic recoveries. However, low prices can also be a sign of a failing company. That's the risk you take.

Trying to decide why certain stock prices are low can be hard, especially if the company doesn't get lots of press coverage. But if value investing appeals to you, it may be worth developing your expertise. The strategy can provide rewards when you get it right.

CONTRARIAN INVESTING

If you're committed to the strategy of concentrating on stocks that other investors are shunning, you're known as a **contrarian**. Using the same approach in a more limited way, you can buy on down days, even in a booming stock market. However, you have to be willing to hold on to a stock even if things get worse before they get better, and you have to recognize that the stock may never make a comeback.

LOOKING FOR BARGAINS

If you're wondering whether it's possible to get stocks on sale, the answer is yes. While stock discounts don't come on schedule, the way furniture sales do, there are always some stocks that are cheaper than others, including stocks that have fallen in price for one reason or another.

Value stocks are stocks selling at a lower price than the company's repu-tation or financial situation seems to deserve. One tried-and-true investment strategy is to concentrate on these opportunities, buying inexpensive stocks with the expectation of selling them when the price goes up.

Sometimes, of course, stocks are cheap because a particular company or industry is in trouble. When times (and sometimes managements) change, you may make a large profit if you buy at or

*Source: Stocks, Bonds, Bills and Inflation 2003 Yearbook, Ibbotson Associates (Annual updates work by Roger G. Ibbotson and Rex A. Sinquefield). Used with permis-sion. All rights reserved. Stocks performance based on the Standard & Poor's 500 Composite Index, bonds on Salomon Brothers Long-Term High Grade Corporate Index, and cash on a US Treasury one-bill portfolio.

Taking Stock

When you know which questions to ask, you'll feel comfortable making stock decisions.

When you're investing in stocks, one of the important things to understand is that what you and other investors buy and sell, and what you're willing to pay, helps determine individual stock prices and the overall performance of the stock market.

If investors are buying a particular stock, the demand increases its price. Similarly, when investors are putting lots of money into stocks, the stock market in general rises. But if they choose other investments instead of stocks, the market in general declines.

One way to invest is to adopt one of the stock-buying strategies that have worked well over the years. You can **buy and hold**, which means concentrating on building a portfolio of stocks with long-term potential for income, growth, or both.

Or you can **trade**, which means you buy when you expect a stock to increase in value, and sell when it reaches a certain price or increases a certain percentage in value. Or you can use both strategies selectively if you have a plan in place.

A TIME TO BUY...

When you're thinking about buying a particular stock, you should seek the answers to several important questions from your own research and your financial advisor.

- **Are the company's earnings growing? At what rate?**
- **Are the revenues and profits up or down?**
- **How much debt does the company have? Why?**
- **Are its products or services competitive in the markets it reaches?**
- **Are new markets available?**
- **What's going on in the economy at large that might make a difference to the company's success?**
- **What are the strengths and weaknesses of the management team?**

To find the answers, you can check investor updates from the company, read financial news and analyses in papers and magazines, research what independent analysts are saying, and consult with your broker or other financial advisor.

WEIGH THE PRICE

In deciding whether to buy a particular stock, you'll have to determine if it's worth the current price. In essence, you're trying to figure out if it's likely to increase in value so you can sell at a profit, or whether the stock will pay enough in dividends to justify the cost.

Although nobody can accurately predict changes in price, your financial advisor can tell you what experts expect, based on the information currently available. And, you can learn to detect recurrent patterns in stock prices. When interest rates are low, and the amount you can earn with other kinds of investments is limited, for example, the price you pay for stocks may be higher than in periods when you can earn high interest rates on bonds.

SET DOLLAR LIMITS

One approach to stock buying is to set dollar limits for your investments and simply not consider stocks that cost more than your self-imposed ceiling. This strategy lets you create a more diversified portfolio for the same investment amount. Here are two ways, for example, to make a $20,000 investment:

200 shares at $100 per share	=	200 at $45 + 200 at $25 + 200 at $15 + 100 at $30

STOCK EXCHANGE

YTD % CHG	52-WEEK HI	LO	STOCK (SYM)	DIV	YLD %	PE	VOL 100s	CLOSE
0.4	53	38.60	NYTimes A **NYT**	.54	1.2	24	6217	45.90
-0.6	16.25	12.26	Newcastle **NCT** n	.51e	3.2	...	500	15.88
-13.2	36.70	24.74	Newell **NWL**	.84	3.2	22	27762	26.32
-9.8	39.24	27.16	NewfldExpl **NFX**		...	20	4712	32.50
-3.1	33.80	22.59	NewhallLd **NHL**	.40a	1.4	17	18	27.85
-15.1	32.75	20.80	NewmtMin **NEM**	.16f	.6	88	65486	24.66
3.0	9.12	2.88	NewpkRes **NR**		...	...	1786	4.48
-9.0	30.89	17.60	NewsCorp ADS **NWS**	.10e	.4	dd	11395	23.89
0.1	28.04	19.79	Nexen **NXY**	.30g	...	...	104	21.70
-24.7	49	18.09	Nicor **GAS**	1.84	7.2	9	4673	25.62
-12.2	78.25	43.75	Nidec ADS **NJ**	.08e	.1			
10.2	64.28	38.53	Nike B **NKE** x	56				
-15.7	33	20.26	99cOnlyStr **NDN**					
-1.5	23.49	16.06	Nippon					

THE P/E RATIO

One way to measure a stock's value is by looking at its price/earnings ratio, or P/E—though you should think of it as one part of the equation, not the only indicator. The ratio is figured by dividing the current price per share by its earnings. Trailing P/Es, shown here, use earnings for the past four quarters, and forward P/Es use earnings for the last two quarters and projected earnings for the next two.

A P/E goes up as investors pay more to own the stock. While no ratio is necessarily too high, some analysts question whether investors can expect a price to continue to rise if earnings don't also increase. This means they would advise against buying stocks with significantly higher than average P/Es.

There are also questions about stocks with lower than average P/Es. These stocks may be good buys because they are undervalued and likely to increase in price over time. But sometimes a stock with a low P/E is in serious financial trouble and therefore a poor investment.

AND A TIME TO SELL

Buying the right stocks could have a major impact on how well your investment portfolio does. But don't underestimate the importance of selling at the right time. In fact, it's just as important to have a strategy for selling as it is for buying. Here's a list of some guidelines that investors follow. Obviously, you can't adopt them all since some contradict others, but you can use them selectively in developing your style of investing:

- **Sell if there's a major change in the company's stability or direction**
- **Sell any investment that gains a predetermined percent in value, because holding out for a higher gain may mean losing an excellent profit**
- **Sell investments that are down at the end of your tax year if you can use the loss to offset capital gains when you file your income tax return**
- **Sell any investment that drops a predetermined percent in value to limit your losses**

LOOK AT BENCHMARKS

One way to gauge how well your stock portfolio is doing is to look at it in relation to the way the stock market in general is performing. One of the best-known measures is the **Dow Jones Industrial Average (DJIA)**, whose ups and downs are always in the news. Since the DJIA monitors 30 major companies, however, it may not reflect your personal portfolio. Broader benchmarks are readily available in the financial pages of your newspaper, in other financial publications, and online.

If most of your stock is in large companies, the **Standard & Poor's 500-stock Index (S&P 500)** is the one to watch. It tracks the performance of a broad base of widely held stocks in different sectors of the economy. And if you have investments in an even wider range of stocks, you can look at the **Wilshire 5000**, which tracks the stocks traded on the NYSE, AMEX, and Nasdaq Stock Market. If your portfolio consistently performs more poorly than the index you're using as a benchmark, it may be time to reevaluate your holdings.

You can also judge the performance of an individual stock by comparing it to an industry-specific index, which companies include in their annual proxy statements. If you discover, for example, that most utility company stocks are prospering while the one you own is not, you may decide to sell and invest your money elsewhere.

The monthly statement you get from a broker or financial advisor may not include index information, but it does give you information that you can use to track performance, including current stock prices and your annual dividend earnings. More comprehensive statements also show the original price you paid and your unrealized gains and losses.

Bonds: The Basics

Companies and governments pay for some of their expenses by borrowing money from investors.

Just as you might borrow money for major expenses if you don't have enough in the bank, so do businesses and governments. Sometimes they borrow from a bank, as you would to get a mortgage for a new home. But they can also borrow by **issuing** a bond that promises to pay investors who buy the bond a fixed percentage of interest for the use of their money.

When you buy a bond, you're really lending money for a certain period of time

The bond issuer agrees to pay you back, plus interest

THE VALUE OF DEBT

From an investor's standpoint, what bonds provide is a steady stream of interest income and return of **principal**. In retirement, your bond interest may be an essential source of income. In fact, that's one reason many financial advisors suggest increasing the amount you have invested in bonds as you get older.

Even if you don't need the income to live on, interest on bonds can provide a regular infusion of cash for your investment account. For example, suppose you had $40,000 in bonds earning 5% interest that paid you $2,000 a year, probably in two $1,000 payments. That money could provide a healthy boost to a mutual fund account or pay for 200 shares of a stock trading for $10 a share.

Reinvesting probably makes more sense while you're building your portfolio than putting the interest you're earning in your checking account and paying day-to-day bills with it.

INFLATION BITES

The chief limitation of bonds, from the perspective of long-term financial security, is that both principal, or the amount you invest, and interest are vulnerable to inflation.

If a $1,000 bond pays 5% interest each year for ten years, the $50 will buy less the tenth year than it did the first. If that's the money you're using to buy athletic shoes, for instance, you might find yourself short at the checkout counter.

One way to minimize the inflation threat is to buy short-term bonds with a portion of the principal you've allocated to fixed-income. Because they mature within a year or less, the buying power of the interest they pay isn't eroded over time.

WHAT BONDS COST

Investing in bonds can help you diversify your portfolio and provide a steady source of income. A bond's initial selling price—usually $1,000—is also known as its **par value**. That's the amount you get back when the bond **matures**, and it's the base on which the interest payments are figured. However, some bonds may require an investment of $10,000 or more. The price tag can make bonds hard to afford, especially if you're just starting to build an investment portfolio.

It can be challenging to diversify your bond investments, since each purchase may require a substantial sum. But there are strategies you can use to build your bond holdings, by channeling earnings on other investments into bonds, or by using one-time windfalls like an inheritance to get you started. Once you have a foot-hold, you can use the principal from a maturing bond to buy another bond.

You also need to understand the relationship between a bond's price and the interest it pays. If bonds being issued pay a higher rate than those already in the market, the older bonds will be worth less than par value if you sell them before maturity. But if the new bonds are paying a lower rate, older bonds will generally sell for more than par. That's because investors calculate the income they will receive in figuring the price they're willing to pay.

BONDS AND BOND FUNDS

Many financial advisors suggest buying **bond funds** rather than individual bonds. One reason is that you usually need less money to invest in a fund than you do to make a bond purchase. And since funds own many bonds, you get more diversification in your portfolio.

You, as an investor, don't actually own the bonds. Instead you own shares in the bond fund. The fund pays you income distributions, or your share of the fund's earnings, based on the interest it receives on its bond holdings.

The fund makes no promise that you'll get your investment back at a particular point in time, the way a bond does. Nor is there a fixed rate of interest, because the fund buys and sells bonds regularly, rather than holding them to maturity. As a result, the fund doesn't earn interest at a single, set rate, but collects from many bonds paying at different rates.

The value of bond fund holdings is affected by changes in the interest rate, just as the market value of individual bonds is.

TYPES OF BONDS

While all bonds raise money in essentially the same way, different types of bonds have different characteristics:

CORPORATE BONDS

These bonds are sold by publicly held companies as a way of raising money for a range of activities, from expanding operations to building new facilities. Many companies prefer borrowing to issuing additional shares of stock, which dilutes the value of the stock already in the market. The interest you earn is taxable, but corporate bonds generally pay higher interest than other types, although they tend to be riskier.

US TREASURY NOTES

The federal government sells two-, three-, five-, and ten-year US Treasury notes to raise money to finance running the government. Since the government doesn't sell stocks (because there is nothing to own), the only way it can raise money is by collecting taxes and issuing bonds. You owe federal income taxes on the interest you earn, but not state or local income taxes.

MUNICIPAL BONDS

Sold by state and local governments, these bonds raise money to pay for a wide array of projects and expenses, and sometimes the actual operation of the government. You owe no federal tax on municipal bond interest, and generally no state or local tax on bonds issued by the municipality where you live.

For example, if you live in New York and buy New York state bonds, you owe no tax on the interest you earn. But if you live in California and buy New York bonds, you will owe tax on your earnings to California.

AGENCY BONDS

These bonds are issued by various government agencies, both in Washington and around the country. Among the best known are mortgage-backed bonds known as Ginnie Maes, or GNMAs. The interest on these particular bonds is taxable, though the interest on some other federal agency bonds is not.

Bond Issues

Whatever your investment goals, there's a role for bonds in your portfolio.

If you buy and hold bonds for the interest they pay, they are an easy investment to manage. They don't require constant attention, and in the era of electronic recordkeeping they can't even get lost. Over time you expect them to provide a dependable source of investment income. Some years, in fact, the return on bonds is better than on stocks.

But you can approach bonds differently. Increasingly, investors buy and sell bonds to take advantage of changing prices that occur because of changes in interest rates. Or you can put money into riskier offerings—known as high-yield or **junk bonds**—as you would invest in more speculative stocks, for the expectation of a higher return.

BUYING TO HOLD

When you buy bonds and hold them until they mature, you know from the start how much you'll earn in interest and when the principal will be repaid.

Only two things can interfere with your expectations: if the issuer **defaults**, or fails to pay the interest or return the principal, or if the bond is **called**, which means the issuer redeems the bond early by paying back the principal. That happens, most often, if the interest rate you're earning is higher than current rates, and the issuer can save money by paying you off and issuing new, lower-paying bonds.

If you're considering a buy-and-hold approach to bonds, here are some suggestions experts make:

- **Investigate a bond's rating and interest rate before you buy to evaluate the balance between risk and reward**
- **Check a bond's earliest call date to determine how long the income is assured**
- **Consider tax-exempt municipal bonds, including tax-exempt zero-coupon bonds, to keep more of your earnings**

MAKING THE INVESTMENT
You can buy bonds through stockbrokers and banks, or in the case of US Treasurys, directly from the government. If you buy when the bonds are issued, there's usually no commission since the borrower pays the expense of bringing the bond to market. To buy new issues you usually need to be the client of one of the brokerage companies that **underwrite** the bonds and bring them to market.

If you buy existing bonds, you pay a commission or a **markup**, though not more than 5%. Brokers should tell you the sales cost, if you ask. But unlike stock transactions, where the broker's commission is shown on the confirmation statement as a separate item, the cost of buying bonds isn't stated directly and can be more than you think.

Transaction markups are generally not disclosed, and the bond price you're quoted by one broker may be different from the price for the same bond quoted by another. That means comparison shopping not only pays—it's a necessity.

You can often get a good price on a bond if your brokerage firm **makes a market in** that bond, which means it has a supply on hand. Or you can buy through a broker who will negotiate the purchase price **over the counter**—which today actually means on the phone or by computer.

BUYING DIRECTLY
If you want to buy US Treasury bills and notes directly from the government, you establish an account with the US Department of the Treasury that's linked to your bank account. When you want to make a purchase you submit an order electronically, by phone, or in writing, and the amount is debited from your bank account.

The interest is deposited directly to your account, as is the principal if you choose not to renew when your investment matures. However, you can renew easily before maturity or make additional purchases once your account has been established. You can ask your bank for information or get it directly at www.treasurydirect.gov.

THE TERM'S THE THING

When you buy bonds, one decision you have to make is how long you want to tie up your money. Unlike stocks or mutual funds, but like certificates of deposit (CDs), bonds **mature**, or end, at a specific time.

One advantage is that you can time bonds to mature when you need the money—to pay your child's tuition bills, for example. And by staggering the maturity dates, you can help ensure that you'll have cash on hand when you need it.

In general, issuers offer a higher rate of interest on **long-term** bonds to offset the risk of tying up your money. That may make them attractive, but you need to evaluate a number of factors, including the potential impact of inflation if you were to hold the bond to maturity and the potential change in interest rates.

You might consider short-term bonds if rates are low, or if you expect to need your principal within a short time to meet a particular goal. You may earn less interest, but the value of the bond is less likely to be affected by rate changes or inflation.

Intermediate- or mid-term bonds typically mature in two to ten years, depending on the bond. Their rates tend to fall in the range between long-term and short-term bonds, and may be a good addition to a diversified portfolio.

BUYING AND SELLING

While you may not have considered **trading**, or buying and selling bonds, you may find you can use this approach to help keep your investment strategy on target. For example, if one of your bonds is called, you'll have the principal to invest in a new bond. If interest rates on new bonds are low, you might prefer to buy an older, higher-paying one in the secondary market, where bonds that have already been issued are traded. Or, if you own a high-interest bond when the rate on newly issued bonds is low, you could sell it for more than you paid and use the money to make a different kind of investment.

Before you trade, though, experts suggest that you:

- ● **Check prices with different brokers to be sure you're getting the best deal**
- ● **Evaluate previously issued bonds as carefully as you would newly issued ones**
- ● **Avoid bonds that change dramatically in price, to prevent big losses if you do have to sell**

NEW YORK BONDS

Bonds	Cur Yld	Vol	Close	Net Chg.
AMR 9s16	8.3	15	108	+ ½
AMR 6⅞24	cv	5	114¾	− ½
ATT 4¾98	4.9	25	97¼	..
ATT 6s00	6.0	25	99¼	..
ATT 5⅛01	5.4	17	94¼	+ ½
ATT 7⅞02	6.9	37	103⅜	+ ⅜
ATT 6¾04	6.7	89	101	+ ½
ATT 7½06	7.1	31	105¼	
ATT 7⅜07	7.2	5	...	

LglsLt 8		
LglsLt 9		
LglsLt †		
Lglsl		
MC		

PRICE AND RATE

If you buy or sell bonds already in the market, you'll find their price, listed here under **close**, is more or less than the par value of $1,000. That's because a bond's price in the secondary market is determined by the interest it pays and its term.

If the interest is higher than what's being offered on newly issued bonds, the price of the old bond will be more than par, since it will be attractive to investors. If the interest is less than the rate the new bonds are paying, the old bond is less attractive and will trade at less than its par value. In this example, the AMR bond paying 9% is selling above par, at 108, or $1,080. The ATT bond paying 5⅛, or 5.125%, is selling below par at 94¼, or $942.50. If you pay more, it's known as **buying at premium**, and if you pay less, it's known as **buying at discount**.

FROM COUPON TO ZERO COUPON

Once upon a time, you collected your bond interest by clipping a **coupon**, or piece of paper, attached to your bond certificate and taking it to the bank. Today, in the age of electronic recordkeeping, you don't have to bother with coupons. Payments are mailed or deposited directly in your account.

But the word *coupon* has stuck as a term for interest. That's why bonds that accumulate their earnings, rather than make periodic interest payments, are called **zero-coupon bonds**, or **zeros**. The catch is, with taxable zeros, you owe income tax each year on the interest you would have earned, as if it had been paid.

Mutual Funds: Investing Together

Mutual funds rely on investor money and management expertise.

When you invest in a mutual fund, you're part of a team that includes investors and an investment company, which can be a mutual fund company, bank, or brokerage firm. You and other investors buy shares in a fund the investment company offers, and your collective assets are invested by a professional manager who decides what and when to buy and sell.

This management expertise is one of the main advantages of investing in a mutual fund, as opposed to buying stocks and bonds on your own.

Another reason for investors to buy mutual funds is that there's something for everyone. Whatever your financial goals, you can find a mutual fund—or a portfolio of mutual funds—to help you meet them, no matter how large or small your investment principal.

BUYING IN, BUILDING UP

Typically you open an account with a mutual fund company by investing in a specific fund. Each company sets its own account minimum, with most falling in the $1,000 to $2,500 range.

Once your account is opened, you can add to it as frequently or infrequently as you like. All funds set a minimum for additional investments, but sometimes it's as little as $50 and rarely more than $100.

Even if you're adding only small amounts each time you invest, your investment has the potential to grow over the years. And, there's nothing to prevent you from putting in substantially more than the minimum whenever you can.

INVESTORS buy shares in a mutual fund

and receive distributions from the fund's profits

WHAT YOU GET

Each time you invest, you buy more shares. As that number increases, you're entitled to a larger proportion of the fund's profits, if it makes money. That happens when it earns interest or dividends from its investments, sells them at a profit, or both. The fund pays you and other shareholders the earnings as income, and the profit from sales as capital gains. Together, they're known as **distributions**.

You can use the distributions from the fund as a source of cash, or you can **reinvest** them. That means you funnel them back into your account to buy additional shares. The advantage of reinvesting, of course, is that you steadily increase the number of shares you own, even if you aren't adding new money to

OPEN-ENDED OPPORTUNITY

In most cases, the sky's the limit on the amount you can invest in a mutual fund. That's because most of the 7,000 funds on the market today are **open-ended funds**. As investors buy more shares, the funds increase the size of their portfolios by making more investments.

In contrast, **closed-end funds** sell a limited number of shares to interested investors. Existing shares are bought and sold on the stock exchanges, like shares of stock.

Sometimes, though, if an open-ended fund is especially successful, and the mutual fund company is concerned that it could lose some of its trading flexibility, the company may close the fund to most new investors—although if you already own shares, you can continue adding to your account.

When that happens, the company may open a second fund with similar objectives—and even the same manager—to capitalize on investor interest.

THE GROWING FUND MARKET

The first mutual fund in the US opened for business in 1924. By 1940, there were fewer than 80 funds, and by 1960 only 161—all of them stock funds. By 1980, there were 564, almost a quarter of them bond funds. In 2003, the number was just under 7,000 funds.

MUTUAL FUND COMPANY

FUND MANAGER

Successful investments add value to the fund

The fund manager buys stocks, bonds, or other investments for their income or growth potential

the fund. And most funds make it easy and cheap to reinvest. All you have to do is choose the reinvestment option when you open your account. The fund takes care of the details—often without charging a fee.

HOW MUTUAL FUNDS WORK

A mutual fund combines your money with the money of other investors and uses those assets to build its portfolio. The manager focuses on investments that match the fund's objectives, seeking to produce the kind of results you were looking for when you selected the fund.

But since you and other investors can **redeem** your shares, or sell them back to the fund at any time, the manager must also keep the fund liquid enough to pay you the current value of any shares you redeem. That means keeping some assets available in cash and holding others that can be traded quickly, perhaps, at a profit.

Funds vary by styles and objectives. For example, some managers emphasize value while others stress growth. Some concentrate on earning dependable dividends. And some trade more frequently than others, and so have a higher **turnover rate**. Because style can affect performance, it's something savvy investors consider when choosing a fund.

UNCLE SAM'S SHARE OF THE PROFIT

You owe income tax on your share of a mutual fund's earnings, including amounts that are reinvested and those distributed as cash, with these exceptions:

- If you invest in **municipal bond funds**, also known as tax-free funds, your dividends aren't usually taxed, but your capital gains are. The fund sends a Form 1099 at the end of the year telling you what's taxable.

- If you buy mutual funds for a tax-deferred or tax-free account, such as a retirement or education account, you owe no tax on any earnings that may accumulate, though you may owe tax when you later withdraw them.

Mutual Fund Marketplace

Whether you like them plain or fancy, you can find funds to match your taste.

The point of investing in mutual funds—like the point of investing in anything—is meeting your financial goals. One major appeal of the mutual fund market is that you can almost always find a fund that appeals to you.

Before you decide which funds to buy, however, it helps to know about the types of funds that exist, and their basic investment objectives. Otherwise, you could end up buying a popular fund that's actually too risky—or too conservative—for your investment plan. Each fund's investment objective, its level of risk, and investment strategy, are explained in the **prospectus** the fund company sends you. It's important to read it before you make an investment decision.

A SHOPPER'S GUIDE

In narrowing your selection, you might choose from a cross section of funds with different objectives.

MUNICIPAL BOND FUNDS buy tax-exempt bonds. Some funds concentrate on bonds issued by a single state, while others buy bonds from many states. You generally don't owe federal taxes on the income earnings from these funds, but you may owe state taxes.

GNMA FUNDS buy bonds backed by a pool of government-insured mortgages. They provide income and return of principal, though what you earn is influenced by changes in interest rates. Since GNMA bonds themselves come in large denominations, funds make them accessible to individual investors.

GROWTH FUNDS are stock funds that invest in growing companies expected to increase in value, thereby increasing the value of the fund that owns shares in them. Some funds concentrate on companies of the same size—large-, mid- or small-cap—and others buy all three sizes. Growth funds are usually most valuable as long-term investments.

AGGRESSIVE GROWTH FUNDS take bigger risks than other growth funds, by investing in startup, small, or mid-sized companies. Even though some investments will fail, others may succeed. These funds, also known as **emerging growth funds**, are best suited for long-term investment.

VALUE FUNDS are stock funds that invest in **undervalued companies**—those whose prices are lower than they seem to be worth, have dropped in value, or are currently out of favor. The fund expects that the prices of its holdings will increase as the companies turn themselves around and resolve the problems that have kept investors away.

THE FIRST CUT

All mutual funds are grouped into three broad categories: stock funds, bond funds, and money market funds. Each type has further subdivisions, to suit different investor goals.

Stock funds buy shares of publicly traded corporations—the same ones you can buy as an individual. But they buy more shares and build more diversified portfolios than you probably could on your own. You can choose funds designed to provide growth, income, or a combination, and reinvest your earnings.

Bond funds buy bonds issued by corporations, federal governments (including the US Treasury), municipal (state and local) governments, and government agencies. Bond funds produce income, but your earnings can be reinvested to buy additional fund shares, so the number you own can grow.

Money market funds invest in short-term corporate and government bonds and other debt. They can usually be used as checking accounts. Some funds set a minimum amount for each check—often $250 to $500—but typically let you write an unlimited number.

INCOME FUNDS invest to produce current income. The amount of income generally reflects the riskiness of the investments the fund is making. The greater the risk, the higher the income. While income funds are frequently bond funds, **equity income funds** and **total return funds** are predominately stock funds, and **balanced funds** are part stock and part bond.

HIGH-YIELD FUNDS are bond funds that invest in low-rated or unrated bonds, sometimes called **junk bonds**. Because they may produce high income, they are frequently appealing to investors who are willing to accept the risk that junk bonds might default.

SECTOR FUNDS are stock funds that concentrate all of their trading in a particular area of the economy, such as utilities, transportation, or technology. A sector fund may perform significantly better—or worse—than other funds, depending on how the particular sector is doing.

GROWTH AND INCOME FUNDS are stock funds that invest primarily in companies poised for growth and paying dividends. Since they seek to buy established stocks with strong performance records, they may provide more consistent returns than funds investing more speculatively.

PRINCIPAL PROTECTED FUNDS combine the potential for long-term appreciation in the value of the underlying stocks with a measure of protection of principal.

SOCIALLY RESPONSIBLE FUNDS invest only in companies whose manufacturing, environmental, social, or marketing policies meet a specific set of standards. A typical socially responsible fund might avoid tobacco company stock or companies with poor environmental or equal opportunity records. These funds, which include stock, bond, and index funds, aren't tracked as a separate category, but promote themselves as being socially conscious.

Specialized Funds

Some funds offer unique investment opportunities.

You can choose specialized funds to meet specific objectives or as a way to invest more broadly, both at home and around the world. New categories of funds and new ways to invest are being introduced all the time. Like all investments, though, specialized funds expose you to certain risks, including the risk that you could lose money.

INDEX FUNDS

One way to evaluate the performance of stock and bond investments is to measure them against the appropriate index. Each index measures the average performance—up, down, or flat—of a certain investment category as a benchmark, or base. Among the best known are the Standard & Poor's 500-stock Index (S&P 500) and the Dow Jones Industrial Average (DJIA).

An index fund is designed to produce results that mirror the performance of the specific index it tracks. To achieve that goal, the fund buys and holds all the stocks or bonds included in that index—or sometimes a representative sample of those securities. The fund portfolio changes only when the makeup of the index changes. That's why these funds are often described as passively managed.

Index funds, especially funds that track the S&P 500, have been popular with investors. With an index fund, you don't have to worry about choosing among the various funds that are available in a certain category, such as large-cap stocks, and you generally pay lower fees than you do with other kinds of funds.

Some financial advisors have reservations about focusing on index funds, especially in weak markets. They suggest that index investors may be ignoring opportunities to take advantage of professional, active management and potentially higher returns. And they point out that not all funds tracking the same index produce exactly the same results.

Other advisors believe that index fund investors should diversify by buying funds that track different indexes. Their argument is that a range of funds, including some linked to international indexes and extended markets, can make your portfolio more diversified.

ALL IN THE FAMILY

Most mutual fund companies sponsor a number of funds. Taken together, a company's offerings are referred to as its family of funds.

As an investor, you can select several funds from the same family or just one or two. One advantage of being part of a family is that you can add a fund to your portfolio or transfer money easily between funds over the telephone or online, and not have to pay additional sales charges. But you can also own funds in several different fund families.

INVESTING AROUND THE WORLD

Most financial advisors agree that it's increasingly important to have money invested in other parts of the world. It may make sense both as a hedge, or protection against downturns in the US market, and as a way to take advantage of strong economies in other regions or countries.

Since funds do the research, handle the buying and selling, and take care of the taxes—all of which can be a hassle for an individual investor—they're often the easiest way to invest overseas. However, remember that investing abroad has certain risks, including the changing value of the dollar and the potential for political or military strife, which can affect the value of your investments.

Many of the large fund companies offer a variety of international and global funds, as well as funds that specialize in particular geographic regions or individual countries.

BALANCED FUNDS

While the majority of funds concentrate on either stocks or bonds, some funds buy both types of investments to seek a combination of growth and income. Balanced funds, in particular, are designed to provide both asset allocation and diversification. The advantage of a portfolio diversified across asset classes is that the bond income may provide some protection against a drop in the value of stocks as markets move through cycles of strength and weakness, and similarly that gains in stocks may offset weak bond yields.

Some advisors suggest that balanced funds are an especially appropriate first investment, as these funds provide immediate diversification. Others suggest that balanced funds continue to be a wise choice as you build your investment portfolio.

Since the stock-to-bond ratio varies from fund to fund, you can find one whose allocation and investing style seems most appropriate for you. Keep in mind that the trade-off for diversification is that balanced funds usually do not perform quite as well as stock funds when equity markets are strong—though they may suffer smaller losses when the markets are down.

EXCHANGE TRADED FUNDS

Exchange traded funds, or ETFs, resemble mutual funds in several ways and differ from them in others.

With an ETF, you buy and sell shares in a fund that owns a portfolio of stocks, such as those included in the S&P 500 or the Nasdaq-100 index. The ETF has a net asset value (NAV) determined by the total market capitalization, plus stock dividends and minus fund expenses, of all the stocks in its portfolio divided by the number of fund shares that investors own.

One difference is that you can buy ETFs throughout the day, as you can stocks, and you can buy on margin or sell short. Mutual fund shares trade only once a day, at the end-of-day price. Another is that the price you pay for ETF shares depends on supply and demand, which isn't the case with open-ended mutual funds. If investors are buying, the share price can be more than the NAV and if they're selling, it can be less—though the differences tend to be quite small.

Buying Mutual Funds

Opening a mutual fund account and investing regularly are easier than you might think.

You can open a mutual fund account by working with your advisor to select the fund and complete the application on paper or online. Or, in some cases, you can purchase directly from the company that offers the fund. Either way, the purchase process is similar.

1. Fill out an application

You complete the application and submit it, either to your advisor, online at the fund's website, or by mail.

2. Make an investment

You send a check with your application or have the amount of your investment transferred electronically from your bank, credit union, or brokerage account. Each fund requires a minimum initial investment, but the amount differs.

3. Keep investing

To buy more shares in the fund, you can send a check or have the amount transferred electronically, either on a regular schedule or when you choose. If your employer offers direct deposit, you can usually arrange to have a portion of your paycheck added to your account.

ASKING THE QUESTIONS

When you're choosing a mutual fund investment for your portfolio, there are five basic questions to ask about each fund you're considering:

- Is the fund's objective suited to my financial goals?
- Is the fund's performance strong in comparison with other funds with similar objectives?
- How do the annual fees and expenses compare with those for similar funds?
- What kind of risk does the fund expose me to?
- Can I live with that risk?

THE COST OF BUYING

With some funds, you pay a sales charge known as a load. The load, figured as a percentage of the amount you invest, may be used to pay commissions to the person or institution handling your transaction. Each fund company sets its own sales charge, up to the legal limit of 8.5%, though most charge much less.

Some fund companies offer a number of alternatives for paying the load, and you can select the method you prefer at the time you buy. **Front-end loads**, which you pay when you make a purchase, are the most common. They're typically known as Class A shares when the company offers more than one payment method. **Back-end loads**, typically known as deferred contingency loads or Class B shares, are subtracted when you sell your shares within a certain period of time after purchase, often the first four to seven years. With **level loads**, typically called Class C shares, you pay an annual sales charge.

In contrast, with a no-load fund, you pay no sales charge when you buy or sell shares. But many fund companies, including some that don't have loads, charge an annual fee, called a 12b-1 fee, of up to 1% of your assets, which is used to pay for commissions and other services.

1. Available to investors only in certain states.
2. Pays dividends on a monthly basis.
3. Subject to availability.

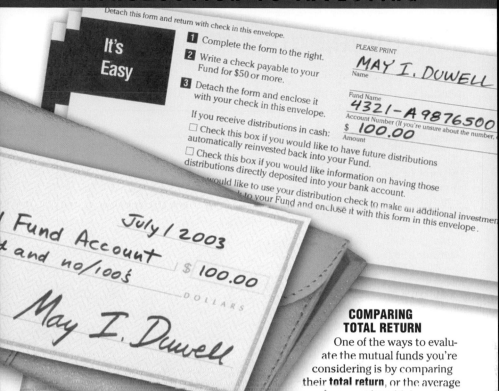

Detach this form and return with check in this envelope.

It's Easy

1 Complete the form to the right.
2 Write a check payable to your Fund for $50 or more.
3 Detach the form and enclose it with your check in this envelope.

If you receive distributions in cash:
☐ Check this box if you would like to have future distributions automatically reinvested back into your Fund.
☐ Check this box if you would like information on having those distributions directly deposited into your bank account.
...would like to use your distribution check to make an additional investment ...k to your Fund and enclose it with this form in this envelope.

PLEASE PRINT
MAY I. DUWELL
Name

Fund Name
4321-A 9876500
Account Number (If you're unsure about the number,
$ 100.00
Amount

July 1 2003
...l Fund Account
...t and no/100$ $ 100.00
DOLLARS
May I. Duwell

The fund's prospectus explains its fee structure, including whether or not there is a sales charge, and how to choose among different classes of shares. You can find the prospectus on the fund company's website.

DIRECT INVESTMENT PLANS

Direct investing can be an easy and smart way to build your mutual fund account. Usually, funds encourage automatic investment by reducing the minimum for opening an account or making additional purchases. Some mutual fund companies, for example, let you open and add to your account with as little as $50 if you use their direct investment plans. The lower minimum can make a big difference if you're ready to start investing but don't have a lot of money.

Direct investing also keeps you contributing, cuts down on check writing, and helps you budget for investing. Since you can stop participating at any time, there's no real drawback to trying it.

COMPARING TOTAL RETURN

One of the ways to evaluate the mutual funds you're considering is by comparing their **total return**, or the average annual amount by which each fund has increased or decreased in value, including reinvested dividends. You get that information from your financial advisor, from the funds themselves, and in the financial press.

A number of factors affect a fund's total return. The most obvious is the performance of its underlying investments, which reflects the strength or weakness of the particular segment of the stock or bond markets they're drawn from. For example, if small-company stocks are outperforming large-company stocks, then funds investing in small companies are likely to outperform funds investing in large companies.

Fees and expenses also impact total return. If you buy a fund with a front-end load—Class A shares—you invest a smaller amount initially than if you bought a no-load fund, so your total return will be lower if the two funds have similar earnings. However, there's historical precedent suggesting that over a period of years the initial difference in investment may diminish and the total return on the two funds may well turn out to be essentially equal.

If you select Class B shares or Class C shares, all of your money is invested from the beginning, but you usually pay a higher asset-based sales charge than with Class A shares. Depending on the fee structures of your specific funds, you may discover that the total return is smaller over a multiple-year period with B or C shares than with A shares because the fees are higher.

Expanding Your Fund Portfolio

As your portfolio grows in value, you can pursue the advantages of greater diversification.

Mutual funds are designed for portfolio building, or increasing the number and value of your investments. Because you can reinvest your earnings easily, you can steadily add to the number of shares you own. And the more shares you have, the more earnings your investment has the potential to generate.

Another advantage of mutual funds is that they're diversified. A stock fund usually owns shares in several dozen companies, known as its underlying investments. That way, if some of a fund's investments aren't living up to expectations, the return on others may be strong enough to offset those losses.

But remember, investing in mutual funds has risks, as any type of investing does. A fund can't do better than the combined performance of its underlying investments after fund expenses.

FINDING THE RIGHT FUNDS

Mutual funds can be excellent tools for building financial security. But as with all investments, you need to select wisely. You can work with your financial advisor to identify types of funds well suited to your goals, and select specific funds to meet your needs.

Before investing, you should always read a fund's prospectus. It provides basic information, including a statement of the fund's objectives, its fees, an analysis of potential risks, and a report on its past performance.

You can compare funds with similar objectives by looking at independent research from firms like Value Line, Morningstar, and Lipper (available by subscription, in libraries, or online). You can also expand your reading to include the financial pages of major newspapers, and business and financial magazines. A qualified financial advisor is also an invaluable resource.

SIMPLIFIED BUYING

One of the most appealing aspects of mutual fund investing is that when you open or add money to an account, you buy the number of full or fractional shares equal to your investment amount minus sales charge, if any. So if a share

Slot your investments into a range of funds, diversifying over time

Invest $3,000 every year for 30 years in a tax-deferred account

costs $20, and you invest $100, you buy five shares. If you invest $250, you buy 12½ shares. That can be a lot easier than saving until you've accumulated the full price of an investment, the way you usually have to do with individual stocks and bonds.

It's also easy to arrange to have any fund earnings and any capital gains automatically reinvested to buy additional shares. The price you pay per share will vary from purchase to purchase, as the net asset value (NAV) of the fund changes. The fund will report the number of new shares you purchased and the price per share on your next regular statement.

* These examples are hypothetical. They do not reflect the past performance of any particular investment or predict future performance.

If you earn 5% annually, the pretax value of your portfolio after 30 years would be $540,770*

THE ADVICE FACTOR
If you're uncertain about which funds to buy, or tend to put off investment decisions, paying a commission to an advisor who helps you make smart decisions can be money well spent.

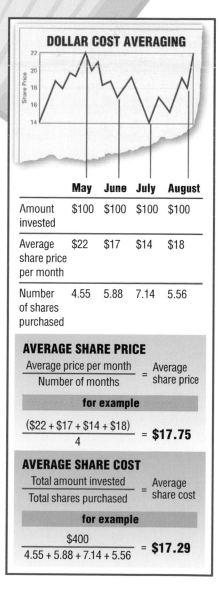

DOLLAR COST AVERAGING

	May	June	July	August
Amount invested	$100	$100	$100	$100
Average share price per month	$22	$17	$14	$18
Number of shares purchased	4.55	5.88	7.14	5.56

AVERAGE SHARE PRICE

$$\frac{\text{Average price per month}}{\text{Number of months}} = \text{Average share price}$$

for example

$$\frac{(\$22 + \$17 + \$14 + \$18)}{4} = \mathbf{\$17.75}$$

AVERAGE SHARE COST

$$\frac{\text{Total amount invested}}{\text{Total shares purchased}} = \text{Average share cost}$$

for example

$$\frac{\$400}{4.55 + 5.88 + 7.14 + 5.56} = \mathbf{\$17.29}$$

DOLLAR COST AVERAGING

One way to increase the number of shares you own and potentially reduce the average price you pay per share below the average cost of the shares is by using a strategy known as **dollar cost averaging**.

That means you invest the same amount of money every month in the same fund, as the price moves up and down—as fund shares tend to do. When the price goes up, you buy fewer shares. When the price is down, you buy more shares. But you have to stick to your plan and continue to invest. If you stop buying when the share price drops, you'll have paid only the higher prices and won't reduce your average cost.

Dollar cost averaging can be an effective and efficient approach to investing, but like all periodic investment plans it doesn't ensure a profit or protect you from losses in a falling market.

Fund Performance

Your goal with mutual funds is steady progress toward your goals, not great leaps and bounds.

As convenient as it is to invest in mutual funds, there are things that you, as an investor, should be doing to ensure that your investments are on the right track.

Mutual fund companies compute the value of each fund at the end of every business day. The information is widely available the next morning in the media and online. That doesn't mean you need to check every day, or even every week. Fund prices and performance change relatively slowly. But over time you want to be sure that your funds' performance is at least as strong as other funds with similar objectives. And you want to be sure that the fund's investments remain consistent with its objective.

TOTAL RETURN

Total return, or the amount a fund increases in value plus the distributions it pays, is one of the clearest measures of fund performance. Both the total return and the **percent return**, or total return divided by the cost of the investment, are reported regularly in the press and in updates your fund sends you.

To see how your fund is doing in relation to others with the same objectives, you can compare the percent return you're getting with the average for all of the funds in the same category. Lipper, Inc., provides those benchmark numbers, which appear regularly in newspaper mutual fund columns.

MARKET CYCLES

Just as stocks and bonds go through alternating periods of gains and losses, so do the mutual funds that invest in them. So while most mutual funds are internally diversified, you'll also want to diversify among fund categories. It's been true historically that the category that's on top one year is unlikely to be there the next.

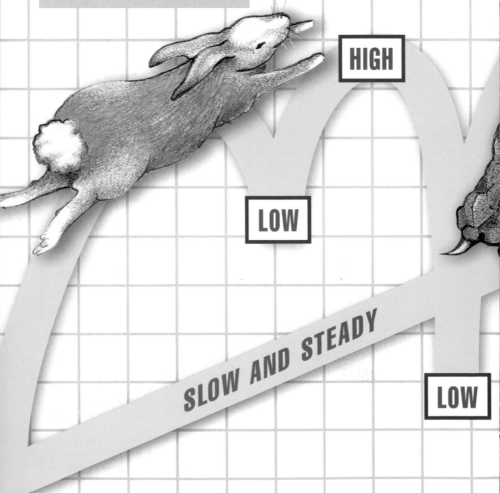

HIGH

LOW

SLOW AND STEADY

LOW

THE IMPACT OF TIME

In judging a fund's performance, it's critical to assess how well it has done, not only in the last year, but in the last five years—and in the last ten if the fund has been around that long. The reason? You want to know how well a fund has done in different economic and market climates. While what happened in the past will not predict future results, it's some indication of the fund's consistency and reliability.

Some funds, for example, do extremely well in **bull markets**, when stocks are booming, but less well in **bear markets**, when their underlying investments lose value. Other funds are better at maintaining a balanced performance—increasing in value when other funds do, and losing less in a downturn.

You can get a sense of the impact a volatile market has on fund returns by comparing the results for several different categories of stock and bond funds between 1997 and 1999 with those for the same funds between 2000 and 2002. However, notice that while stock fund losses in those years pulled five-year total returns down, many funds were still in positive territory over ten or more years.

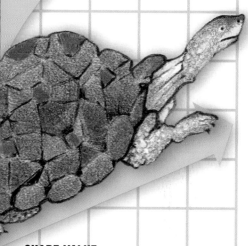

SHARE VALUE

A mutual fund's share price is known as its **net asset value (NAV)**. It's the value of the fund's net assets, divided by the number of outstanding shares. You pay the NAV for each share of a no-load fund, and NAV plus sales charge for a load fund. The load price is known as **MOP**, or **maximum offering price**.

You can use changes in a fund's NAV to track performance. But the NAV isn't as reliable an indicator as total return. One reason is that it decreases when distributions are made to shareholders.

FEES

All mutual funds have annual management fees, and some have marketing fees known as 12b-1 fees, as well as administrative fees. Most financial advisors suggest looking for funds with average or below average costs.

The reason is simple: The more you pay in fees, the more your fund has to earn to provide the return you want. For example, if two stock funds earn the same 8% return, but Fund A has expenses of 2.5% while Fund B has expenses of 1.5%, you come out ahead with Fund B.

The good news is that you can easily check most fees before you buy. Both a fee schedule and **expense ratio**—annual operating expenses divided by average net assets—are shown in a fund's prospectus, along with an estimate of the fees you can expect to pay while you own the fund.

The exceptions are sales charges and trading expenses, which aren't included in the expense ratio.

TURNOVER RATES

Another factor that may affect return is a mutual fund's **turnover rate**, which is the percentage of the fund's assets that changes every year. For example, if a fund owns 48 stocks on January 1 and replaces half of them by December 31, it has a turnover rate of 50%. Some funds have turnover rates of 10% or less, and others have rates of 500% or higher.

Though some funds with a high turnover rate provide strong returns, frequent turnover can be a drag on a fund's results because it is spending more than low-turnover funds on trading commissions and other transaction costs. You can find the turnover rate in a fund's printed and online financial statements and prospectus, and the amount it spends on commissions in the annual statement of additional information.

Another potential consequence of a rapid turnover is more capital gains taxes for shareholders if the fund sells holdings at a profit. Any capital gains may be distributed and taxed at the appropriate rate—either short term if the fund held the asset less than a year or long term if it was held longer than a year. However, funds that have sold assets at a loss can use those losses to offset future gains.

LOOKING AHEAD

Most financial experts stress that mutual funds are best suited for long-term investing. They believe you should be less concerned with short-term peaks and valleys, or with the top performing funds of the year, than with sticking with funds that perform consistently and fit your investment strategy.

Figuring Your Return

The bright side of taking investment risks is the potential for reaping rewards.

Successful investing is usually the result of making educated decisions and taking calculated risks. Nothing brings that essential combination into clearer focus than evaluating the **return**, or rewards, of your portfolio.

Total return, or the amount your investment increases or decreases in value plus the earnings it pays, is the most accurate measure of an individual stock or mutual fund performance.

The best way to evaluate an investment's performance against other investments is by calculating **percentage return**, or total return divided by initial cost. And since the most accurate comparisons are on a yearly basis,

you can find the **annual percentage return** by dividing the percentage return by the number of years you've owned the investment.

Remember, though, that comparing returns as a way to decide which investments to keep and which to sell works best if you compare similar investments or investments with similar goals.

For example, if you compare the total return of one small-company stock fund with another fund investing in the same kinds of companies, you can tell which fund is performing better. The same is true for two bond funds, or other investments of the same type.

CALCULATING RETURN

When you invest for long-term growth, as you do, for example, when you buy stocks and stock mutual funds, one measure of your success is the **return**, or the amount you get back, in comparison to what you invest. With a little calculation, you can use return figures to evaluate the performance of investments in relation to each other.

for example

In the hypothetical case used in this example, an investor bought 200 shares of a stock for $25 a share and sold it ten years later for $35 a share, a gain of $10. The stock paid a steady dividend of $1 per share, or $200 a year.*

TOTAL RETURN

is the amount your investment increases in value plus the dividends it pays.

	Dividends
+	Gain in value
=	TOTAL RETURN

The information you need to figure your return is all part of your tax records.

	$2,000	($200 per year x 10 years)
+	**$2,000**	($10 per share x 200 shares)
=	**$4,000**	Total return

PERCENTAGE RETURN

is the total return divided by the cost of the investment.

	Total return
÷	Price of investment
=	PERCENTAGE RETURN

In an actual case, the gain in value would be reduced by the cost of commissions.

	$4,000	Total return
÷	**$5,000**	(200 shares @ $25 a share)
=	**80%**	Percentage return

ANNUAL PERCENTAGE RETURN

is the percentage return divided by the number of years you held the investment. That's the number you need to make your comparisons.

	Percentage return
÷	Years you held investment
=	ANNUAL PERCENTAGE RETURN

When you're making long-term investments, a decline in value in one or more years may be offset by stronger performances in other years.

	80%	Percentage return
÷	**10**	Years you held investment
=	**8%**	Annual percentage return

COMPARING RETURNS

Figuring out the actual return on your investments can be difficult. And you can't expect to compare the performance of different kinds of investments solely on their return. Here are some of the reasons:

- The amount and makeup of your portfolio changes. Most investment portfolios are active, with money moving in and out.

- The time you hold specific investments varies. When you buy or sell can have a dramatic effect on your overall return.

- The return on some investments—like real estate holdings, zero-coupon bonds, and limited partnerships—is difficult to pin down, partly because they're more difficult to liquidate easily. You have to evaluate them by different standards, including their tax advantages.

- The method of computing return on different investments may vary. For example, performance can be averaged or compounded, which changes the rate of return dramatically.

* These examples are hypothetical. They do not reflect the past performance of any particular investment or predict future performance. Sales charges and taxes are not included.

HOW MUCH IS ENOUGH?

How much return do investors expect? It changes over time, if the market price of stocks is any indication. One explanation seems to be that investors demand returns on their equity investments that beat the yields on government bonds. In some but not all market environments, investors will pay more for equities as the interest rate drops than they'll pay when yields are high.

KEEPING UP TO DATE

You don't have to wait until you sell an investment to get a sense of the kind of return you're getting. If you're tracking a stock's performance, total return isn't reported in the press, but you can use the current price of the stock to estimate your unrealized gain in value. (It's unrealized because you still own the stock. When you sell, you realize the gain.) Then use the formula on the opposite page, just as you would if you'd sold.

If you're tracking mutual fund performance, you can find updated information on every fund's total return—which includes earnings and increases in value—regularly in the financial pages of your newspaper, in magazines, or on financial websites or the fund company's website.

Your financial advisor, the brokerage firm where you have an account, or your mutual fund company also may include information on the return of various investments in your portfolio in their monthly, quarterly, or annual reports. If they don't provide what you want to know, you can ask for it.

USING BENCHMARKS

While it's useful to compare the return on an investment with what you might have earned on a similar investment, you may also want to compare individual investments, such as stocks or mutual funds, with an appropriate unmanaged benchmark index, even though you can't invest directly in the index.

For example, you might use the Lipper mutual fund index that tracks the performance of a group of funds with the same characteristics as the one you own. Or you might compare a stock's performance to the most appropriate stock market index. For a small-cap stock, that could be the Russell 2000, and for a large-cap stock, it could be the S&P 500.

Many indexes give more weight to securities with the largest market capitalization. That means the results may indicate a greater gain or larger loss than would be the case if all the securities were equally weighted.

PERCENT

12 —

10 —

8 —

6 —

4 —

2 —

0 —

Searching for Yield

Yield measures your investment income against the price you paid.

If you're earning $500 a year from a bond fund in which you invested $10,000 and another $500 on a certificate of deposit (CD) with a balance of $20,000, you should be aware that the first investment is doing twice as well as the second.

The difference between the two is the **yield**, or what you're making on your investment. Even though the income from each is the same, you need twice as much in the CD to produce the equivalent amount. That's because you're earning 2.5% on your savings, but 5% on the bond fund. If all your money were in an investment yielding 5%, your income would be $1,500 rather than $1,000, or 50% more.

When It's Simple...

You figure yield by dividing the amount you receive annually in interest or dividends by the amount you spent to buy the investment.

For example, if you spend $1,000 on a bond and get $50 in annual interest, the yield is 5% [$50 ÷ $1,000 = 5%]. And if you hold onto the bond until it matures, you should go on collecting a 5% yield until you redeem the bond and get your $1,000 back.

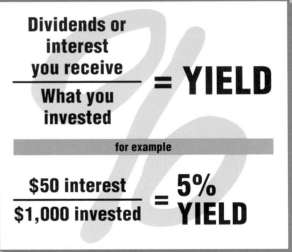

$$\frac{\text{Dividends or interest you receive}}{\text{What you invested}} = \text{YIELD}$$

for example

$$\frac{\$50 \text{ interest}}{\$1,000 \text{ invested}} = 5\% \text{ YIELD}$$

TIME AND YIELD

The yield that's reported in the stock and bond pages of the financial section of the newspaper is actually **current yield**, or what you're receiving in relation to the current price of the investment. For US Treasury bonds and notes, the current yield is reported as **ask yield**, or the yield based on the price that sellers are asking for the bond.

You'll also sometimes hear about a bond's **yield to maturity**, a more accurate estimate of what it will be worth to you over time. It's figured using a complex formula involving the interest rate, the price you paid, the par value, and the years to maturity. Although it's rarely reported in bond tables, you can ask your financial advisor for the information.

If you have a bond that you bought when it was issued, and intend to hold until it matures, you don't have to worry about current yield. But if you're thinking about buying or selling bonds, current yield is one way to estimate what you'll get back on your investment.

YIELD DOLLARS AND SENSE

Paying attention to yield is smart, since it is a measure of how well you're doing in building your assets. But there are some danger zones:

● Small differences in yield are usually not worth chasing, unless you have large amounts invested

● Yield alone can't tell you as much about how well an equity investment is performing as total return can

● Risky investments promising high yields may be tolerable in small doses, but as a regular diet, they can be big trouble. That's especially true with many **derivatives**, or investments whose values depend entirely on the way other investments are performing, and with junk bonds, because of the risk that the issuer will default

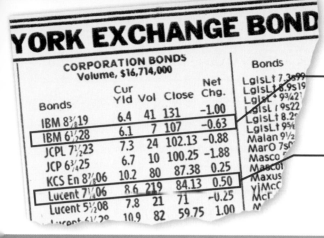

CORPORATION BONDS
Volume, $16,714,000

Bonds	Cur Yld	Vol	Close	Net Chg.
IBM 8⅜19	6.4	41	131	−1.00
IBM 6½28	6.1	7	107	−0.63
JCPL 7¼23	7.3	24	102.13	−0.88
JCP 6¾25	6.7	10	100.25	−1.88
KCS En 8⅞06	10.2	80	87.38	0.25
Lucent 7¼06	8.6	219	84.13	0.50
Lucent 5½08	7.8	21	71	−0.25
Lucent 6¼29	10.9	82	59.75	1.00

Bonds
LgIsLt 7.3s99
LgIsLt 6.9s19
LgIsl 93s42
gIsL 9s22
LgIsLt 8.2s
LgIsLt 9⅝
Malan 9½
MarO 7s0
Masco
Masco
Maxus
yiMcC
Mcf

CHANGING YIELDS
Yield changes when the price of an investment changes. For example, the IBM bond paying 6.5% interest is currently yielding only 6.1% because the price is $1,070 (107), or $70 (7) above par. In contrast, the Lucent bond paying 7.25% interest is currently yielding 8.6% because the bond is selling for $841.30 (84.13), or $158.70 below par.

When It's Not So Simple...

Your life as an investor isn't always simple, and neither is figuring yield, especially if you're trying to evaluate the performance of an investment that:

- **Changes in price**
- **Pays no interest or dividends until you sell**
- **Earns interest at anything other than a straight annual rate**

INTEREST VS. YIELD

ONE YEAR CD
ANNUAL PERCENTAGE YIELD **3.25%**
INTEREST RATE **3.00%**

It's easy to confuse the interest rate an investment is paying with its yield, since they're both stated as a percentage of the amount of the investment. To complicate matters further, there are times when they are the same. The best examples are CDs that pay simple interest and bonds that you buy at **par value**, or the price at which they are issued. Then a 5% rate means a 5% yield.

However, if interest is **compounded** (added to your balance), or if the price of a bond moves higher or lower than par, the yield will be different than the interest rate. Of the two, yield is the one that matters when it comes to figuring out how well you're doing with your investments.

STEPPING UP YOUR STRATEGY

When interest rates are high, as they were during the early 1980s, it's easy to get used to healthy yields on even the most conservative investments. But what happens when a five-year CD that's been yielding 6% matures, and the best you can find is one yielding 3%?

One solution for many fixed-income investments—specifically CDs and bonds—is to use a technique known as **laddering**. Instead of putting $30,000 in a single 10-year bond, you can buy three bonds, each worth $10,000, that

mature two years apart. Each time one matures, you reinvest that amount. That way, if you have to settle for a lower rate for that part of your money, you'll still be earning the higher rate on the rest. And when the next bond matures, the rates may be up again.

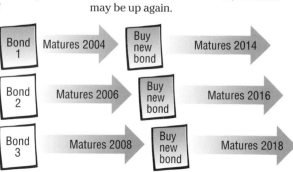

Bond 1	Matures 2004	Buy new bond	Matures 2014
Bond 2	Matures 2006	Buy new bond	Matures 2016
Bond 3	Matures 2008	Buy new bond	Matures 2018

Financial Planning

A strong financial future begins with a sound financial plan.

Your sense of what it means to be financially secure is likely to have certain things in common with the way other women in your family, at work, or in your circle of friends define that phrase:

- **Being comfortable that there's enough income to pay regular bills**
- **Saving enough to cover unexpected expenses**
- **Having the right types and amounts of insurance to protect your dependents and your assets**
- **Owning a home**
- **Paying for your children's education if you're a parent**
- **Affording a comfortable retirement**

But it's also likely that your special situation—whether you run your own business, are a single parent, care for aging parents or a special needs child, or are still finishing your education—determines where most of your energy goes and how your immediate and long-term goals differ from other people's.

How do you achieve both the more universal goals and those that are uniquely your own? The answer is, you plan ahead, you define your goals, and you learn from your own and other people's mistakes.

SHORT-TERM PLANS
- Emergency fund
- The right insurance

THE STARTING POINT

Developing a plan that will help put you on the road to financial security is easier than you may think. The place to begin is by evaluating where you are now, what you want to achieve, and how much each of those goals will cost.

As part of creating your plan, you'll also need to develop a timeline and a set of priorities. Although some of the things you'd like to accomplish are right around the corner, others may be 30 or 40 years in the future. Similarly, you may decide that while some of your goals would be nice to achieve, others are absolutely essential.

Avoid debt bumps. If you're still paying for purchases you made weeks or months in the past, it will be harder to afford what you want in the future

WHEN SILENCE ISN'T GOLDEN

Since the point of financial planning is setting goals and finding ways to achieve them, you need to decide what's important to you personally and how you plan to make it a reality.

If you're on your own, the next step is beginning to invest, perhaps with the assistance of a financial advisor. If you have a husband or partner, you'll be ready to put your heads together about the goals you share and those that are more important to one or the other of you.

If asserting yourself about how money gets spent, how much you should be investing, or which investments you're making is hard for you, you may want to make an extra effort to say what you think. You don't want to risk being frustrated, or even angry, about not being able to afford something in the future because nobody knew it mattered to you.

MID-TERM PLANS
• Buy new home

Retirement Reservoir

Midway Lake

Starter's Pond

LONG-TERM PLANS
• Retirement
• Travel

• Pay for kids college
• Start my own business

KEY TO FINANCIAL PLANNING

You need to know how to read the signs on the road to financial security, and know which turns to take to arrive where you want to be.

Understand risks.
Investments can shrink in value as well as grow. You need to learn about the different types and levels of risk and why some risks may be worth taking

Anticipate inflation.
You need to be prepared to pay gradually increasing prices for almost everything, almost every year

Allocate assets.
You don't want to make the mistake of putting too much money into one single category of investment, even your home

Diversify investments.
You're probably better off in the long run with several different stocks, bonds, or mutual funds rather than just one of each

Take a Closer Look

Is it time to give your financial profile a new look?

If you're concerned that you'll have to give up on some of your financial goals because they'll cost more than you can afford, think again. You may have to make certain changes in the way you spend money now. You may have to postpone some of your less time-sensitive objectives to meet those that are more time-specific. You may even decide to sacrifice something you'd been excited about to achieve an objective that seems more urgent. But before you can make any of those decisions, you do have to know where you stand now, and what change you may have to make in the way you spend money.

IN THE BLACK OR IN THE RED?

If you're serious about meeting your goals, the place to begin is by looking at your cash flow. Cash flow is the relationship between the money you have coming in and the money you're spending, on a weekly, monthly, or annual basis. The bottom line is that if you're paying all the bills that are due and regularly have money left in your account, your cash flow is positive.

If you're always short of cash, if you skip payments even occasionally, or you have to borrow regularly from savings to meet your obligations, your cash flow is negative. Persistent negative cash flow has two inevitable consequences: You fall into debt, and you don't make progress toward meeting your financial goals.

The good news, though, is that there are solutions to negative cash flow. You can increase your income or reduce your expenses—or both. The first may sound better, but the second is actually easier and is probably more important to long-term success.

PUTTING SAVINGS TO USE

When you've got your cash flow in the black, you'll probably want to think about creating an **emergency fund**. That's savings you can use while you're between jobs or to see you through an illness, the aftermath of an accident, having to replace the roof, or buy a new car unexpectedly.

Advisors typically suggest you keep at least three to six months of living expenses in your emergency fund and that you choose fairly liquid investments. Liquidity, in this sense, means that you can withdraw cash easily or sell investments without having to worry about losing money. That's why money market mutual funds or short-term bond funds are considered more liquid than stocks.

The more money you keep in your emergency fund, the more types of investments you may want to make. The cost of even a serious emergency tends to be spread out over several months or longer, giving certificates of deposit (CDs) and US Treasury bills—which generally pay higher interest rates than savings accounts—time to mature before you need the cash.

EVALUATING YOUR SPENDING

Though everyone allocates her income a little differently, depending on what she earns and what her priorities are, some basic expenses are unavoidable.

You need a place to live, food to eat, clothes, transportation, and money for medical expenses. You need insurance. You have to pay taxes on your income, on your real estate if you own your home, and, in most states, on some or all of the purchases you make.

So how do you spend less? Again, individual choices will differ. But if you're serious about living within your means, you have to look seriously at every category. Assume, for the sake of argument, that your housing and health-care are fixed costs. Where else can you trim—and by how much?

NUMBER GAMES

It's probably easiest to evaluate your cash flow on a month-to-month basis since so many bills are due every 30 days or so. You can also get a good sense of how holidays and vacations affect your spending. But be sure to account for payments you make quarterly or less often—such as insurance premiums or taxes that aren't withheld—by dividing the total due by 12.

Then figure out what difference those savings are making in your bank balance each month.

Could you reduce your food and transportation costs by 15%? Could you do the same with the money you spend for clothes? Could you still have a good time if you cut your entertainment budget by 15% or more? If a 15% cut seems unrealistic, try 10% to start.

Then figure out what difference those savings are making in your bank balance each month.

MY BUDGET

Evaluate your spending

Set up an emergency fund

Allocate for investment

LOOKING TO THE FUTURE

Once your emergency fund is set, it's time to invest, a critical step on the path toward realizing your financial goals. Just as you allocate a percentage of your cash flow to pay the mortgage or your life insurance, you can allocate a percentage of your income to one or more investment accounts.

Here are some techniques for boosting the amount you're investing:

Don't buy the next thing you plan to put on your credit card. Put what it would have cost in an investment account.

Pay off the balance on your credit cards and start investing an amount equal to your average monthly payment.

Have a percentage of your salary deposited directly into a tax-deferred or tax-exempt investment account each pay period.

Invest some—or all—of any extra money you earn or receive as gifts or bonuses.

Avoid having too much withheld for taxes and invest the difference between your old and new withholding each pay period.

Reinvest all the dividends and interest you earn, preferably automatically, so you're not tempted to spend it.

Sign up for a retirement savings plan that's offered through your job as soon as you are eligible.

Managing Debt

You don't want debt to be a stumbling block
that trips you up.

When you're using money that could otherwise go into your investment account to pay interest that's accumulating on old debts, it's time to take a hard look at your spending plan. And if you're wondering what **spending plan** that might be, it's probably time to put one together.

When you construct a spending plan, sometimes called a budget, you divide up your income so that it covers your regular expenses—both essential and nonessential—always including some for your emergency fund and ideally some for your investment account.

Some people use what they spent last year as a starting point—though last year's spending may be what got you into debt. Or you may prefer to check the Bureau of Labor Statistics website (www.bls.gov) for the average nationwide expenditures for housing, food, and other costs. You'll have to modify that information to reflect local costs and your own situation. But it's a place to start.

KEEPING ON TRACK

If you're determined to stick to your plan, it helps to keep careful track of where your money goes. Get into the habit of writing down the cash you spend and where you spend it. Then, once a month, using those notes, your bank statement, and your credit card bills, analyze where your money went.

You may find you've underestimated some essential costs and overestimated others. But since a spending plan is an evolving document, not a set of rules, you can always adjust it if necessary. For example, heating your home and buying gas for your car may jump in price at certain times, or you may have unusual medical expenses in some years. You may also be spending much more than you thought on something you consider expendable.

Following a plan doesn't guarantee you'll stay out of debt. But it does mean you're less likely to be taken by financial surprise if you follow the guidelines you've set for yourself.

DON'T GET DETOURED

If you simply can't pay your credit card bills in full each month, even with a spending plan in place, you may have to take radical action. Consumer debt can create major problems, even if you are meeting your other obligations on time.

Try substituting a debit card when you shop. Though there's no guarantee that you won't overdraw the bank account it's linked to, especially if you have a line of credit that gives you overdraft protection, you'll know you've spent too much the next time you check your balance.

Give up all but one of your credit cards and use the one that's left only for emergencies. While using a credit

A WORD TO THE WISE

Beware of anyone who promises to fix your credit rating. It will cost you money, and you'll have nothing to show for it.

FACING A TIDAL WAVE?

If you owe more than you can comfortably repay with your current income, an informal spending plan may not be enough to solve the problem.

Rather than risk losing your home or your car, having your electricity and telephone turned off, or your insurance canceled, be proactive. Ask your creditors to change the terms of your loans. They may agree to add the amount you're behind to the end of the loan, reduce your monthly payment, or both. It will extend the payback period and cost you more in finance charges over the long term, but it may keep you from drowning in debt.

You may also decide to seek professional help from an accredited credit counselor, who will help you change the way you spend and create a repayment plan. Check with the National Foundation for Credit Counseling for a not-for-profit center near you. You can call 800-388-2227 or find them on the Web at www.nfcc.org.

As part of choosing a credit counselor, ask how he or she will work with you, and how your collaboration may affect your credit report. Ask, too, whether there is a charge for the assistance. Payment arrangements vary from center to center.

AUTOMATIC PAYMENTS

If part of your debt problem is the result of not paying on time, you may want to consider automatic bill payment arrangements that help you avoid hefty late fees. For example, many utility, telephone, and cable companies make it easy to sign up, and they debit your linked bank account each month. Some credit card issuers also offer automatic payment plans, which give you the choice of paying as little as the minimum balance or as much as the full bill.

Of course, there has to be money in your account, or enough overdraft protection, for the debit to go through. But you can time automatic payments to coincide with the direct deposit of your paycheck—also usually a good idea.

DON'T PANIC

While it's possible to slide slowly into debt, you're actually more likely to face serious problems as the result of illness, an accident, or unemployment. That's why having an emergency fund is so important, along with adequate health-care, disability, and life insurance.

card is a good way to build a strong credit history, it's also one of the easiest ways to end up with a poor one. Once your finances are under control, you may be confident enough to return to plastic. But you may also find you can live without it most of the time.

Avoid buying on impulse. You may lose out on a good deal or two, but you'll strike a major blow against finance charges.

Creating a Plan

Required equipment: blank paper, sharp pencil, eraser, and commitment.

Getting your goals down in black and white helps you focus on what's really important to you. Nothing is too trivial or too fantastic, at least in the initial planning stages. And creating the list will probably help you clarify your priorities.

DEFINING FINANCIAL PLANS

The term *financial plan* has more than one meaning. Informally, your **financial plan** is a list of the things you'd like to be able to afford in the future, and the steps you'll take to obtain them.

A formal financial plan is a document prepared by a financial advisor that provides an analysis of your current financial situation, explains financial planning strategies, and identifies specific goals and the steps to take to reach them. You may pay a one-time fee for a formal plan—typically somewhere between $1,000 and $5,000—or it may be part of the advisor service you receive for an annual asset-based fee.

All financial plans—informal and formal—come to the same conclusion: The difference between just keeping your head above water and moving closer to realizing your financial goals is how much, how well, and how soon you invest, and how you protect what you already have.

WHAT IF YOU DON'T PLAN?

If you sometimes think that what you want out of life is so normal that it will happen in the regular course of events, you're being lulled by a false sense of security. Most advisors agree that goals become realities only when you have invested enough to make them happen.

Ask yourself, for instance, if you'd have enough money for a down payment if your ideal house were for sale right now. Or whether you'd be able to pay a $30,000 tuition bill if your child had just been accepted to college. If your answer is yes, you can breathe more easily. But if it's no, then this is the time to act.

To have money available when you need it, you have to develop a plan for making the kinds of investments that are most likely to produce what you'll need. Identifying what those investments are, learning how to put money into them—and then doing it—is precisely what planning for the future is all about.

FINANCIAL PLANNING WORKSHEET

Short-Term Goals

Make specific investing decisions for the next few years

Mid-Term Goals

Sketch the major expenses you visualize for the next ten years

Long-Term Goals

Commit a percentage of your income to tax-deferred investments

THE IMPACT OF TIME

Timing is an important part of financial planning. If you identify when you'll need investment income, you can select investments designed to produce it at the right time.

You also have to keep track of when you make certain investments and when you sell them. For example, you must

INVEST IN YOURSELF

To build a strong enough financial base you'll need two things: money and time.

Sometimes, though, you may have financial opportunities, like buying a home or building up a business, before you have enough cash to afford the investment.

That's why financial plans often include borrowing to meet your more immediate goals. You can think about paying off these loans as the equivalent of putting money into an investment account—except you're already enjoying the benefits. The only caution is that you should also be investing to meet future goals.

TYPICAL GOALS	POTENTIAL CHOICES
New car	☐ Treasury bills
Down payment on home	☐ CDs
Extra education	☐ Money-market funds
Establishing a business	☐ Short-term bonds
	☐ Balanced funds

TYPICAL GOALS	POTENTIAL CHOICES
Education for children	☐ High-rated bonds or bond funds
Larger home	☐ Stock in well-established companies
Second home	☐ Stock mutual funds
Travel	☐ Treasury notes
	☐ Zero-coupon bonds

TYPICAL GOALS	POTENTIAL CHOICES
A comfortable retirement	☐ Growth stocks
Affording travel, hobbies	☐ Real estate
Security for long-term care	☐ Stock mutual funds
Helping children	☐ Long-term bonds
Inheritance for heirs	☐ Zero-coupon bonds

COMPETING FOR YOUR DOLLARS

In many cases, your goals will be competing with each other for your investment dollars. By planning ahead, you can develop strategies for resolving the conflicts without having to abandon your goals along the way.

For example, if you start a retirement savings plan when you begin your career, you can contribute part of every paycheck to your savings, year in and year out. Even if you miss a year or two, when you're buying a house, or paying college tuition, for instance, the money you've already invested is available to grow.

put money into an IRA by April 15 for it to qualify as a contribution for the previous year. Or, if you want to sell a stock that's lost value and use the capital loss to offset capital gains, you must act by December 31.

Every year you should also revise and update your financial plan and the investment strategy you're following. For one thing, you probably won't have exactly the same goals today that you had a couple of years ago, or that you will have a couple of years from now.

What's more, investments change in value, depending on what's happening in the economy, within a certain industry, or with a particular mutual fund. You may want to adjust your plan to take advantage of those changes.

Tailoring a Plan

Work with your advisor in creating a financial plan.

Financial planning is the cornerstone of successful investing. And you can get help developing your plan when you work with a financial advisor.

In looking for a person to work with, you'll discover that some advisors do planning exclusively, and refer you to other experts when you're ready to put your plan into action. Others incorporate planning into the services they provide, like handling your investment orders or preparing tax returns.

A RANGE OF GOALS

One part of financial planning is developing strategies to reach the goals that are most important to you—perhaps owning your own home, enjoying a secure retirement, or paying for a college education for your children or grandchildren. Since these are ambitions many women share, anticipating them puts you in good company. It means that as you begin the planning process, you can benefit from what others have learned about getting your priorities in order, balancing competing demands, and selecting the right places to put your money to work.

Another reason you plan is to be prepared for events that may happen unexpectedly. Some of these possibilities are exciting, such as the opportunity to go into business for yourself or the pleasure of hosting your child's wedding. But you will have to identify the resources to pay for them.

Other surprises, such as a suddenly widowed parent or a serious car accident, may threaten financial hardship. If you've established a sound plan, you're more likely to survive these challenges without incurring long-term debt.

A FORMAL PLAN

A professionally prepared financial plan is sometimes a formal document that describes your current financial situation and goals and provides an overview of investing strategies. It also proposes several different types of investments, as well as insurance, tax planning, and other financial advice. If a planner suggests a formal plan, you'll ask to see a typical one, so you'll have a clear sense of what you'll be paying for.

Advocates claim that a formal plan will tell you where you stand, focus your investment strategies, and help keep you on track.

WHERE TO GO FOR HELP

While sometimes financial planners come looking for you, the more customary approach is for you to make the first move. If you're not sure where to start, here are some ideas:

1 Go to seminars offered in your local library, bank branch, or community center. Some organizations and independent advisors specialize in presentations for women.

2 Most banks, but not all their branches, offer basic planning services. Pick up information in your branch, or ask someone you've worked with there about whom you should talk to.

3 Look up financial firms and life insurance companies in the yellow pages. Those that offer planning advice may advertise it.

4 Take advantage of information that's available on your job, or through religious, social, or civic organizations.

A PLAN THAT WORKED

In 1944, when Anne Scheiber retired from the IRS, she'd saved $5,000. But when she died in 1995, at age 101, she left an estate worth more than $22 million to Yeshiva University. Scholarships in her name ensure that many young women can afford the educations they seek.

How did someone whose top annual salary was $4,000 build such an impressive fortune? She had a strategy: invest in stocks you believe will grow in value, reinvest your dividends, and be patient. And she worked at it diligently. Of course, a buy and hold strategy doesn't guarantee a strong return. But Ms. Scheiber's success can be the inspiration you need to get started.

A LESS FORMAL PLAN

Advocates of less formal financial plans maintain that you don't need a costly, multipage document to summarize personal information you provided in the first place, or to describe investment opportunities that are regularly discussed in books, newspapers, and magazines.

Instead, they suggest you ask your financial advisor to write a follow-up memo, or report, of your initial meeting, outlining your assets, goals, and willingness to take risk. That memo can serve as the foundation for building an investment strategy.

TAILOR-MADE PLANS

One of the major advantages of working with a financial advisor to develop an investment plan is having it custom-fitted to your needs and goals. The more experience your advisor has working with women clients, the more precisely he or she can tailor a plan to suit you.

Woman-centered plans are important for several reasons. For one, you have a longer life expectancy. This means you'll have to emphasize growth investments that will enable you to live comfortably for 20, 30, or more years after retirement. Your life insurance needs are also different from many men's, since you're less likely to have to worry about providing security for a surviving spouse.

A BUYER'S MARKET

As an investor, you're the one who decides which plan to adopt and which investments to make. But that control comes with responsibility for making the wisest choices. As you invest:

1 Ask for an evaluation of the costs of each investment, including what you would pay if you changed your mind or wanted to sell it in the future. The advisor will know the answer, or can find it for you. If it's a mutual fund, you can check the prospectus.

2 Do some comparison shopping before you make your decision about annuities, insurance policies, bonds, and other investments where the cost depends in part on the seller's commission. That will tell you if the price you're being quoted is competitive.

3 Don't act quickly on recommendations. Most of the investments that you'll be considering change price slowly, so you can take time to think it through, or ask for more information. The only time speed pays for the average investor is in trading stocks, and then you're probably working with a familiar advisor attuned to your wishes.

Getting the Money Together

Accumulating and allocating investment money is a key part of your plan.

With your financial plan in hand, you can turn your attention to getting the cash together to make the first investment, and the next one, and the ones after that.

You don't need much money to open an investment account. And once it's opened you can add to it easily, often as little as $50 to $100 at a time. You can have money directly deposited from your paycheck or transferred from your checking account, or write a check yourself.

You can also accumulate money in a savings account and plan to transfer lump sums to your investing account. But you should compare what you'd earn there with what you have the potential to earn by investing right from the start. You may find investing makes more sense for no more effort.

KEEP IT SEPARATE

If you're building an investment account, it makes a lot of sense to keep it separate from your checking account. One reason it can pay off is that you probably won't be as tempted to spend your investment money on everyday expenses.

NEW MONEY should be added regularly to investment accounts

INVESTMENT ACCOUNTS

Minimum opening deposit
One of the factors you may consider in choosing an account that you'll use to accumulate investment principal is its minimum opening deposit. Some accounts may require as little as $100 while others have a floor of $1,000 or more. Each institution that offers such accounts sets its own minimums.

Minimum balance
Some accounts require that you maintain a minimum balance to be eligible for earnings or avoid maintenance fees, or both. If you plan to be moving money in and out of your account, you may want to choose one with the most flexible minimum balance rules.

Costs and fees
Most investment accounts have a range of fees and expenses that are explained in detail in the account materials the sponsor provides. Some fees are asset-based, calculated as a percentage of your account value, while others are transaction fees or penalty fees.

Average return
If you're using your account primarily to accumulate assets you intend to invest rather than as an investment itself, you may not be concerned with the return on investment the account provides. But the longer you leave money in the account, the more important potential return may be.

Insurance
Investment accounts are not insured against losses and do not guarantee a return. When you withdraw, your account may be worth more or less than the amount you deposited.

REINVESTING YOUR EARNINGS

One of the most reliable ways to build your assets is to reinvest the money you earn from the investments you already have. You can do that directly and easily with all mutual funds and some stocks because the company will handle the transaction. All you have to do is participate in the company's reinvestment plan.

With bonds and some stocks, the interest or dividends you earn are paid to you (or your brokerage account) directly, and you have to decide how to reinvest. That's where having a financial plan can make a big difference: If you know what you want to do next, you can act promptly—for example, putting the earnings into a mutual fund where you hope they will generate earnings to help you accumulate money for a bigger purchase.

INVESTMENTS
are purchased with the funds you accumulate

MUTUAL FUNDS

Once you've made an initial investment in a fund, you can add to it any time you have the minimum amount, usually $50 to $100. From nearly 7,000 funds available, you can choose stock or bond funds in tune with your goals, which may range from current income to long-term growth.

STOCKS

You can buy stock through a broker or, in some cases, directly from the company. Prices range from less than $1 to more than $100 a share. You can sell stocks you own and buy others. Stocks may provide growth, income, or both. But earnings are not guaranteed.

BONDS

Bonds generally cost $1,000 each and may require a minimum purchase of $10,000 or more. Once you have invested, you can use money from maturing bonds to buy new ones. Bonds generally provide income, but the income and principal are not guaranteed on most bonds.

CERTIFICATES OF DEPOSIT (CDs)

You can open a CD with as little as $250 and earn a guaranteed rate of interest. You can invest for periods of three months to five years, and decide either to withdraw your money at the end of the term or reinvest. CDs are income, not growth, investments.

EARNINGS
can be reinvested

THE ACCUMULATION PHASE

You can build an investment account from money you're earning by adding a certain amount every paycheck or every month.

If you stick to the guideline of investing 10% of your annual salary, you're talking about $250 a month if you're earning $30,000 a year, and $1,042 a month if you're earning $125,000 a year. You can find the monthly amount you're aiming for by dividing your annual salary by 12 and multiplying by 10%.

If you don't have a steady income, and you're building your investment assets in bursts rather than in regular installments, there may be an added incentive for using an account that puts your money directly into investments. But remember that these accounts do not assure you'll have a profit or protect you from losses in a declining market.

IT'S NOT PIN MONEY ANYMORE

A woman's right to control money of her own has a long history, though in the past it rarely made her financially secure. In Europe, cash, commonly known as **pin money**, was allocated for her incidental expenses by a marriage contract. In the original Greek, the term was *paraphernalia*, or things outside the dowry. And in the US, where dowries were not the norm, farm women traditionally controlled their **butter and egg money**, or what they earned selling the products they gathered or made.

Choosing Growth or Income

Growth means an increase in value, and income means money coming in.

Growth Investments

You buy a **growth investment** anticipating that it will increase in value over time, though there's no way to predict the rate of growth or the change in value. Shares of stock, shares in a stock mutual fund, and real estate (land and the buildings on it) are typical growth investments.

An investment grows in value when its price increases, and you can sell it for more than you paid for it. For example, suppose you buy 100 shares of stock at $10 a share and hold it ten years. If its price goes up to $18 a share over time, you profit from that growth in value.* The risk you take is that the price will fall when you want to sell. That would result in a **capital loss** rather than a **capital gain**.

BUY

100 shares of stock at $10 per share

$1,000

Year 1 **Year 2**

Income Investments

Income investments usually pay interest or dividends, depending on the kind of investment they are.

Interest is a percentage of the price of the investment. For example, if you buy a ten-year $1,000 bond that's paying 5% interest, you earn $1,000 x .05, or $50 a year.* Investments that pay interest are known as **fixed-income investments**, and include bonds and similar investments.

The risks you take are that the bond issuer will default on its promise to pay, and that the bond price will fall, perhaps because of an increase in interest rates. Changing bond prices don't affect you, though, if you hold the bond to maturity.

BUY

$1,000 bond at issue paying 5% interest and hold to maturity

$1,000 **$50** **$50**

Which to Choose

How can you decide between growth and income investments? Here are some things to consider, based on advice from investment experts:

* This hypothetical example is for illustrative purposes only and does not represent the return on any specific investment or predict future performance.

SUIT YOUR CHOICE TO YOUR GOALS

The longer your time frame, the more sense growth may make, since you can ride out possible downturns in the value of your investment.

The whole point of investing is making money. That may happen if an investment grows in value or pays you income. But while growth and income may seem equally appealing, they aren't interchangeable goals.

You may emphasize growth when you are investing to meet long-term goals. That way you'll have time to weather a downturn in the markets and not have to change your plans. On the other hand, if you're counting on cash from your investments to pay for living expenses or to meet short-term goals, you may be more likely to make income investments.

Or, you might look for investments, typically specific stocks and mutual funds, that provide a strong total return. That's the combination of growth and income.

YOU REALIZE A GAIN OR LOSS ONLY WHEN YOU SELL

SELL

$1,800
Sell now and realize a profit

MARKET VALUE OF STOCK

A stock's price may increase if one or more of the following occur:

- Strengthening of the overall market
- Increased earnings
- Positive management changes
- More competitive products
- Expanding markets

$500
Sell now and take a loss

| Year 3 | Year 4 | Year 5 | Year 6 | Year 7 | Year 8 | Year 9 | Year 10 |

YOU ARE PROMISED INCOME FROM INTEREST AS LONG AS YOU OWN THE BOND

REDEEM

$50 $50 $50 $50 $50 $50 $50 $50

$1,000
Get par value back

PAR VALUE OF BOND

The price of a bond, called its **par value**, is usually $1,000 at issue and at redemption. However, its market price moves up and down during the term.

CONSIDER THE TAX IMPLICATIONS

You may have to pay taxes on distributions, whether or not you reinvest them, and when you sell your investments.

BALANCE YOUR RISK

If you have a variety of investments, you aren't as vulnerable to the economic ups and downs that are sure to come.

MONITOR YOUR INVESTMENTS

As your financial situation changes, be prepared to adjust your portfolio to switch the focus from growth to income, or vice versa.

Basics of Investing

If you concentrate on the principles, you'll have the elements of an investment strategy.

As you make individual investment decisions, you'll want to ask where the investment fits in your overall **asset allocation** and **diversification** strategies. You'll want to evaluate the **yield** the investment may provide and the level of **return** it's reasonable to expect. And you'll want to assess how **volatile** the investment is likely to be and what **risks** you'll be taking in adding it to your portfolio.

VOLATILITY

is how much and how quickly the value of an investment changes

RISK

includes all the reasons you may have a loss or a weak return

DIVERSIFICATION

is making several different types of investments rather than just one or two

GROWTH

INCOME

ALLOCATION

is deciding what percentage of your portfolio goes into which categories of investments

PLANNING AND MONITORING

An important part of financial planning is anticipating how well investments will perform. That means weighing the risks you're taking against the rewards you can potentially receive. In addition, you need to monitor return and yield so you can judge how well you're actually doing.

Another key to successful investing is having a broad perspective. This means looking at a range of investments in relation to one another rather than zeroing in on one or two. You also have to set your sights on long-term rewards, ignoring the inevitable short-term swings in the marketplace.

TWO STRATEGIC APPROACHES

You might decide that the way to meet your long-term goals is to put money into equities you expect to grow in value. This strategy helps you concentrate on specific types of investments, first on equities and then more narrowly still on those that seem likely to perform best over the long haul.

If you are investing to meet both long- and short-term goals, you might select stocks and stock mutual funds that strive to provide both growth and income, in addition to those emphasizing growth alone. By reinvesting your dividends and any other gains, it's possible to build your investment base more quickly. Of course, stocks and stock mutual funds are more volatile than some other types of investments. So you may lose money if the market takes a sharp downturn.

If you've retired and want to begin collecting income from your portfolio, you may want to shift some of your assets to income-producing investments, such as bonds.

Any strategy, however, requires attention to basic details: understanding risk, volatility, diversification, asset allocation, and how to measure and evaluate yield and return.

RETURN

is what you get back, based on what you invest, usually measured on an annual basis

Total Return

1 Yr		5 Yr-R		10 Yr-R	
−1.2	E	+3.5	C	+8.7	B
−0.9	E	−3.9	E	+6.1	D
+2.3	B	NS	..	NS	..
+9.5	A	+9.1	A	+10.2	C

YIELD

is the income you receive as a percent of what your investment cost you

FIVE YEAR CD

ANNUAL PERCENTAGE YIELD
3.20%

INTEREST RATE
3.15%

KEEPING ON TRACK

Picking the right investments is only the first step in achieving your financial goals. You also have to monitor their performance regularly, asking whether these investments are still right for your portfolio as your goals shift and your life style changes. And—this is where many investors falter—you have to be ready to make adjustments, sometimes even major changes, when you redefine your goals, or when the investments you've made aren't performing the way you expected.

It can be hard to move in new directions. If you feel comfortable relying on the investments you already know—perhaps CDs, money market accounts, or stock in the company you work for—there's always the temptation to stick with them. And while they may have their place in your investment plan, tying up your money in one or two places exposes you to greater investment risk.

A DISTINCTIVE DIFFERENCE

Saving and investing both have a place in your financial plan, but they're not the same:

Saving is holding money, usually in bank accounts or money market funds, for a specific *short-term* purpose.

Investing is buying things of intrinsic value—particularly mutual funds, stocks, and bonds—that have the potential to provide income or increase in price over the *long term*.

Though your savings earn interest, they may actually shrink in value over time. That's because the interest you earn is rarely more than the rate of inflation. On the other hand, insured savings, such as money market accounts and certificates of deposit (CDs), are well suited for meeting short-term goals, such as the down payment on a home you hope to buy within a year, since your principal is safe.

There's also a middle ground between saving and investing, where short-term bond funds and US Treasury bills fit. You generally earn more than on insured accounts, but the market value of these investments fluctuates as interest rates change.

Understanding Investment Risk

The springboard to successful investing is balancing risk and return.

If you want the rewards of successful investing—financial security and the confidence that comes with taking important steps toward meeting your goals—you have to be willing to take some risks.

That doesn't mean you have to take flying leaps into untested waters. But it does mean you should consider venturing into growth investments, usually stocks and stock mutual funds, even when they lose value in certain periods. The greatest risks novice investors face are concentrating too much on investment income and putting too much money into just a few investments.

HIGHER RISK

- Putting all your money in one investment
- Investing in products you don't understand
- Concentrating on investments that can be eaten away by inflation
- Focusing on quick profits
- Investing money you cannot afford to lose in riskier ventures

- Putting money into newer, untried funds or companies
- Taking more risk with a small percentage of your portfolio
- Expanding your investment portfolio into new or different areas
- Allocating the largest portion of your portfolio to equities

- Investing in a balanced portfolio
- Selecting investments suited to meeting specific goals
- Emphasizing long-term growth

LOWER RISK

WHAT RISK MEANS

Though the biggest investment risk you take is doing nothing at all, the risk you may be most worried about is the possibility of losing your money.

With some investments, the risk of loss can be minimal. If you buy a ten-year US Treasury note when it is issued and keep it until it matures, you'll get back all the money you invested. Plus, you'll have earned ten years of interest.

Sometimes the risk of loss is greater because the investment may not live up to its promise. Buying stock in a start-up company, for example, increases your risk since, statistically, new ventures are more likely to fail than established ones.

While you'll need to take some risk if you're going to invest seriously, you can minimize it by **diversifying**, or spreading your investments around, a principle that's discussed later in this chapter.

STAYING TUNED IN

You can get a better handle on risk by keeping an eye on your investments. You have to evaluate the performance of each investment separately, and be prepared to make adjustments to your portfolio, all the while sticking with your long-term investment plan. All the evidence suggests that starting early and staying with it are crucial to investment success. But the role of individual investments can change, either because they become riskier, provide lower returns, or because they no longer fit into your plan.

RISK MEASUREMENT

You may be willing to take a certain amount of risk if you expect that the long-term return on the investment you're making will be greater than the return on a risk-free investment.

The risk-free investment you typically use as a benchmark in making this comparison is the 13-week US Treasury bill, also referred to as the 90-day bill. A **T-bill** is considered risk free on two counts: Its status as a federal government issue makes it free from the risk of default so you won't lose your principal if you hold it to maturity. And its relatively short term means it's not as vulnerable to inflation as longer-term notes or bonds. The only risk with a T-bill is the possibility that you might have a loss if you sold in the secondary market before expiration.

You can calculate the risk premium over a series of years, though the formula varies for different types of investments. For large-company stocks, for example, you divide the annual total return for that category by the annual total return for Treasury bills. In some years the results are positive—meaning taking the risk paid off—and in some years, they're negative.

One reason experts encourage you to invest in stocks is that in 48 of the 77 years between 1926 and 2003, or roughly 62% of the time, stocks had a positive risk premium. In the other 29 years, the risk premium was negative, though overall, gains have outweighed losses.

Suppose you put money into a global growth fund, with holdings in both US and overseas markets, early in your investing career. As your equity portfolio grows, and you seek more diversification, you might want to invest a larger percentage in overseas markets. So, you might consider moving assets into an international fund and building your US investments separately.

THE RISK OF SAFETY

If you're so worried about the possibility of losing money that you put your money only into investments you consider absolutely safe—like insured CDs or US Treasury bills—you're investing to **preserve principal**. Basically, that means you expect to get back what you put in, plus the interest you earn.

For many people, bank CDs seem the safest investments because they're FDIC-insured. Unlike other investments, where you risk losing money, most bank deposits, including CDs, are guaranteed by the Federal Deposit Insurance Corporation for up to $100,000 per customer. (Remember, though, that the insurance doesn't cover other investments you buy at banks, including mutual funds and annuities.)

As an investment strategy, preservation of principal has its own serious risks. First, insured investments often pay less than uninsured investments. Then, the double blow of taxes and inflation steadily erodes your **real return**, or the purchasing power of what you get back in relation to what you invest.

Preservation of capital may be an appropriate short-term strategy. But for the long term, you probably want to focus on growth.

Managing Risk

Risk won't take you by surprise if you
know where and when to expect it.

The one thing about risk you can be fairly sure of is
that it will pop up from time to time. But when you
accept risk as a normal part of investing, you
can figure out ways to keep the lid on. In fact,
you can come out ahead as a savvy investor
by balancing the various risks you
take to produce a potentially
greater return.

RISK TOLERANCE

Risk doesn't mean the same thing to everybody. That's
because some people can live with—or can afford—more
risk than others.

There's no way around the fact that most investments
will drop in value at some point. That's what risk is all
about. Knowing how to tolerate risk and avoid panic
selling is part of a sound investment strategy.

For example, if your portfolio includes a mutual fund
that concentrates on small companies, it's likely to drop
in value—perhaps significantly—during a market downturn since small-cap companies tend to be among the
most volatile equity investments. But if you switch money
out of this fund in a down period, you lose the potential
increase in value if stocks rebound. You may lose money
as well.

You can build your tolerance—or compensate for
it—in several ways:

1 Remember that over the long haul, taking some risk
may increase return.

2 Maintain a well-diversified portfolio to offset
potential losses.

3 Keep the bulk of your money in investments that
don't require constant monitoring.

4 Discuss any change in investment strategy with
your financial advisor.

BANG FOR YOUR BUCK?

RISK ASSESSMENT

Risk is too complex to measure by any one standard. For example, there's the risk of not earning as much in one place as another, or having an investment do less well than you expected.

When you're trying to figure out how risky an investment could be, you have to factor in a number of different elements.

Management risk exists because the way a mutual fund, a corporation, and even a government performs is often a reflection of the way it is managed. Change in management often signals a shift in strategy. Sometimes that can turn around an ailing company. Or, it might mean abandoning a formula that has worked well for years.

Currency fluctuations affect the value of your overseas investments. While having international holdings in your investment portfolio balances other risks, owning them means you're affected by changes in the value of that currency.

Political climates around the world influence the risks you face in making certain investments. A period of instability in an overseas country, for example, can drive the value of investments in that market down, while political stability and growth can increase value.

MARKET RISK

Market risk is what can happen in the stock and bond markets. If you invest in a profitable stock mutual fund, and the stock market declines, the value of the fund will drop. You might lose money if you have to sell at that point. If you wait until prices rebound and move upwards, you may avoid a loss.

RECESSION RISK

A **recession**, or period of economic slowdown, means investments of all kinds can lose value and make investing seem riskier. Of course, the opposite is true, too. Things seem less risky during periods of prosperity.

INTEREST RATE RISK

Interest rates create several potential risks. When interest rates go up, the price of your existing fixed-income investments, like bonds, declines since they're paying less than newly issued bonds. The money you're earning on those investments will buy less. Plus, higher rates may also mean that stock prices decline as investors put more money into interest-paying investments.

DEFAULT RISK

A bond issuer may **default**, or fail to pay interest on schedule or repay principal at maturity. Since most bonds are not insured, and an issuer who defaults is likely to have massive financial problems, you may never fully collect on the debt. Buying only high-rated bonds limits but doesn't eliminate risk.

DUD

Time and Risk

Quick changes can speed you forward or take the wind out of your sails.

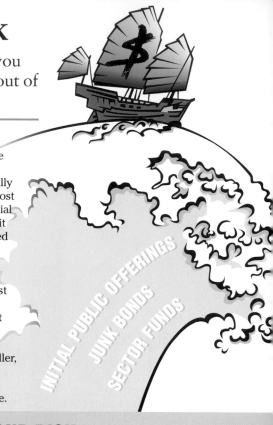

Volatility is the degree to which an investment gains or loses value and the frequency of those changes. The more volatile it is, the more you can potentially make or lose in the short term. But in most cases, if you have a sense of the potential risk involved and the confidence to wait for prices to stabilize, you'll be prepared to ride out the storm.

For example, **equities** (specifically stocks and stock mutual funds) tend to change price more quickly than most **fixed-income** investments (bonds and bank deposits). But it's not always that simple. The price of stock in large, well-established companies tends to change more slowly than stock in smaller, or newer, companies. And the more predictable a company's business, the slower the price fluctuation is apt to be.

Similarly, low-rated, high-yield bonds, often known as junk bonds, and some bond funds fluctuate in price at least as much as stocks, offering some of the same opportunities for gain—and loss. Junk bonds may provide higher income than other bonds in the short term but are more likely to default on their obligations to pay principal and interest, just as some speculative stocks may lose all of their value.

TIME AND RISK

Volatility poses the biggest investment risk in the short term. If you wait, and hold onto your equity investments—specifically your stocks and stock mutual funds—until a market downturn ends and recovery begins, its effect may be reduced. Similarly, if you hold your bond investments until maturity, changing market values have no impact on their par value or their interest payments.

Volatility may pose several serious problems, though. If you have been planning to sell an investment to pay for the down payment on a home, college tuition, or any other goal, you may not have enough to cover your costs if its price has fallen dramatically. Or, you may be so concerned over the falling value of your investment that you sell. Not only does that lock in your loss, but you'll no longer own the investment. If its price rebounds, you can't share in its potential recovery. And, of course, your investment may not recover even if the market rebounds.

Historically, major drops in the stock market—including market crashes and **bear markets**, when the value of stocks drops 20% or more—have been ultimately followed by a period of recovery.

NO PAIN, NO GAIN

Illogical as it may seem, what seems like predictability is sometimes a bigger stumbling block to achieving your long-term investment goals than volatility.

For example, the rate of return on a bank-issued certificate of deposit (CD) is predictable. The problem is that while what you earn on that CD in the short term may be higher than the return on a stock, bond, or mutual fund during a market downturn, it doesn't have the potential to increase in value.

When the CD matures, you can roll the principal and interest into a new CD at whatever the current rate is. But you can't sell the CD for more than you paid for it, and you can't earn more than the current rate that's being offered. What's more, while what you earn on a CD increases when interest rates are high, the real rate of return, after taxes, is rarely greater than the rate of inflation.

WATCHING THE MOVEMENT

If you recognize a certain trend in stock prices, you can turn it to your advantage. For example, some investments, known as **cyclicals**, move in identifiable patterns, up in certain economic climates and down in others.

If you invest when a cyclical stock is down and sell when it's up, you benefit from the movement. One problem, of course, is knowing when to get in and out. Your advisor can help you decide.

Other investments are more volatile and less predictable. For example, technology stocks (and the mutual funds that invest in them) jumped dramatically in value between 1995 and 2000. But in the years before that many of them performed rather poorly. And in 2000, after they hit their peak, many technology stocks plummeted.

If you look at the big picture, you'll discover that what seems to be a huge drop in price often evens out when it is part of a longer-term pattern.

Another way to deal with volatility is to capitalize on it. If an equity increases dramatically in value, you can sell it and make another investment. Then, if the price of the equity you sold drops, you might buy it again and wait for the cycle to repeat itself. The one investment strategy that's pretty much doomed to failure is trying to **time the market**, or predict what the stock and bond markets are going to do in the next day or next week, so you can be in the right place at the right time. It can't be done. Or at least nobody has been able to do it successfully over a period of time.

READING THE WIND

The range between an investment's high and low price over a period of time—often a year—is one measure of its volatility. The smaller the percentage of change, the less volatile the investment.

In this example, you can see that the average year-to-date percentage change (YTD % CHG) has been more dramatic for some stocks than others, as have the differences between high and low prices over the past 52 weeks.

One strategy some investors use to avoid volatility is to sell stock when its price increases or drops a predetermined percent, often in the range of 15% to 20%. One way to handle this approach is to give a **stop** order, instructing your broker or advisor to sell any investment automatically when it drops below the level that you set. However, once the price drops below the stop price, the order becomes a market order, and you may sell for less than you'd like.

TWO FACES OF VOLATILITY

Don't get the mistaken impression that volatility is to be avoided at all costs. It can work in your favor at least as dramatically as it can work against you. A strong stock market may produce rapidly increasing prices in a relatively short time. But, of course, there's no guarantee those prices will hold.

LEVELING OUT YOUR RISK

While the prices of most investments fluctuate, adding volatility to individual and mutual fund portfolios, some investments are more price stable. Sometimes called **noncyclicals**, they include stocks issued by companies whose products and services continue to be in demand whether the economy is expanding or contracting.

Many financial advisors suggest including some of these stocks or mutual funds that emphasize them in your portfolio, both on their own merits and as a counterweight to market ups and downs.

Keeping Ahead of Inflation

You have to be prepared for costs that keep going up.

If your investments are going to help you achieve your financial goals, they have to beat **inflation**, the rate of increase in the cost of practically everything.

FINANCIAL FACTS OF LIFE

The truth about inflation is that you usually need more money every year to pay for the same things. And while you're probably resigned to increases in the cost of dry cleaning, running shoes, or pizza, you've also got to plan for inflation's longer-term effects on the cost of shelter, food, healthcare, or the cost of college.

The higher your **real rate of return**, or what you earn after inflation, the better off you'll be in the long run. That's one reason financial advisors encourage you to include equity investments in your portfolio. While they may disappoint you in some years, their returns have historically outpaced inflation.

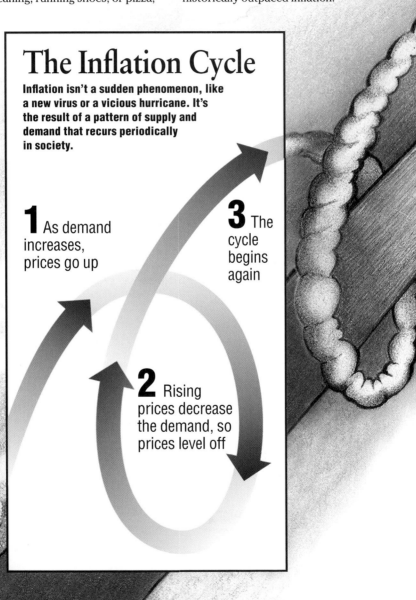

The Inflation Cycle

Inflation isn't a sudden phenomenon, like a new virus or a vicious hurricane. It's the result of a pattern of supply and demand that recurs periodically in society.

1 As demand increases, prices go up

3 The cycle begins again

2 Rising prices decrease the demand, so prices level off

The inflation rate varies from year to year, and since 1980, has averaged

3.8% a year

according to the US Bureau of Labor Statistics. In 1980 it hit 12.5%, and for several years it was less than 2%.

GETTING PERSONAL

It's not that inflation affects you, as a woman, more than it affects a man. But, statistically at least, gradually rising prices will affect you longer because women live, on average, more than five years longer than men. While you're working, what you earn may increase fast enough to offset inflation's bite. Or you can take a second job. But when you retire, you'll still need an ever-larger cash flow to maintain your lifestyle, and do the things that are important to you.

That's one of the reasons that investing in a diversified portfolio of stocks, bonds, and mutual funds is so important. While investment income isn't predictable, any amount that supplements Social Security and a potential pension will be a welcome addition to your retirement budget.

UPS AND DOWNS

As time goes by, the buying power of the dollar declines. That means that if you have the same amount of income each year, your purchasing power gradually shrinks. While stamps aren't the most expensive thing you buy or the most inflationary, the gradual increase in their prices gives you a sense of shrinking buying power.

RISING COST OF POSTAGE

1965	5¢	1985	22¢
1968	6¢	1988	25¢
1971	8¢	1991	29¢
1974	10¢	1995	32¢
1975	13¢	1999	33¢
1978	15¢	2001	34¢
1981	18¢	2002	37¢
1981	20¢		

MEASURING INFLATION

The Consumer Price Index (CPI) is the most widely used measure of inflation. The Bureau of Labor Statistics figures the index each month by computing the percentage of change for a market basket of 80,000 goods and services. The CPI is measured against the reference period 1982-1984. The CPI determines adjustments in Social Security payments, federal income-tax brackets, and a host of other payments and charges.

Building Your Portfolio

As you increase the number and variety of your investments, you're also building your confidence as an investor.

You begin to create a **portfolio**, or collection of investments, the moment you open your first mutual fund account or buy your first stock or bond. If you invest money regularly, you'll be able to diversify your holdings, which allows you to spread your risk. If your investments produce the returns you expect, you can reinvest any income in additional investments. If the returns are negative, you'll need to decide whether it's an opportunity to buy or time to sell.

As you continue to invest, you can gradually buy more stocks, bonds, and mutual funds. You'll also discover newer products, such as managed accounts, which may be well suited to your goals and risk tolerance. The more you know, the more confident you're likely to be in making selections and deciding how to **allocate**, or divide up, the total value of your assets among various investments.

INVESTMENT STYLES

You can invest **conservatively**, which means you expect there's less chance you'll lose what you already have, though your return is likely to be less than with the other alternatives. You can invest **moderately**, which means you may come out with substantially more than you started with, but may also lose some of your investment. Or you can invest **aggressively**, which means you could make a bundle, but could also have big losses.

Or you can do a little of each.

HOW TO BUILD A PORTFOLIO

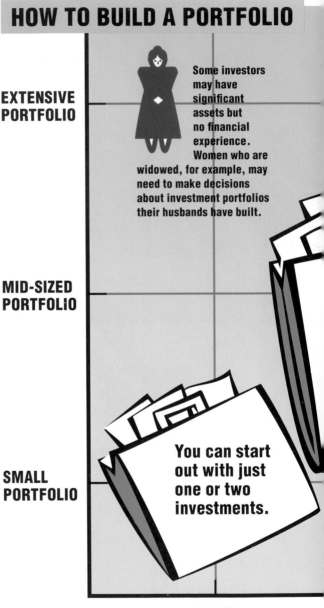

EXTENSIVE PORTFOLIO

Some investors may have significant assets but no financial experience. Women who are widowed, for example, may need to make decisions about investment portfolios their husbands have built.

MID-SIZED PORTFOLIO

SMALL PORTFOLIO

You can start out with just one or two investments.

NOVICE INVESTOR

If you're at the beginning of the investor learning curve or just starting your career as an investor, you may want to move slowly. Whether you're investing money you're accumulating yourself or a lump sum you've just received, it's time to begin building your assets. Many advisors suggest novice investors buy mutual funds.

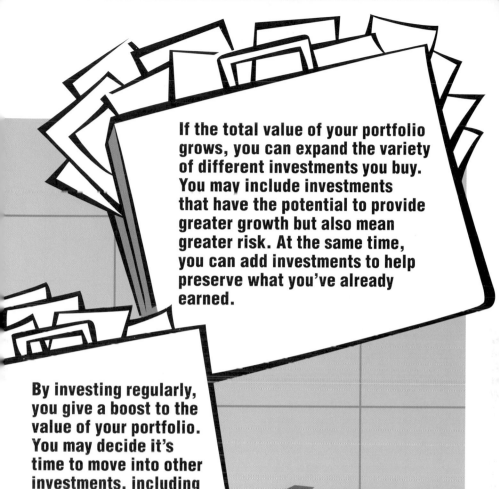

If the total value of your portfolio grows, you can expand the variety of different investments you buy. You may include investments that have the potential to provide greater growth but also mean greater risk. At the same time, you can add investments to help preserve what you've already earned.

By investing regularly, you give a boost to the value of your portfolio. You may decide it's time to move into other investments, including those in international markets.

Some investors begin to develop their financial plans before they have much money to invest. But even small amounts have the potential to grow into sizable portfolios, especially if you add money regularly.

INTERMEDIATE INVESTOR

With your assets and your investing experience growing, you may be ready to make purchases that require larger sums of money. It's also time to work toward a balanced portfolio that includes a variety of different mutual funds, stocks, and bonds. You may be developing your own investment style, too, that reflects your time frame and your tolerance for risk.

EXPERIENCED INVESTOR

The more you know about investing, the greater the challenge—and the fun—of choosing where to put your money. The more money you have to invest, the more diversity you can achieve. With a secure base, you may be ready to try more speculative investments, although the core of your portfolio is likely to be a balance of stocks, bonds, cash, and mutual funds.

Allocating Your Assets

Divide and conquer is often the best way to win your investment battle.

In the end, **asset allocation**—the way you divide your portfolio among **stocks, bonds, and cash**—has the greatest impact on reaching your financial goals. Stocks include stock mutual funds. Bonds include bond mutual funds. Cash is usually invested in money market funds, CDs, and Treasury bills.

Here's why asset allocation is such a critical principle of sound investing:

- **No single investment produces the best return year in and year out**
- **Stocks have historically turned in a strong performance in some years and a weak one in others**
- **Bonds produce better returns in some years and weaker returns in others**
- **Cash usually provides the smallest but most consistent returns**

One word of caution: These results reflect the performance of an entire **asset class**, or group of investments. They don't report the return of any individual stock or bond.

CREATING A FORMULA

As the evidence piles up on the importance of asset allocation, financial experts have devised some formulas for dividing up your overall portfolio.

Don't be confused if you encounter a range of suggested allocations. Brokerage firms and other advisors, for example, modify their recommendations regularly, though rarely dramatically, in response to changes in the economy.

Any standard allocation can be modified to suit your own financial situation

AN AGGRESSIVE APPROACH

80% STOCKS

15% BONDS
5% CASH

and your tolerance for risk. For example, you may decide on a single allocation model—say 60% in stocks, 30% in bonds, and 10% in cash—and stick with it. Or you may decide to modify your allocation over time, perhaps increasing your stock holdings to 80% earlier in your financial life, and reducing them to 40% after you retire.

THROUGH THICK AND THIN

Seeing the wisdom of using an allocation model is the easy part. Sticking with it is often more difficult.

Let's say you divided your $10,000 portfolio into a 60%-30%-10% stock, bond, and cash allocation a year ago.

MARKET UPS AND DOWNS

You can get a sense of the impact of market downturns as well as long-term historical results by considering a hypothetical unmanaged $100,000 portfolio invested 60% in stocks, 30% in bonds, and 10% in cash for one year. The first column shows the result based on the average annual rates of return between 1926 and 2002. The second shows the return for 2000 to 2002.*

	1926 – 2002	2000 – 2002
Stocks	60% @ 10.2%	60% @ −14.4%
Bonds	30% @ 5.9%	30% @ 13.3%
Cash	10% @ 3.8%	10% @ 3.8%
Average Annual Earnings	**+$8,270**	**−$4,270**

*Source: Computed using data from Stocks, Bonds, Bills & Inflation 2003 Yearbook, Ibbotson Associates, Chicago (Annual updates work by Roger G. Ibbotson and Rex A. Sinquefield). Data is based on the S&P 500 Composite Index for stocks, Salomon Brothers Long-Term High Grade Corporate Index for bonds, and a US Treasury one-bill portfolio for cash. Securities in an index are unmanaged and as such do not account for sales charges or management fees. An investor cannot invest directly in an index. Past performance does not guarantee future results.

Since then, the bond market has been booming, and the stock market has faltered. If you add up the value of your investments, your portfolio may have 55% of its value in stocks, 40% in bonds, and 5% in cash.

If you're committed to your strategy, you can either put new investment money into stocks and cash equivalents, to bring the value of your overall holdings back into balance. Or you might sell off some of your bonds or Treasury bills and buy stocks with the proceeds to return to the original balance.

A MODERATE APPROACH

60% STOCKS

30% BONDS

10% CASH

AN EASIER APPROACH
If juggling your investments to keep your allocation mix the way you want it seems complicated, there's an easier strategy. If you're using the moderate approach suggested above, for example, each time you have money to invest—say $1,000—you could put $600 into a stock mutual fund, $300 into a bond fund, and $100 into a money market fund toward the purchase of your next CD or T-bill.

While your overall portfolio may never be allocated as precisely as a hypothetical model, perfection isn't what you're after. But by adding money to all three investment categories, in the approximate proportions you've decided on, you've made asset allocation easier to keep on top of.

And remember, while it may seem smart to keep investing in whichever asset class is hot at the moment, you may increase your risk over time by tampering with your asset allocation.

INTO THE FUTURE
It's just as important to allocate the investments in your retirement funds as it is to direct the money you're investing on your own. That may mean putting a substantial part of your 401(k) or IRA account, for example, into stocks and some into fixed-income investments, though probably little or nothing in cash.

And it also means looking at the bigger picture of your retirement and non-retirement investments together. For example, if you're putting most of your 401(k) money in stock mutual funds, you may want to balance that by putting a larger share of your nonretirement money into fixed-income investments.

Or, if you know you're eligible for a specific, fixed-income pension when you retire, you may want to invest more heavily in stocks on your own. Sorting out all the details and figuring out the best overall allocation is one of the ways working with your financial advisor may make a real difference to your bottom line.

A CONSERVATIVE APPROACH

40% STOCKS

40% BONDS

20% CASH

ADDED FLAVORS
While stocks and bonds are the meat and potatoes of asset allocation, many financial advisors suggest adding a little spice. You could put some money in gold, or funds that invest in gold, some in real estate, and part of your stock allocation in emerging companies.

Branching out can be an acquired taste, though. As you learn more about investing, and have more money to invest, you may decide you're ready for more adventure. Or you may prefer to draw the line at investments you're already comfortable with.

Diversification
Smart investing requires variety and balance.

ONE MODEL OF DIVERSITY

If you woke up one morning $250,000 richer, how would you invest the money? Here's one hypothetical solution that could provide both diversity and balance. You should work out an appropriate model with your financial advisor.

If there were a single, perfect investment, your life as an investor would be a lot easier. But since it doesn't exist, the next best thing is to build your portfolio by balancing a variety of investments that together will help you achieve your goals. As a group, a portfolio of investments can help offset some of the risks that an investment might pose individually. That's what the principle of **diversification** is all about.

GROWTH INVESTMENTS

Blue Chip Stock		Dividend-paying Stock	Emerging Market Fund
International Stock Fund	Stock B	Equity Income Fund	Aggressive Growth Fund
Growth and Income Fund	Index Fund	Stock A	Balanced Fund	Specula-tive Stock

SPECIFIC INVESTMENTS

Step 3: Divide the money allocated to each level of risk among several different investments. You'll find plenty of choices with moderate risk.

ALLOCATION

Step 2: Divide both stock and fixed-income investments into three parts—putting most into moderate-, some into low-, and the least into high-risk investments.

60% MODERATE RISK

30% LOWER RISK

10% HIGHER RISK

GROWTH VS. INCOME

Step 1: Decide how much to allocate to stock and how much to fixed income.

70% STOCK INVESTMENTS

TOTAL WORTH

Creating a diversified portfolio means putting money into a variety of investments following a well-thought out plan.

$250,00

DIVERSITY VS. CHAOS

You won't achieve diversity by buying impulsively when an investment sounds intriguing, or by increasing the sheer number of your investments. If you buy different investments randomly rather than striking a balance, you're more likely to create chaos than diversity.

Strange as it seems, diversity has to be planned with an eye to the present and the future.

For example, if you expect a substantial pension from your employer when you retire, you may not be as concerned with

FINDING THE RIGHT BALANCE

Just as there's no ideal investment, there's no ideal formula for diversifying your investments. What you're looking for is balance.

Some that produce growth	Some that produce income
Some that protect principal	Some that outstrip inflation
Some that do well in economic booms	Some that do well in slow times
Some that are US companies	Some that are international

INCOME INVESTMENTS

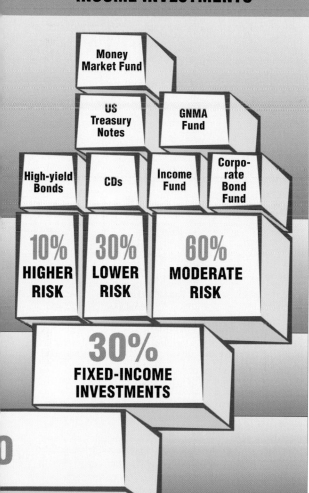

Money Market Fund

US Treasury Notes

GNMA Fund

High-yield Bonds

CDs

Income Fund

Corporate Bond Fund

10% HIGHER RISK

30% LOWER RISK

60% MODERATE RISK

30% FIXED-INCOME INVESTMENTS

income-producing investments as someone who has no pension. But if the company's retirement plan is invested heavily in its own stock, your personal investments probably should be spread around among a broader range of equity and debt.

UNTYING THE KNOT

Single-minded devotion has no place in investing. Loyalty to an investment can hinder you from making intelligent investing decisions. You're especially vulnerable if you concentrate all of your money in one kind of investment—the proverbial risk of putting all your eggs in one basket.

If all your money is in bank CDs and money market mutual funds, for example, you're limiting yourself to lower-yielding, income-producing investments that may lose the battle with inflation.

But it's also risky to buy shares in a half-dozen mutual funds that specialize in small-company growth, or stocks in six pharmaceutical companies—however well they're doing at the moment. The more narrowly focused you are, the more vulnerable you are to changing market conditions.

TOO MUCH OF A GOOD THING

While you can never have too much invested, you can own too many different investments. One clue is having a hard time keeping track of what you have. Many financial advisors suggest that five to eight mutual funds is a reasonable range.

Investing, Tax-Wise

Be tax-smart. Do tax-preferred investing first.

Inflation nibbles away at your investment earnings over the years, but taxes can take big bites every year. The solution isn't out of reach: You can include some tax-saving strategies in your overall financial plan.

Many of these strategies involve long-term investments. But there are other ways to keep a bigger share of your earnings. Your tax advisor can explain how to bunch or defer income into a single tax year, for example, or take advantage of tax deductions and credits.

PERSONAL INCOME TAX

TAX ON INTEREST AND DIVIDEND INCOME

SUPPLEMENTAL INCOME AND LOSS

Tax-Deferred Investing

You can invest money you've earmarked for your long-term goals through a **tax-deferred** retirement account, and postpone paying taxes on your earnings. The account can be a plan your employer provides, one you set up yourself, or a commercial offering like a deferred annuity or certain kinds of life insurance, as long as it meets IRS requirements.

In some cases, tax-deferred plans have the added advantage of reducing your current income, and therefore your taxes, either because your contribution is excluded from your income, or because you can deduct the amount of your contribution when you figure your taxes.

That's why most financial advisors agree that you should probably participate in any tax-deferred retirement plan that's available at your job, even if it's the only investing you're doing. However, there are some contribution limits on the amount you can put into many of your tax-deferred accounts each year. And you will pay a penalty in most cases if you withdraw the money before age 59½.

BITING BACK AT TAXES
One of the least effective tax strategies is having too much withheld from your earned income. If you get a big refund when you file your return, don't think of it as a bonus. Think of it as a tax-free loan you've made to Uncle Sam. You can solve the problem easily by revising your W-4.

TAX EFFICIENCY
When you make investments that are neither tax deferred nor tax exempt, you can still limit the amount of income tax you owe.

- If you hold an investment for more than a year before you sell, you'll owe tax on any increase in value at the lower long-term capital gains rate

- Most domestic stock dividends are taxed at the long-term capital gains rate of 15% or 5%, depending on your tax bracket

- If you own an investment that's worth less than you paid for it, you can sell, take the loss, and use that amount to offset capital gains

- You may also be able to use excess capital losses to offset up to $3,000 per year in ordinary income

PAPER PROFITS

Another way to avoid current taxes is to put some of your money into investments that pay little or nothing now, such as certain stocks, managed accounts, and real estate, but may be valuable later.

There are ways to pass these investments to your heirs without owing tax on the full increase in value. But of course, there is also the risk that your investment will shrink rather than grow in value.

TAX RELIEF

A long-term **capital gain** is the profit you make on an investment you hold for at least a year. Taxes on most long-term capital gains and qualifying stock dividends are figured at the long-term capital gains rate, which is 15% or less, depending on your tax bracket.

TAX ON RETIREMENT INCOME

TAX ON LUMP-SUM DISTRIBUTION

SELF-EMPLOYMENT TAX

SCHEDULE C-BUSINESS INCOME

TAX ON REAL ESTATE INCOME

AND MANY MORE

Tax-Exempt Investing

One way to pay less in income taxes is to invest in tax-exempt **municipal bonds**, or **munis**. They're bonds issued by states, or local governments, usually to raise money for building or improvement projects or to pay for day-to-day operating expenses.

Munis usually pay less interest than comparable taxable corporate or Treasury bonds, but you usually don't owe federal tax on your earnings, though they may be vulnerable to the alternative minimum tax (AMT) and any capital gains may be taxed. Your earnings are often exempt from state tax if the bonds are issued in the state where you live.

Tax-exempt investments can make a lot of sense, especially if you're in the higher tax brackets or if you live in a state with high income tax rates.

CAPITAL GAINS AND LOSSES

You can also open federally tax-exempt investment accounts aimed at meeting specific goals, such as paying education expenses or providing retirement income. But there may be limits on what you can invest, and you must follow the withdrawal rules to enjoy the tax exemption.

TAXABLE EQUIVALENT YIELD

There's an easy formula you can use to figure out how much you'd have to earn on a taxable investment to equal your tax-exempt earnings. Suppose, for example, you can earn 5% tax exempt and you're in the 35% tax bracket. You would need to earn 7.7% on a taxable investment to have the same return.

$$\frac{\text{Tax-exempt yield}}{100 - \text{your tax rate}} = \text{Taxable equivalent yield}$$

for example

$$\frac{5}{100 - 35} = .07692$$

Taxable equivalent yield = 7.7%

Leaving a Legacy

Being able to provide for your loved ones is a major benefit of good financial planning.

A critical part of financial planning is deciding how to share the assets you accumulate during your lifetime with your loved ones and your favorite charities. That includes making gifts to people and institutions, choosing beneficiaries, writing a will, and perhaps creating one or more trusts to establish a legacy for the future.

The more you have acquired, the more important it is to think long term. Not only do you need to decide how to allocate your wealth among the possible recipients. You must also determine whether your assets will be vulnerable to federal and state estate taxes. Part of that process involves estimating what your assets are worth now and what they are likely to be worth in the future.

A TAXING OVERVIEW

The federal government taxes estates whose value is greater than the exemption limit that Congress has established. The good news is that most estates aren't large enough to be taxed. In 2003, you can leave an estate worth $1 million after all tax-free bequests and the costs of settling the estate are deducted. That amount is scheduled to increase gradually through 2009 and be eliminated in 2010, though it may happen sooner. What's more, even if you have sizable assets, there are many legitimate ways to reduce your estate value that may bring it below the taxable level. The complicating factor is that if Congress doesn't act to end estate taxes permanently, they return in 2011 and the tax-exempt limit will go back to $1 million. That uncertainty makes it hard to know what steps to take.

However, a well-drawn estate plan, which you develop with attorneys and accountants who specialize in this area, should allow you to achieve the results you want at the same time it helps protect your assets for your heirs.

MAKING PERSONAL GIFTS

Making tax-free gifts is the simplest and most popular way to reduce your estate, making it less vulnerable to estate taxes—though of course you don't want to give away so much that you leave yourself short of cash.

You can give up to $11,000 a year in cash or property to each person you choose—sometimes called a **donee** or a **beneficiary**—and, if you're married, you and your husband can double that amount. What's more, there's no cap on the number of people to whom you can make annual gifts. For example, if you have 15 grandchildren, you and your husband could give them as much as $330,000 in a single year (15 gifts times $22,000 a gift) without going over the tax-free gift limit. In addition, you could make as many other $11,000 gifts to other people as you wanted to make.

You can also pay medical bills and college tuitions for anyone you choose, provided that you write the checks directly to the institution. Those amounts don't count against the annual per person cap or as income to the beneficiary.

You are also entitled to give away up to a total of $1 million during your lifetime, over and above any annual tax-free gifts, without owing federal gift tax.

Individual states may impose estate taxes on the value of the assets you leave at your death. Rules and rates vary significantly from state to state, so you'll want to ask your legal advisor or estate planner what steps you can take to minimize the taxes that may apply.

DOING WELL BY DOING GOOD

Another way to reduce your estate is by making charitable gifts either during your lifetime, through your will, or with a trust. There's no estate or gift tax on any amounts you give to a legally recognized charitable organization.

Better yet, you can generally deduct cash gifts and the fair market value of property gifts on your income taxes, reducing your current tax bill. But there are limits on what's deductible, so you should talk to your accountant or attorney before you decide on large gifts.

You may also want to discuss **Charitable Remainder Trusts (CRTs)** and **Charitable Lead Trusts (CLTs)** with your attorney. These trusts let you balance or split your gifts between a charity and yourself or your family. With a CRT, you can retain an income from the trust for life with the remainder going to the charity. With a CLT, the charity gets an income for a period of years with the remainder going to your family.

A MARITAL ADVANTAGE

Any gifts you give your husband are also exempt from taxes, provided he is a US citizen. (If he's not, the tax-free cap is $112,000 a year as of 2003.) The same is true of gifts he makes to you. Some attorneys suggest using this rule to equalize the value of what each of you owns individually, potentially allowing both of you to take full advantage of the estate tax exemption by using an exemption equivalent trust to benefit your children.

WHAT'S IN AN ESTATE?

Your estate is the value of what you leave at your death. It includes essentially everything you own individually and your share of anything you own jointly, including:

- Real estate
- Personal property, such as cars, furniture, jewelry, and collectibles
- Retirement plans, including IRAs and annuities
- Bank accounts
- Stocks, bonds, and mutual funds
- Life insurance policies you own
- Income tax refunds you're entitled to
- UGMA and UTMA custodial accounts for which you are the custodian, if you created the accounts

Financial Advice

Expert advice is the key to making strong financial decisions.

If you'd like to have your investments working harder for you, ask yourself if you'd be making better decisions if you were getting professional advice. For most people, the answer is yes.

That's because the difference between getting advice and doing without it is often the difference between moving toward your goals and being stuck where you are.

Financial advice isn't something you save for emergencies. And it's not an admission of ignorance. Rather, advice works best when it's ongoing and goal-oriented, helping you to increase your confidence and your investing skills as you develop a financial strategy and put it into action.

WHAT FINANCIAL GUIDANCE CAN DO

If you work with a financial advisor, what should you expect to gain?

- **Help in defining your goals**
- **Help with understanding and managing risk**
- **Explanations of investment opportunities and common mistakes**
- **A structured, individualized strategy for investing**
- **Advice on specific investments**
- **Help with evaluating how well your investments are meeting your goals**
- **A system for recordkeeping**

FINDING THE RIGHT ADVICE

When you're ready to choose an advisor, you should look for one who'll help you move toward your goals. To make the search easier, it helps if you've thought about the kind of advice you're looking for and the things you want to accomplish. And remember, the choice is yours: Clients pick advisors, not the other way around.

Always ask potential advisors to explain specifically how investments and financial planning strategies they recommend may help you accomplish your goals. The more direct the answer, the better you'll feel about following the advice and developing a working relationship with that advisor.

Look for advisors and financial organizations that stress your investment

ALL IN THE FAMILY

Whether you share an advisor with your husband or companion or choose your own is a matter of personal choice, just as your other financial decisions are. Some couples, for example, keep separate accounts and divide household bills. Others pool their money in a joint account. Both ways work.

Sharing an advisor might make it easier for both of you to balance your portfolios and simplify tax planning. On the other hand, if you're used to making separate financial decisions, or if you feel that your partner's advisor is not interested in your concerns or your questions, finding your own advisor might be the right thing to do.

Your age, the length of your relationship, and other factors can also influence whether it's important to get separate advice. But remember that you're likely to be managing all the investments alone at some point. You don't want to face that responsibility without financial advice from an advisor you know and trust.

WHEN TO GET ADVICE

There's no right time for starting to work with a financial advisor—like your 35th birthday or the day you find the first gray hair. It's one of those situations when it's never too soon—or too late.

But there are occasions that might encourage you to talk to an advisor, either because things are going well or because they're not:

WHEN TIMES ARE GOOD	WHEN THEY'RE NOT SO GOOD
The balance in your savings account is more than three months' salary	You're afraid of losing your job, or don't expect a salary increase
You just received a big raise or a large bonus	You're facing the likelihood of divorce, and you're not sure where you stand financially
You inherited some stocks and bonds, but you don't know whether to hold onto them or sell them	You don't have a savings account or a money market fund
You have several large CDs that are about to mature, and the new interest rate is low	You know you'll need money for certain expenses—like education—but don't know how you can manage it
Your investments are doing well	Your investments have lost value, and you're concerned about future losses

and financial planning concerns. Be alert to advisors who may promote investments or stategies that you don't understand and which they can't explain clearly.

If you use the guidelines for choosing an advisor that are suggested in the following pages—with their emphasis on asking direct questions and checking references—you should be able to find a qualified advisor interested in building a long-lasting relationship that's centered on your goals. If you have specific planning needs—as a business owner, for example—seek an advisor with relevant experience. Professional associations may be a good source of leads.

Sources of Help

If you're looking for professional advice, you can find it.

As you look for expert guidance to help answer your investing, insurance, and tax-planning questions, you may want to consider a team of professionals that includes people with different specialties and different sets of credentials.

For example, you may want to work with a financial planner, an insurance agent, and an accountant to talk about investment strategies, risk management, and the potential tax consequences of your financial decisions. Your team might include three different people, or you might find someone who is licensed to provide both planning and insurance or planning and accounting assistance.

As you look for help, you can use the chart below to get a sense of the primary roles different professionals play and other services they may provide.

HOW ARE THEY PAID?

The way a financial professional is paid depends on the services she provides, which in turn depends on the licenses or other qualifications she has. For example, financial planners who aren't licensed to sell investments may charge an hourly fee. A stockbroker who buys and sells investments for you may charge a commission figured as a percentage of the transaction or an annual fee figured as a percentage of your account value.

Experts you're working with should be willing to explain how they're paid, what the charge covers, and how much you should expect their services to cost.

TYPES OF ADVISORS	PRIMARY ROLE
ATTORNEYS (Specializing in estate planning, tax law)	Provide legal advice as it relates to estate planning, taxes, or other financial matters
BANK INVESTMENT REPRESENTATIVES (Account executive, Financial consultant)	Advise clients on investments through the bank, including annuities, mutual funds, CDs, and money market funds
CERTIFIED PUBLIC ACCOUNTANTS (CPA, PFS)	Provide tax planning, some provide financial planning and investment advice
FINANCIAL PLANNERS	Provide financial planning and investment advice
INSURANCE AGENTS	Provide insurance needs analysis and product recommendations
STOCKBROKERS (Broker, Financial consultant, Financial advisor)	Buy and sell stocks, bonds, and mutual funds

PROFESSIONAL STANDARDS

While some excellent financial advisors have no formal credentials, you can often learn about an advisor's education and experience by his or her professional designations and association memberships. Here are five of the most common and respected ones:

Certified Financial Planner (CFP) from Institute of Certified Financial Planners, Denver. Experience and code of ethics required. Ten-hour exam. Thirty hours continuing education every two years. About 30,000 certified. 888-237-6275 or www.cfp.net.

Chartered Life Underwriter (CLU) and **Chartered Financial Consultant (ChFC)**, designations granted by the American College, Bryn Mawr, PA. Experience and code of ethics required. Thirty hours continuing education every two years. CLUs are insurance agents who offer financial planning, and may qualify for ChFC with additional exams. 888-263-7265 or www.amercoll.edu.

Personal Financial Specialist (PFS) Granted by the American Institute of Certified Public Accountants. Highly selective. Accredits CPAs as financial planners. Involves eight-hour exam. About 3,100 accredited. 888-777-7077 or www.cpapfs.org.

Fee-Only Advisors
National Association of Personal Financial Advisors provides listing for comprehensive fee-only advisors. Almost 1,000 members listed. 800-366-2732 or www.napfa.org.

Masters of Science in Financial Services (MSFS), granted through an accredited master's program in advanced financial planning offered by the American College, Bryn Mawr, PA. Designed for financial service professionals. Thirty-six course credits. 888-263-7265 or www.amercoll.edu.

OTHER SERVICES	WHERE THEY WORK	HOW THEY GET PAID
Prepare legal documents, such as wills, trust documents, and business ownership plans	Private practices, usually law firms	Hourly or flat fee
Referrals for day-to-day banking assistance, like reinvestments, loans, transfers, check orders	In most banks and bank branches, increasingly by phone and computer	Salary, and sometimes commissions on sales of annuities and mutual funds
Offer tax preparation, some licensed to sell securities and insurance	Private practices, ranging from sole practitioners to international companies	Hourly or flat fee
Offer ongoing evaluation of strategy, referrals to other experts	Individually or in local or nationwide planning companies	Fee only, or sometimes commissions if licensed to sell products
Registered representatives licensed to sell investments	Individually and at a wide range of companies and in banks	Primarily commission
Offer advice about specific investments, sometimes as part of an overall financial plan	At brokerage firms, which can be either local or a branch of a national firm	Commission, often based on the number or volume of trades, or annual fee

The Price of Advice

If you know what investment advice costs, you can make better decisions about what you're spending.

A smart consumer knows what things cost, and is willing to pay the price to get what she wants and needs. That attitude is just as important in investing as it is in selecting food, shelter, and clothing.

You can evaluate the advice you're paying for by weighing what it costs against what you gain. If you know, for example, that you'd still be putting off financial planning if you weren't talking regularly to your advisor, you're probably convinced that you're getting your money's worth. Or if you've had help choosing between two insurance alternatives or dividing your investment principal among different asset classes, you're probably well aware of the benefits of professional advice.

Of course, there are times when even the best advice doesn't work, or when investments don't make money. You have to pay for that, too. But over the long haul, most people find that the cost of professional help pays for itself.

FIVE WAYS TO PAY

You pay for financial advice and for the investments you make in one of five ways, depending on the advisor you use and what you buy. Sometimes the cost is built into the price of the investments, sometimes it is added to the cost, and sometimes you pay for advice separately. You should ask for a statement of costs from those advisors who don't provide one automatically.

FEE-ONLY
Fee-only planners charge a fee but don't sell investments or insurance.

FEE-BASED
Fee-based advisors charge a fee and may earn commissions if licensed to sell investments or insurance.

THE COST OF COMMISSIONS

The advantage of up-front sales commissions is that you know from the start what the price will be.

For example, you may pay a commission each time you buy and sell stocks. It's rarely more than 2% of the price for listed stock and can be as little as a flat $9.95 for an online transaction. The charges are added to the purchase price or deducted from the selling price and printed clearly on your confirmation statement.

Commissions on load mutual funds vary from company to company and from fund to fund, and are clearly stated in the fund prospectus. The charges may range up to the NASD limit of 8.5%, though they are typically less. You may also pay marketing and promotion fees on certain mutual funds, known as 12b-1 fees. Typically, the charges are subtracted from the amount you invest to buy or receive when you sell.

Insurance companies also pay salespeople a commission on annuity and life insurance products. The amount is built into the premium you pay.

HANDS-OFF INVESTING

For some extremely wealthy investors, managing a portfolio is a full-time job—for someone else. Well-compensated financial advisors known as money managers are authorized to make all decisions related to their clients' portfolios, including buying and selling investments. These are known as discretionary accounts, and the fee for this advice is usually a percentage of the account value.

DOING IT YOUR WAY

Can you do your planning on your own and use a licensed broker only to buy and sell? Certainly. You'll have no trouble finding someone ready to work with you in that capacity. The biggest problem you may have, if you're like other self-directed investors—especially those that are just starting out—is following through on your intentions.

On the other hand, there's lots of excellent information available about financial planning and investing in books, newspapers, and journals, from mutual fund companies, online over the Internet, and in other computer programs. You can use this information to develop your expertise, define your strategy, and choose investments.

Your investment costs, if you do the spadework yourself, will come from paying the sales commissions on investments that have them, plus management and other fees when they apply.

HOURLY RATES

Some planners charge hourly rates but not annual fees.

SALARIED

Some advisors are paid a salary no matter which investments they sell.

COMMISSIONED

A person who works on commission earns a percentage of any sale as payment for handling the transaction.

CAVEAT EMPTOR

BUYER BEWARE

Some financial professionals who earn high commissions on certain products they sell may not always reveal the amount they stand to gain. In fact, a commission may never be mentioned at all.

Commissions on some types of insurance, for example, may amount to 100% of the first year's premium. However, those costs are often built into the cost of the policy, so you won't know what they are unless you ask. It's not rude to press your questions about costs. It's the only way to decide whether the cost of a product is justified by its value to your plan.

Some investments pay high commissions to the people who sell them:

- **Some fixed-income investments**
- **Some tax-deferred annuities**
- **Unit investment trusts**
- **Limited partnerships**

Set Your Standards

There are some easy steps to follow in hunting for a financial advisor.

Once you've decided to get financial advice, it's time to look for the right person for the job. Where you look—and the advisor you choose—will depend on your goals and the kind of relationship you want to develop. But there's no lack of choice.

Some advisors help you define your financial plan and then refer you to other professionals to put the plan into action. Others specialize in buying and selling financial products you select. And still others are involved in every phase of your financial life.

While the selection process may sound like a lot of work, it really isn't. A good way to begin is by making a list of people to consider for the job:

1 Ask your family, friends, colleagues, or employer if they would recommend the advisors they work with.

2 Consult your accountant or attorney. Someone you already have a good working relationship with may be qualified to provide financial advice or can refer you to people who are.

3 Go to seminars, classes, professional meetings, and community events on managing your financial affairs.

4 Contact the branch manager at brokerage firms, life insurance agencies, or banks. Be sure you make your requirements clear, so that you're directed to advisors with the qualifications you're looking for.

Qualifications to Look For

Just as you would with any person you plan to hire, determine the qualifications your advisor must have.

EXPERIENCE

While new advisors deserve a chance to prove themselves, they don't have to learn at your expense. Make up your mind that anyone you're paying for advice has to have experience.

Five years is a sensible minimum, as is experience working with people whose professions, incomes, or lifestyles are similar to yours. The newer you are to investing, the more important an experienced advisor may be.

REPUTATION

Any advisor you're considering ought to have a good reputation in the field. Referrals from people you trust are important, especially other professionals. Plus, you can—and should—ask for the names of an advisor's current clients with financial situations similar to your own who are willing to act as references.

References are important because there is no complete listing of qualified advisors. Nor does listing, by itself, provide all the information you want.

AFFILIATION

Since well qualified advisors may work independently, for a local firm, or as part of a large regional or national organization, you probably won't end up judging an advisor strictly by his or her affiliation.

Experts don't agree on which affiliation provides the strongest resource. Some point out that large companies provide superior training programs, supervision, and access to research. Others advocate smaller firms where an advisor may be more likely to offer independent advice. They all agree that a proven track record for the person or the firm is critical.

A CALL'S THE WAY

You can telephone each of the people on your preliminary list, explaining that you're looking for a financial advisor. The tone of the conversation and the kind of information you're given can help you decide whether to schedule an interview.

QUESTION: What if you get called by salespeople you don't know with offers of financial advice and investment opportunities?

ANSWER: If their offers seem to fit your overall plan, you could ask them to send you more information. The only thing you should never do is transact business on the spot. And no legitimate advisor expects you to.

SEVEN WARNING SIGNS

Be wary of any advisor who:

- Guarantees you're going to make lots of money
- Insists that an investment has little or no risk
- Doesn't arrange for you to receive official statements showing the current value of your investments
- Advises you to put all of your money in one type of investment or pressures you to act quickly
- Recommends investments you don't recognize and doesn't try to explain them clearly, or says they're too complicated for you to understand
- Argues with or ignores your instructions
- Is vague about the amount of commission or fees he or she will earn

COMPATIBILITY

You've got to be confident in your advisor's skills and feel comfortable working together. Those are judgments you can usually make accurately based on a face-to-face meeting and conversations with some of the advisor's clients.

Some of the things you may find important are building a strong bond with an advisor, being encouraged to ask questions, getting clear explanations about investments and investment costs, being listened to and taken seriously, and being treated with respect.

EXPERTISE

Can you imagine buying glasses from your dentist or letting your travel agent fix your car? The same respect for expertise is important in managing your financial affairs. Your advisor may suggest you consult a CPA, for example, or a retirement planning specialist. He or she can recommend a broker to buy and sell stocks. Expertise does cost money. But it can make a big difference in carrying out your plan.

REGISTERED ADVISORS

Anyone who gets paid for providing investment advice must register as an investment advisor, either with the Securities and Exchange Commission (SEC) or with his or her state securities agency. The exceptions are advisors whose investment advice is incidental to their main business, such as stock-brokers, insurance agents, attorneys, and accountants.

Registered advisors file Part II of Form ADV, which contains a summary of their background and fees. If your prospective advisor is registered, you can ask to see his or her full form by calling the SEC Public Reference Branch (202-942-8090) or going to www.sec.gov. Part I will report certain disciplinary actions against the advisor, but not current complaints, if there are any.

To sell securities, an advisor must be licensed as a registered representative. To get information from NASD about any registered representative, you can call 800-289-9999 or go to www.nasdr.com.

Conduct an Interview

Ask better questions to get better answers.

An interview can make or break any business relationship—especially one that depends on the interaction of advisor and client. But you have to know what you want to find out before the interview starts. And you need a clear sense, afterward, of what was said and promised.

1. Make a List of Questions

Make a list of the questions you want to ask—and be sure you ask them. You don't want to be so distracted or nervous that you miss the information you'll need to make a decision.

Here are some basic questions you might want to include in each interview:

- **What experience do you have, and what is your educational background?**
- **What types of investments do you sell the most?**
- **Who are your typical clients, and what kinds of investments do most of them make?**
- **How will you help me plan for my retirement (or other goals)?**
- **How often will you review my plan?**
- **How will you keep me up to date on my investments?**
- **What continuing services will I get, and how much can I expect to pay each year?**
- **How are you paid for the service you provide?**
- **How are your fees calculated?**
- **What are your ideas about how someone like me should be investing?**
- **Do you have clients who would agree to be references?**

WOMEN AND ADVISORS

As recently as a decade ago, many financial service companies and advisors dismissed women investors as overly cautious, slow decision-makers with few assets and little investing knowledge.

It has become increasingly clear to the financial services industry that women investors want what any investor would want: knowledgeable advisors, clear explanations, time to evaluate their options, and planning. Today, most financial advisors view women investors as valuable clients who deserve their attention and their best efforts.

WEB CHECK

Be sure to ask potential advisors if they have websites. By paying a visit before your interview, you can get a sense of how comprehensive the advisor's services are and how much support material you'll have access to if you decide to work with that person. Being able to talk about what you found there may also make it easier to make conversation as you start the interview.

2. Take Notes

Take notes during the discussion. They'll help you remember what's said—and the very act of taking them may encourage more precise answers.

TEAM EFFORT

Investment groups need financial advisors, too. If you're in the process of setting up a group, you should put together an interview committee to meet with prospective candidates and make recommendations to the whole group. You'll want to ask most of the same questions you'd ask if you were looking for investment guidance for yourself. In addition, discuss the advisor's experience in working with groups, especially groups of women. Among the things you might expect your advisor to provide are seminars on specific topics, as well as investment strategies and specific recommendations for implementing them.

When the client is a group, it's also critical to decide from the start who will give the buy and sell orders, and who will act as liaison to the advisor.

3. Evaluate

Prepare a summary of your impression right after the interview and keep it with your notes. The summary will be especially helpful if you interview advisors over several weeks. Check each advisor's references.

4. Choose

You may find that your decision is obvious, even before you've finished the search. Or you may have to draw up a balance sheet to choose between two candidates. If it's that close, you may find that the reputation of the advisor's firm tilts the scale in one direction or another.

Here are some questions you might want to ask yourself as part of the decision process:

DID THE PERSON I INTERVIEWED

- Treat me with courtesy and respect?
- Listen carefully to my questions and answer them candidly?

DID THE PERSON FIND OUT ABOUT ME AS AN INVESTOR BY

- Asking what my financial goals are?
- Asking about my income and assets?
- Discussing my tolerance for risk?

A TWO-WAY STREET

Interviews are conversations, not performances. The more you know about your goals and your current financial situation, the better you'll be at discussing what you need. And the more eager a qualified advisor will be to work with you.

THE REFERENCE QUESTION

Checking references should be an essential part of your decision-making process, as it should be whenever you hire someone. But knowing you should do it doesn't always make it easier to ask for references or check them.

When you ask your prospective advisor for names, be sure to specify that you want to talk with other clients like yourself—women with similar financial experience, circumstances, or goals. You can expect the advisor to refer you to people who have agreed to talk, presumably because they are pleased with the advice they're getting. You might get the most useful mix, though, if you ask for a list that includes both recent and long-term clients. You should be aware, however, that advisors are not legally required to provide references for potential clients.

When you call, ask each person specifically how she's better off as a result of working with the advisor. Her answer should help give you a sense of the kind of investment or financial planning advice she has received as well as how it meets her goals.

Build a Partnership

When your search for an advisor ends, the work of building a partnership begins.

If the energy you've spent in finding the right financial advisor is going to pay off, it's important to get off to a good start.

Above all, that means being candid about about your goals and your assets. The more specific you can be, the better.

AVOID MISUNDERSTANDINGS

From the outset, you should put a high premium on clear communication. The best way to ensure that you and your advisor understand each other is to put things in writing.

After you meet, ask your advisor to send you a letter summarizing your goals, your willingness to take risk, and your overall financial situation. If the letter reflects what you've said, you should sign and return it, keeping a copy for your records. If the letter is vague or leaves things out, let your advisor know and ask for a more detailed revised statement.

While the misunderstanding may be something your advisor got wrong, you might also have second thoughts about your own instructions when you see them in black and white.

WHAT TO DO

✔ **Insist on periodic meetings to review your plan**

✔ **Read the financial press and material you're given**

✔ **Be inquisitive and ask questions**

✔ **Take a long-term view and give decisions a chance to pay off**

Your part in maintaining a relationship with your advisor means staying actively involved. If you don't stick with your investment program or keep an eye on how effectively your plan is working, nothing will happen. And that won't be your advisor's fault.

You should let your advisor know when you anticipate major changes in your goals or circumstances, since they may require changes in your investment plan. Any advisor will tell you that financial planning is much harder—sometimes even impossible—after the fact.

If you want your advisor to buy or sell investments in your portfolio, you have to give clear instructions. Don't assume your advisor is going to

DO YOUR SHARE

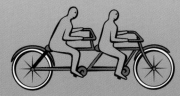

intuit what you want. In any case, you're the boss. It's also a good idea to keep a file of the letters you exchange, your financial statements, and all trade confirmations.

Above all, never hesitate to ask questions, and insist on clear explanations. Part of the advisor's job is to evaluate investments in relation to each other. But you might want to know what the advisor's stake is if you make one investment rather than another. Most important, be sure the recommendation makes sense for you.

LONG-TERM RELATIONSHIPS

Your work together doesn't stop after your initial meetings with your new advisor. After you put your financial plan into action, you'll want to set up regular reviews to reassess your plan. Once a year may be enough. But if you're actively investing, you may want to meet or talk more frequently.

For example, you may want to review the monthly or quarterly reports you receive from your mutual funds, managed accounts, annuity providers, and brokerage firm with your advisor and alter your portfolio when appropriate. And you'll certainly want to discuss any major changes in your personal life that might mean you need more insurance, a college savings plan, or a new estate plan.

TRY AN EXPERIMENT

As you test your new relationship, you might consider starting with a fairly narrow focus. Ask your new advisor to help you invest for a specific purpose, like your daughter's education, or with a specific amount, like your retirement plan payout. Most advisors will be willing to work on a specific assignment.

Of course, you'll have to assess and act on the advice you're given. But you can also evaluate the way in which the advisor makes investment recommendations and explains them to you. If you're satisfied, you can then make a longer-term arrangement to work together.

WHAT NOT TO DO

✓ **Don't be passive**

✓ **Don't agonize**

✓ **Don't have unreasonable expectations**

✓ **Don't expect to have your hand held**

Although you may work with only one professional advisor, some people are more comfortable using more than one. The reason is access to greater expertise.

For example, you may want to talk to a special advisor about your retirement plans. In most cases, your employer sponsored investments will be managed separately from your other investments. However, your retirement portfolio can influence the investment decisions you make elsewhere. For example, if your retirement funds are invested in your employer's company stock, you might decide to avoid buying stocks in the same industry for your personal investment accounts.

You may also work with an accountant or tax attorney, to make certain investment decisions to reduce the amount of tax you or your heirs will owe. Accountants, especially those with financial planning expertise, can also provide a valuable second opinion if you have questions about what other advisors are suggesting.

However, if you're working with an advisor to create a long-term financial plan, it doesn't make sense to keep secrets about decisions you have already made, or the other advisors you're consulting.

CONSIDER A TEAM

Starting to Invest

Advisors can help with both parts of the investment process: choosing investments and making them.

With your goals defined and your plan in place, you're ready to invest. But that doesn't mean you're on your own. Investors and advisors often work together on investment decisions.

First, you have to decide what to buy. Among the things that will influence your decision are the amount of money you have to invest, your tolerance for risk, and the information you have about various investments.

THE RIGHT STUFF

Are you wondering if you have what it takes to invest? Then take another look at the qualities that many financial experts consider crucial to investment success:

● Willing to admit what you don't understand

● Ready to ask questions and look for the answers

GROUP DYNAMICS

You can invest individually, with another person, or as a member of an investment club. Several heads may be better than one, and pooling your money may give you more capital to invest. If you're interested in joining or establishing a club, you may want to visit www.better-investing.org, the website of the National Association of Investors Corporation. Or you can call 877-275-6242 toll free.

● Open to professional advice

● Deliberate in making a long-term plan and sticking to it

● Disciplined enough to invest regularly and reinvest your earnings

● More concerned with meeting your goals than getting rich

PUTTING THE TRADE THROUGH

You may invest by calling your broker—or sometimes a mutual fund or discount brokerage house. You can invest by mail. And, of course, you can join the many people who invest online.

To invest online, you can open a new account with an online brokerage firm, mutual fund company, or other financial institution. Or, if the institution that you currently use offers online trading, you can expand your existing account. Here are some of the benefits of online trading:

● **Lower sales charges**
● **Regularly updated account information**
● **Immediate access to market prices, research, and relevant news stories**

● **Price alerts on investments you own**
● **Opportunity to place buy and sell orders 24 hours a day**
● **Ability to create model portfolios**

One of the potential downsides of online investing, though, is that you don't get the benefit of professional advice when you're ready to authorize a purchase or sale.

COORDINATING YOUR EFFORTS

One advantage of working closely with your financial advisor in making investment decisions is that you'll have help coordinating your various accounts. These might include your retirement and regular portfolios, or the investments you and your husband or partner are making together.

Your advisor can also help you avoid one pitfall that many investors face, by ensuring that your holdings aren't concentrated too heavily in just a few investments. For example, your advisor might suggest ways to balance long-term investments in stocks and stock mutual funds with investments better suited to achieving your more immediate goals.

WRAPPED PACKAGES

Your advisor may offer you a package of services to encourage you to do more business with the company.

Banks often reduce the amount you pay for checking and borrowing if your combined accounts and investments hit a specific level. Typical incentives include no-fee credit cards, free ATM transactions, and lower loan rates. Brokerage firms may offer a package of banking services, including checking accounts, credit cards, and access to loans. They're sometimes referred to as **asset management accounts** and generally include an annual fee based on the value of your account.

ADVICE AND ACTION

While you can make some investments directly if you choose—including US Treasury bonds, some mutual funds, and stocks offered through reinvestment plans—much investing is done through an intermediary. Any investment traded on an exchange, for example, is handled by a licensed broker. Mutual funds and annuities are sold through licensed bank investment representatives, investment or insurance company representatives, and stockbrokers.

If you're an active investor and develop specific criteria for making buy and sell decisions with your advisor, he or she may keep in touch with you regularly, updating you on the overall financial markets and offering specific investment advice. With a cooperative arrangement like that, you can take advantage of opportunities that you might otherwise miss.

Resolving Problems

Being prepared for problems can help you resolve them.

Whenever money is involved, things can go wrong. By knowing the potential for problems in the relationship you have with your advisor, you can minimize the hassle of dealing with them if they do occur.

GETTING THINGS STRAIGHT

When you and your advisor disagree about investment decisions, there are two questions to resolve before you go any further:

- Have you been misled by the information you've been given, or did you misunderstand it?

- Did your advisor misinterpret your wishes, were they ignored, or was there an honest error?

If it was your fault, you'll know better next time. But if the problem is with your advisor, you should act to correct it as quickly as possible.

IF IT'S BROKE

Mistakes do happen when you give buy or sell orders. For example, your stock broker might buy a different stock from the one you intended. Or the money in a mutual fund could be incorrectly transferred. If you catch the error and report it promptly, it may be corrected, or **busted**.

You should call your advisor or broker as soon as you're aware of any problem, ask what happened, and say you want it resolved. That may be all you need to do, especially if it was a misunderstanding. It's always smart, though, to write a letter confirming your call and indicating the resolution that you've agreed to.

If the problem isn't settled promptly, write to your advisor's supervisor. Explain exactly what went wrong and how you would like it corrected. The larger the amount of money involved and the more serious the problem, the more likely it is you may have to seek an outside remedy.

If your complaint isn't handled promptly, you can go to your state's securities division. If that doesn't resolve

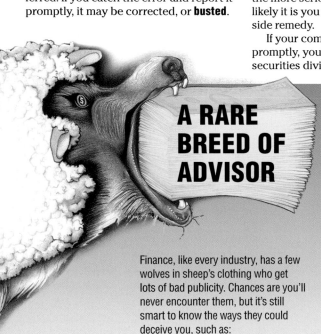

A RARE BREED OF ADVISOR

Finance, like every industry, has a few wolves in sheep's clothing who get lots of bad publicity. Chances are you'll never encounter them, but it's still smart to know the ways they could deceive you, such as:

- Lie about the risks in particular investments

- Buy and sell without your permission

- Sell phony or unregistered investments (which you'll know only when you try to sell them later on)

- Steal from your account (which you'll only know if you read your monthly statement carefully)

- Provide false information about pending lawsuits or other legal matters

BINDING ARBITRATION

Arbitration means that you present your complaint, either on your own or with a lawyer's assistance, to a panel of **arbitrators**, or decision-makers, put together either by one of the securities exchanges (such as the New York Stock Exchange) or by the American Arbitration Association.

The arbitrators use the evidence you and your advisor present to make their decision, which is based on their sense of fairness rather than on legal precedent. In most cases the decision is **binding**, which means it can't be appealed. If you're bringing a case, it pays to be prepared with all the supporting documents you can muster. The better your evidence, the stronger your chances of prevailing.

There's a modest fee for arbitration hearings, usually based on the amount of the claim you're making.

TAKING NOTE

Keep track, in writing, of all the conversations and correspondence with your financial advisor about investment decisions. If your relationship goes sour, you'll have material to bolster your claims. It's easier and more credible than a record you try to create after the fact.

your problem, you may be able to use mediation and finally **binding arbitration**, where a panel of experts will rule on your claim. If you have an unresolved problem with an insurance agent, begin with the agent's supervisor. If unsuccessful, contact your state's insurance commission.

If enough money is involved to make it worth your time and expense, you can take a case to court. But before you decide on arbitration or a lawsuit, you should get good legal advice from a specialist in securities law.

PREVENTABLE PROBLEMS

While it doesn't happen often, sometimes investors have to deal with problems created by their advisors. You can usually avoid these situations, especially if your advisor knows you're paying careful attention to detail and asking hard questions.

That's why many experts suggest you keep your eyes open for these three warning signs:

1 An advisor who urges you to make unsuitable investments or put most of your principal into high-risk stocks or bonds. Although knowing what's unsuitable means being aware of what each type of investment is designed to do, that shouldn't stop you from questioning your advisor's recommendations. Nor should it deter you from investing.

2 An advisor who buys and sells too frequently **churns** your account. It's hard to say what's too frequent, but if you're paying as much or more in commissions as you're making on your investments, that's a sign to act.

3 An advisor who urges you to buy too much on **margin** by borrowing against your account assets.

Insuring the Future

Insurance is part of a complete financial plan.

When you invest, you put part of your income into stocks, bonds, mutual funds, or other assets to help you meet your financial goals. But what happens if you can no longer provide income to invest or even to pay everyday living expenses?

Your illness, disability, or death could radically change your dependents' quality of life and expectations for the future. If you have young children, who will pay their daily expenses and college tuitions? You and your husband or partner may have a mortgage and car payments that neither of you could afford alone. Perhaps your elderly parents depend on your support.

As you create your financial plan, you should consider these risks. To make sure those who depend on you are taken care of, you can buy life insurance and disability insurance to replace your income, and long-term care insurance to pay for extended health-care costs.

LIFE INSURANCE

Life insurance is designed to replace the financial support you would have provided over your expected lifetime. At the minimum, a policy can help your dependents cover immediate costs associated with your death, such as funeral expenses. But life insurance can do more by allowing them to maintain their quality of life and invest for future goals.

Besides using life insurance to provide for dependents, you can explore ways to use the savings component of cash value life insurance to supplement your retirement income. If you plan to leave assets to anyone other than your husband, insurance can be a vital part of your estate plan, to minimize taxes or to make sure heirs receive equal shares of an inheritance.

If you own a business, you can use life insurance to secure your company's finances and future if something should happen to you. You can also offer life insurance as a benefit to attract and keep valuable employees.

Of course, not everyone needs hundreds of thousands of dollars of life insurance in her financial plan. If you're single with no dependents, or if you're older and have met most of your financial obligations, your life insurance needs may be minimal.

STAY AT HOME?

If you're not the family breadwinner, you may still want to consider life insurance to replace the value of the services you provide at home. For instance, if you're a stay-at-home mom, how much would it cost your family to hire someone to do the work you do now?

ESTATE TAXES EXTINCT?

If the value of your estate when you die is above the exemption limit set by law—in 2003, $1 million—your estate owes estate taxes to the IRS. That tax is almost half the value of the taxable estate. Many people have traditionally purchased life insurance to help pay the tax so that assets such as a home or business don't have to be sold to cover the bill.

However, the 2001 Tax Act gradually phases out the estate tax by increasing exemption limits and reducing the tax rate until 2010, when the estate tax is scheduled to be completely repealed—but for one year only.

That's because the law includes a **sunset provision**, which means that in 2011 the exemption limit will revert to $1 million, and the rate will be reinstated as it was in 2001, unless Congress passes new legislation to make the changes permanent. Because at this point there's no way to tell whether the tax will be permanently eliminated, you may want to consider how it could affect your financial plan.

PREPARE FOR SETBACKS

If a disability or serious illness strikes, it can have lasting effects on your finances. If you have dependents, the consequences may be even greater, since you'll still have to provide for their basic living expenses while you're sick.

To prepare for this possibility, you can buy disability insurance to replace a percentage of your income. Without disability insurance, a serious medical condition could make it difficult to pay the bills, and it could throw off your entire financial plan. Not only might you have to stop contributing to your retirement and college investments, but you may find it necessary to plunder them to make ends meet. Even after you go back to work, you may have difficulty restoring your accounts to their previous levels, and you'll have lost any potential earnings you would have received by leaving the money invested.

Furthermore, your financial security could be at risk if you develop a medical condition that leaves you unable to perform the basic, everyday activities of life on your own. Unfortunately, long-term care can be expensive and generally isn't covered by traditional health insurance. You may want to consider buying long-term care insurance, which can help pay for these costs.

Life insurance companies originally did not insure women. When they began doing so in the late 1800s, they charged women higher premiums than men, due to the higher mortality rates associated with childbirth. Today, because women tend to live longer than men, they pay equal or lower life insurance premiums.

A GENDER GAP

53%

47%

While women outnumber men in the US population 51% to 49%, they buy fewer life insurance policies, and their policies have a smaller death benefit, on average, than the policies bought by men. According to a 2003 LIMRA study, men own 53% of the policies that cover adult lives while women own 47%. The average **death benefit** on the policies insuring women is just slightly more than half the face value on the policies insuring men.

Types of Life Insurance
Should you get coverage for a term or for a lifetime?

Before you decide what kind of life insurance policy to buy, you should have a clear picture of what you need the coverage for, how long you'll need it, and how much you can afford to spend on it.

Otherwise you may buy a policy that's ill-suited to your financial plan.

There are two basic kinds of life insurance: term and permanent.

TERM INSURANCE

Term insurance is the simplest type of life insurance. You pay **premiums** to the company that issues the policy you buy, and if you die during the specified term, the company pays a **death benefit** equal to the **face value** of your policy to your **beneficiaries**. If you're alive at the end of the term, the company pays nothing.

Because a term policy provides only insurance coverage, its premiums are much lower than for a permanent policy with an equivalent death benefit. However, there are many kinds of term insurance, so be sure to know what your needs are.

Decreasing term insurance pays a larger death benefit at the beginning of the term and less near the end. It's often sold as mortgage protection, since the benefit decreases with your mortgage balance. Premiums stay the same throughout.

Level term insurance pays the same death benefit if you die at any time during the policy's term, and the premiums stay the same throughout.

Convertible term insurance lets you switch your term policy for a permanent policy with an equivalent death benefit without proving you're in good health. You do pay higher premiums for this flexibility.

Renewable term insurance guarantees you can renew the policy without having to prove you're in good health. However, premiums go up with age.

HOW LONG A TERM?

Annually renewable term is a kind of term insurance that you can renew indefinitely at a higher rate each year. Its initial premiums are low, but if you need term insurance for several years, you're usually better off buying a level term policy.

For example, suppose a 45-year-old woman in perfect health applies for $250,000 in term insurance. One company offers her two term options: a level term policy for ten years with a $338 annual premium and an annually renewable term policy with a $300 initial premium.

While the annually renewable policy looks like a bargain, its premiums will go up every year, at different rates each year. The tenth year, the company will charge her a premium of $468 for the annually renewable policy, while the level term policy premium would remain $338. Over ten years, the annually renewable policy would cost $468 more.

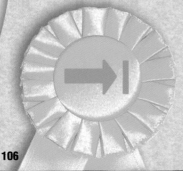

PERMANENT LIFE INSURANCE

While term insurance covers you for a specific period, permanent life insurance covers you for a lifetime. In the beginning, premiums are much higher than they would be for an equivalent amount of term coverage. However, while term insurance gets more expensive each time you renew, permanent insurance premiums are guaranteed as long as you hold the policy.

Furthermore, permanent insurance offers more than a death benefit. Part of your premium pays for insurance coverage and administrative fees, and the rest goes into an account known as the **cash value**, which accumulates tax deferred.

The cash value is your money. You can borrow against it, and in some instances make a withdrawal. However, withdrawals and outstanding loans reduce the death benefit that's paid to your beneficiaries. If you cancel the policy, the company will subtract any charges and fees and pay you the balance as the **cash surrender value.**

Although companies have tailored a vast array of permanent policies to match the complex needs of buyers, there are just a few basic types:

1. Whole life, also known as **straight life**, is the most traditional type of permanent life insurance. Your premiums are guaranteed and may be level, increasing, or decreasing. The insurance company controls how your cash value is invested—usually quite conservatively.

2. Universal life gives you more flexibility with face amount and premium. You can pay a higher premium one year and use the extra cash value to cover the premium another year. You can also increase or decrease the death benefit. Universal life usually involves higher administrative fees than whole life.

3. Variable life is like whole life with a twist: You allocate your cash value among investment options offered by the company. While this gives you the chance to increase your cash value by investing it in the financial markets, it ties the cash value of your policy, and in some cases your death benefit, to the performance of those accounts.

4. Variable universal life has the flexibility of universal life and the investment options of variable life. You can change your level of coverage, vary your premiums, and invest your cash value among the accounts provided by the company. The policy's cash value, and in some cases the death benefit, is based on the performance of the accounts.

5. Survivorship life, also known as **second-to-die**, insures the lives of two people and pays a death benefit only after the death of the second person. Married couples often use survivorship life insurance to cover estate taxes.

YOUR MONEY BACK?

Some insurance companies are **mutual**, meaning they're owned by policyholders, not shareholders. When mutual insurance companies take in more money than they need to cover the cost of providing insurance, they report a **surplus**. In that case, the company decides how much of the surplus to return to owners of participating policies as **dividends** (not to be confused with stock dividends, which are a portion of a corporation's profits). Policy dividends can be used to pay premiums or to buy more coverage. You may also take them as cash. However, dividends aren't guaranteed.

A HOST OF RIDERS

If you have special needs and are willing to pay an extra premium, insurance companies offer **riders**, or options, to customize your policy. Here are a few common riders:

Spouse and children's insurance riders add life insurance coverage for your spouse and children.

Waiver of premium allows you to keep your insurance in force without paying premiums if you have a qualifying disability.

Accidental death or **double indemnity** riders usually pay double the face amount if you die in an accident.

Accelerated death benefit riders give you access to your death benefit while you're alive, to pay for long-term care or treatment for a terminal illness.

How Much Life Insurance?

The right coverage can secure your family's financial future.

You may have heard that your life insurance policy should replace five to seven times your annual income. However, this kind of rough estimate is no substitute for a thorough analysis of your needs. Your insurance agent can help review your life insurance options with you to be sure you buy a policy that fits your financial plan.

First, you should determine what expenses the policy should cover. For most people, the death benefit should pay immediate costs related to your death, help meet your dependents' daily living expenses, and set aside money for college or other needs. Of course, your dependents may need more or less, based on your existing assets, their own income and assets, and whether they'll receive income from Social Security or other sources.

As you get older, your life insurance needs will probably change. For example, having children and buying a home can increase your need for coverage. But as you pay off your mortgage and your kids graduate from college, you may need less. Or you may want to convert to a permanent policy to lock in lower premiums if you know you'll need life insurance later for estate planning purposes. So, it's a good idea to review your life insurance and your financial plan regularly, to be sure you're on track to meet all of your goals.

CALCULATE YOUR NEEDS

Add up the immediate and long-term expenses your death benefit should cover, and subtract other income, as in the following example:

IMMEDIATE AND ONE-TIME EXPENSES

Funeral expenses, costs of settling the estate, unpaid medical bills	**$10,000**
Your outstanding debts (minus mortgage)	**+ $20,000**
One-time contribution for college fund	**+ $120,000**
Total immediate costs	**= $150,000**

DEPENDENTS' ONGOING LIVING EXPENSES

Dependents' annual living expenses (include mortgage payments)		**$85,000**
Subtract spouse or partner's take-home pay	**−**	**$50,000**
Subtract Social Security survivorship benefit	**−**	**$5,000**
Subtract investment income	**−**	**$3,500**
Dependents' annual need for additional income	**=**	**$26,500**
Multiply by the number of years they would need the income	**X**	**20**
Total death benefit for living expenses		**$530,000**
Add immediate costs to amount needed for living expenses		**+ $150,000**
Death benefit needed		**$680,000**

ADD OR SUBTRACT

A life insurance calculator can help you come up with a ballpark figure for your life insurance needs. But it can't take you as an individual into account. You should modify the basic coverage the calculator suggests to come up with a more precise amount—by adding money for special purposes or subtracting things that don't apply. Here are some things you may want to consider:

Some life insurance calculators list your mortgage balance as a one-time expense. If your dependents plan to sell the house at your death, you may want to provide a lump sum to pay off the mortgage. But if they'll continue living in the house, you can include the mortgage payments in your living expenses calculation, as above.

When you calculate your college fund contributions, you may not have to provide enough to pay for a full four years of college if your family invests some of the death benefit in a special education-savings account. And if your children are of widely differing ages or have extraordinary expenses—say, you're supporting a world-class ballerina in the making—you might want to take the extra step of calculating costs for each child separately.

The way your beneficiaries receive the death benefit could also have an impact on the amount they need. While they may choose a lump-sum payment, the insurance company may give them the option to invest the death benefit in an **annuity**. Annuities pay out income based on the amount you invest. There are several annuity options. Beneficiaries receive a fixed amount based on age, paid monthly or annually for life, or an amount that varies with the performance of the investment options you select.

You also need to fit the premiums into your budget. If you buy a policy with premiums you can't afford, you're more likely to let the policy lapse, leaving your dependents' financial security at risk. But if you buy too small a policy, you still leave your dependents' security at risk.

SPECIAL LIFE INSURANCE NEEDS

There are some extraordinary situations that require a more detailed life insurance needs analysis than you can do easily on your own with a basic calculator. If you're facing one of these potentially complex

PAY THE BILLS

Some states are community property states in which married couples share debt. If you live in one of these states, your husband could be liable for your outstanding debts upon your death, or you for his, if he dies first. In other states, your estate is responsible for paying what you owe.

life insurance issues, you may be more comfortable working with an experienced life insurance agent who can suggest solutions that fit in with—and strengthen—your overall financial plan.

For example, if you have a child with special needs, you should consider consulting an agent who has experience working with families like yours and can describe how you can provide for your child's future medical care and quality of life with life insurance and special-needs trusts. You may also want to discuss providing for elderly parents or a spouse whose health may require special care. If your family runs a business, you may also want to talk to an agent who specializes in working with family-run businesses.

Whatever your circumstances, if you have questions about the right amount of life insurance for your needs, you can talk to an agent who can help you understand your options.

SWEET CHARITY

For many people, life insurance is used to comfort and protect family. If you no longer need the policy for your family, you might consider naming a charitable, nonprofit organization as your beneficiary.

You might be able to donate more money through a death benefit than you could afford to give in your lifetime. There may be tax benefits, too, since if you assign complete ownership of your policy to the charity you can deduct the cash value and premiums from your income tax.

Be sure to consult with the charity about your gift, since organizations have different preferences. Some can afford to wait years to collect a death benefit, but others may prefer to use the cash value now.

Qualifying for Coverage
What kind of life insurance risk are you?

Applying for life insurance can be complicated. Often, you need to answer a long list of questions about your medical history and lifestyle and undergo a physical exam. Sometimes you may need to provide blood or urine samples for testing. It may seem intrusive, but it's necessary.

RUNNING THE NUMBERS

Everyone dies eventually. The question is, when? Life insurance is based on a company's ability to calculate the answer, not for you individually, but for all the people who have medical histories and lifestyles similar to yours.

A **mortality table**, created by statistical experts called **actuaries**, shows how many people out of a large, defined group with similar risks can be expected to die this year, next year, and each year after that. Using these tables, insurance companies calculate how much money they will need to pay **claims**, which dictates the premium rates they charge.

If your medical history and lifestyle put you in a group that tends to live to a ripe old age, the company charges you a lower rate, since they expect you to live to pay premiums over a longer time than a high-risk person. If your life expectancy is too short, the company may turn your application down. This evaluation process is called **underwriting**.

IF YOU LIVE TO BE 100

Premiums for traditional permanent life insurance policies were often priced so that the cash value would equal the death benefit at age 100. If the insured person lived to be 100, the policy would end, and the company would issue the policyholder a check for the cash value. Now that more people are living to 100, many policies promise that you can keep them in force no matter how long you live.

FACTORS AFFECTING RISK

Life insurance companies typically consider the following risk factors:

Age: The older you are, the higher your risk.

Sex: Except in states with unisex life insurance laws, most companies consider women a lower risk than men.

Current health: You may have to undergo a medical exam.

Personal health history: The insurer can request your medical records from your doctor.

Family health history: The insurer can also request your family's medical records.

Finances: Your tax records and investment and bank account statements may be up for review.

Personal habits or character: Among other things, the company may check for a criminal record and run a credit check.

Occupation: Some jobs, like coal-mining or stunt work, are considered high risk.

Hobbies: High-risk hobbies, like scuba diving, can affect your rating.

HIGH-RISK WARNINGS

While each company's standards are different, most of them pay close attention to the following warning signs:

Smoking: Tobacco companies may claim their product doesn't cause disease, but life insurance companies beg to differ. Almost every company will charge higher rates if you smoke.

Serious medical conditions: Heart disease, cancer, diabetes, and AIDS, for example, are red flags for insurance companies. Depending on how serious your condition is, the company may agree to insure you at regular rates, higher rates, or not at all.

Sickness in the family: Some serious diseases tend to run in families, such as Huntington's disease, heart disease, stroke, and sickle cell anemia.

IN THE GENES

When an insurance company tests a medical sample, what are they looking for? Naturally, the company is interested in determining if you have any illnesses now. Some companies also test for genetic predisposition to diseases that you may have in the future. For example, you may have a gene that has been linked to an increased risk of breast cancer or Alzheimer's disease.

Is it legal for companies to deny you coverage because of your DNA? While most states prohibit or restrict health insurance companies from denying coverage because of genetic risks, few states have passed similar restrictions for life insurance. To know whether your genes are up for review, check your state's law.

RISK CATEGORIES

The following are the basic risk categories, although many companies divide these into subcategories:

Preferred risk applicants have the longest life expectancy and pay the lowest rates.

Standard risk applicants have average life expectancies and pay standard rates.

Substandard risk applicants have lower life expectancies and pay the highest rates.

Declined or **uninsurable** applicants pose more risk than the company's underwriting standards allow it to insure.

HONESTY IS THE BEST POLICY

Whatever you do, don't lie on your life insurance application. It's illegal, and if the company finds out, it can refuse to pay a claim. However, don't give up if you've been turned down for coverage or rated substandard. You may still be able to obtain life insurance.

For example, you may be eligible for group insurance through an employer or association that guarantees life insurance coverage up to a certain limit without underwriting. You may also be eligible for coverage through your spouse or partner's group policy. Be sure to check your existing policies for options that can increase your coverage. If you have an existing permanent life insurance policy that pays dividends, you may be able to use those dividends to buy more coverage without underwriting.

Also, remember that risk ratings are variable. Sometimes additional information can improve your chance of getting a better rating. For example, a company may lower your rating because you've gone scuba diving. But if you tried it once and hated it, your agent or broker can attach an explanation to your application. You may also be able to improve your rating by changing your lifestyle and reapplying later. You might also get a better rating from another company. Of course, if the rating is too good to be true, be wary, since lax underwriting could put a life insurance company out of business, making your policy worthless.

Ownership and Beneficiaries

Decide carefully who will own your policy, and who will benefit.

If your life is insured by a policy, you're known as the **insured**, and the death benefit goes to your **beneficiaries**. If a policy belongs to you, you're the **policyowner**, which gives you the right to change the beneficiary, assign ownership rights to others, and use the cash value.

While you may prefer to keep the rights of ownership yourself, you may find that you're better off if someone else owns your policy. You should also examine how to divide the proceeds among the beneficiaries to make the most of your life insurance plan.

OUT OF YOUR HANDS

Although you may think estate planning is only for the very rich, if you own your house, a car, investment accounts, assets like jewelry and collectibles, or a business, your estate may come closer to the estate tax exemption limit than you think. If you also own your life insurance policy, when you die the proceeds will be considered part of your estate. Unfortunately, if you haven't planned carefully, the death benefit might push the value of your estate over the exemption limit, triggering estate taxes that could cut into your heirs' inheritance.

You can do three things to keep the death benefit out of your estate and away from estate taxes. You can name your husband as sole beneficiary, since the estate tax doesn't apply to assets you leave your spouse. You can assign ownership of the policy to someone else. Unmarried couples often own each other's policies to avoid estate taxes. You can also assign ownership of the policy to a **trust**.

Experts strongly recommend that if you're considering a trust you get professional help from a lawyer who specializes in estate planning.

THREE-YEAR RULE

If you die within three years of assigning ownership of your existing life insurance policy to a trust, the death benefit is still part of your estate. But if the trust buys a new policy on your life, the three-year rule doesn't apply.

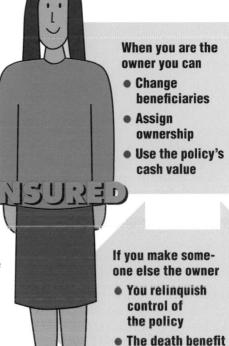

When you are the owner you can
- Change beneficiaries
- Assign ownership
- Use the policy's cash value

If you make someone else the owner
- You relinquish control of the policy
- The death benefit is not part of your estate

INSURABLE INTEREST

To buy an insurance policy on someone's life, you must have an **insurable interest** in that person, which means that you would suffer a financial loss if he or she died. The law assumes you have an insurable interest in your own life and the lives of your spouse and dependents. Others must prove they have an insurable interest if they want to buy a policy on your life.

The buyer only needs to prove an insurable interest at purchase. If circumstances change—such as through divorce or the dissolution of a business partnership—the person named as beneficiary, even if he or she is also the policyholder, can still collect a claim at the death of the insured.

In the days before insurance regulation, anyone could buy a policy on anyone's life, whether that person was family, friend, stranger, or foe. These policies could be morbid wagers, as some people hoped to cash in on the deaths of celebrities and casual acquaintances. Ethics prevailed, and states banned this practice.

Estate taxes may reduce benefit amount

BENEFICIARY

OWNER

No estate taxes will be due on benefit amount

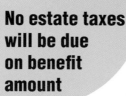

You may also want to use life insurance to equalize inheritances, especially if you'd like to leave assets to children from a previous marriage, or if you have material assets that can't be split evenly. For example, suppose you own a valuable grandfather clock that your daughter has always admired. You'd like to leave it to her but don't want to play favorites. Life insurance can provide an inheritance to your other children equal to the value of the clock. Or you may own a business that you'd like to keep in the family, although some of your children want nothing to do with it. You can leave the business to the children who want it, and provide for the others with life insurance.

If instead you designate your estate as your beneficiary, you can address the death benefit in your will. Estate planning is complicated, and regulations differ from state to state. An estate-planning lawyer can help make sure your arrangements are sound.

DOING THE SPLITS
Some families and corporations divide a life insurance policy's ownership and death benefit to help children or employees buy more coverage than they could afford on their own. This arrangement, called **split-dollar life insurance**, has many variations. In one version, your parent or employer pays the part of the premium that goes into the cash value, and you pay the rest, which covers the cost of term coverage on your life. The parent or employer owns the cash value, and you name beneficiaries. Should you die, the death benefit would pay back your parent or employer for the premiums they put in, and the rest would go to the beneficiaries.

Taxation of split-dollar life insurance is complicated and subject to IRS review, so experts recommend you consult your attorney and financial advisors about current regulations.

WHO GETS THE BENEFIT?
When you name the beneficiaries of your life insurance policy, you should consider how the death benefit will supplement other assets you leave to your heirs, and what the effect will be on the people who receive the money.

You may feel comfortable leaving everything to your husband or partner. But you may want to choose secondary beneficiaries, in case that person is no longer living—if you die together, for example. If the beneficiaries are under 18, a guardian, custodian, or trust must manage the money for them until they reach 18. So if you name children as beneficiaries, you must consider designating someone to manage funds in their interest.

GIVE YOUR LIFE TO CHARITY
The portion of your death benefit payable to a nonprofit charitable organization is deducted from the value of your estate.

Advanced Planning with Life Insurance

If you make the right legal arrangement, you can use life insurance more effectively.

Sometimes complex financial needs call for complex financial planning. Perhaps your assets are substantial and complicated, or you own your own business. You can work with financial advisors and lawyers to use life insurance in legal arrangements that give you more control, reduce potential estate taxes, and accomplish more of your goals.

LIFE INSURANCE TRUSTS

By assigning ownership of your policy to an **irrevocable life insurance trust (ILIT)**, or by having the trust purchase the policy with money you gift to it, you can take the death benefit out of your estate and maintain control over how it's used. You must give up complete ownership to remove the policy from your estate. If you think you may need to use the cash value or want to reserve the right to change beneficiaries, you probably don't want an ILIT.

But, by assigning ownership to a life insurance trust, you gain another kind of control: the ability to specify how the trust distributes the death benefit. If you want part of the death benefit to fund your

child's college tuition, you can instruct the trustees to maintain funds for this purpose. You can also leave the death benefit money in the trust with instructions to provide income to your husband or partner, which keeps the assets out of his or her estate. However, establishing an ILIT is something you don't want to do without legal and tax advice.

How ILITs Work

1 You, the **donor**, set up the trust. You name the trust as the life insurance policyowner and beneficiary. You provide the trust with enough money to pay the premiums. In the trust document, you specify the beneficiaries of the trust.

2 Your **trustees** control the property in the trust, paying the premiums while you're alive and managing the death benefit and distributions after you die. The trustees are generally paid a fee for their services. You can choose to give your trustees wide discretion in managing the trust or restrict their actions.

3 Your **beneficiaries** get their share of the death benefit from the trust.

X

BUY-SELL AGREEMENTS

One of the biggest investments you ever make could be in your own business. You might own a business by yourself, with a partner, or as a **closely held corporation**, which is owned by a limited group of stockholders. If so, your death could throw the company's future into uncertainty. The surviving owners and your heirs would have to determine who gets your share in the company. Discussions could turn into long legal battles that sour relationships and drain money from the business and your heirs. To make the transition easier, you can work with an attorney to create a **business continuation plan**, which irons out what happens to a company if an owner dies.

One popular business continuation plan is a **buy-sell agreement** funded with life insurance. There are several ways to structure a buy-sell agreement. Basically, the agreement ensures that if an owner dies, the surviving owners must buy the deceased person's share of the business at a set price. For example, suppose you own a business with a partner. Your buy-sell agreement could set the value of each share of the business at $500,000. Each of you would buy a life insurance policy on the other's life with a death benefit of $500,000. That way if you died, your business partner would immediately have the money to buy out your share of the business, and vice versa.

You can also set up a buy-sell agreement with a chosen successor, such as an employee or relative you trust to run the business after you're gone. In that case, your successor would be the beneficiary of a policy on your life that pays out enough to buy your share of the business at your death. Here, too, you'll want professional advice before signing any documents.

KEY EMPLOYEE INSURANCE

What if one of your employees is so valuable and irreplaceable that his or her death would spell financial disaster for your company? You can buy life insurance on a **key employee** to protect your business from that financial risk.

Just remember to approach your employee first. Most states require either that you notify your employee about the reasons for the insurance coverage or that you get your employee's written consent.

TIME MATTERS

When you move assets into a trust to take them out of your estate, the three-year rule applies. In brief, that means the transaction must have occurred at least three years before your death to be effective. Otherwise the assets are considered yours.

DEFERRED COMPENSATION

Deferred compensation is a way to offer an incentive for employees to stay with the company. The employee agrees to defer income now and receive benefits later.

Unlike benefits such as a 401(k) plan, deferred compensation isn't a qualified plan. You can offer it to some employees and not others, and you can choose when to start paying benefits.

For example, you may have a well-compensated employee you'd hate to lose. You can set up a plan in which she agrees to freeze her salary in exchange for $5,000 a month after age 65. By forgoing raises, she stays in a lower tax bracket.

To make this plan work, you can buy a large permanent policy on her life. When she retires, you use the cash value to pay the deferred compensation. If she dies before retirement, her beneficiaries get the death benefit. However, if she leaves the company, she forfeits the future income. That's why deferred compensation has been nicknamed *golden handcuffs*.

Tax rules that apply to arrangements like this are complex, though, so be sure to consult a qualified advisor.

115

Disability Insurance

Disability insurance replaces part of your income if you're unable to work.

As you set your financial and investment goals, it's natural to assume you'll earn a steady income and make regular investments over time. But what happens to your goals and even to your day-to-day financial security if you're disabled and unable to work?

Disability can be a double-edged sword. It reduces your income, and it may also increase your medical expenses. If others depend on your income, your disability may end up affecting their quality of life and prospects for the future as well. To protect your financial security and the people who depend on you, you can buy **disability insurance**, which replaces part of your income while you're unable to work.

Your employer may offer disability insurance at a low group rate or at no cost to you. You may also be eligible for coverage through your husband's or partner's employer, and vice versa. Either way, a group plan is usually the most economical solution. However, if there's no plan at work, or if your employer's disability policy won't cover your total expenses, you may want to consider an individual policy.

HOW BENEFITS WORK

Most disability policies pay a percentage of your monthly salary, usually between 50% and 70%, up to a **cap**, or limit. If you make $7,000 a month and your policy pays 60% of your income, you'll receive a disability check of 60% of $7,000, which is $4,200. However, if the policy caps payments at $10,000, you won't receive more than $10,000 a month, no matter how high your salary is.

Disability policies also offer varying periods of coverage. You could buy insurance that would provide income for a year, two, or up to five years, or one that would pay benefits until age 65. Such added benefits usually increase the cost of the premiums.

ESTIMATING EXPENSES

To get a rough estimate of how much income you would need to replace, add up your expenses and subtract the amount that would be covered by your spouse or partner's income and by investment income.

Among the expenses to consider are:

- Mortgage or rent, including any property tax
- Food
- Clothing
- Medical expenses
- Car payments
- Credit card payments
- Loan payments
- Utilities
- Insurance premiums (home, car, health, and life)
- Monthly savings and investment contributions

WHAT'S A DISABILITY?

Insurers and the government are strict about what constitutes disability. To collect Social Security disability benefits, you must be unable to earn more than $800 a month at any job, and your disability must be expected to last at least a year or to end in death. Some insurance policies apply stricter rules, but some are more flexible.

One type of disability policy called **own-occupation** or **own-occ** will pay benefits to you if your condition prevents

you from doing your own skilled work. So, if you're a doctor, you can start receiving benefits if you're unable to practice medicine, even if you're able to do other types of work. For that reason, own-occ policies are popular among skilled professionals and executives who are willing to pay the higher premiums. Other policies will not pay if you're able to do any work at all.

If you're considering any policy, read it carefully to find out what it does and does not cover. Many policies exclude disabilities that are the result of drug abuse, attempted suicide, or criminal actions on your part, and some may refuse to cover disabilities that result from a pre-existing condition.

WHILE YOU WAIT

It takes a while for disability benefits to kick in—usually 90 days—but you can buy policies with shorter or longer waiting periods. The longer the waiting period, also known as the **elimination period**, the lower the cost of insurance. You'll receive your disability checks at the end of the month, so a 90-day waiting period may translate into four months between the first day you're considered disabled and when you receive the check. That's why experts recommend keeping some of your cash in liquid accounts, so you can use it in an emergency.

COMPARE POLICIES

Check for the following features as you compare policies:

Renewability. Some policies allow you to renew at the end of your coverage period.

Cost of living adjustments. Consider whether the policy increases benefits as the cost of living goes up.

Waiver of premium. This feature allows you to stop paying premiums on your disability policy while you're receiving benefits.

Residual or partial disability. If you're partially disabled and lose some, but not all, of your salary, this feature allows you to collect a portion of your benefits.

IF YOU'RE SELF-EMPLOYED

If you're self-employed or own your own business, you can imagine the effect your disability might have on your business, especially if your participation is so vital that day-to-day activities would be disrupted. Unless you have low-cost group insurance, your medical costs could be higher too.

If your business isn't incorporated and you can't pay your bills, creditors may have the right to repossess your personal property. In short, disability insurance can be especially important for the self-employed.

Besides the usual income-replacement insurance, you may want to buy **business overhead expense insurance** to cover your business's normal operating expenses in case of your disability. That way your business may pay bills and even maintain normal operations while you recover. By keeping it solvent, you may also make the business more attractive to buyers if you decide to sell.

TAX FACT

If you pay your disability insurance premiums, your benefits aren't taxable income. But if your employer pays your premiums and doesn't include those premiums in your annual income reported in your W-2, the benefits are taxed.

Long-Term Care Insurance

Women are at greater risk of needing long-term care.

Long-term care (LTC) is a broad term, covering everything from around-the-clock nursing home care to once-a-week assistance from a relative. Long-term care is **custodial care**—help with ordinary, everyday activities—not medical care. As such, traditional health insurance and Medicare don't cover it. It can be expensive. The average cost for a year of nursing home care is $56,575, though it's significantly higher in some areas. For home care, the average annual cost is $47,800. Those costs rise about 7% a year.

If you're in the prime of life, planning for long-term care might seem less urgent than investing for your child's college tuition, a down payment on a home, or retirement. You might assume you'll never need it. You may be right. If so, you're luckier than most women. Studies show that over 50% of women will need nursing home care after they retire, and many others will need some kind of care at home. By contrast, only one out of three men will need long-term care.

There are four ways to address long-term care in your financial plan:

1 You can plan to pay for care yourself, which may be easiest if you have over $2 million in assets.

2 You can rely on Medicaid after you've exhausted your own assets.

3 You can count on family members or friends to provide care for you.

4 You can buy long-term care insurance to help pay for care.

Long-term care insurance can help you protect your assets, maintain independence, and expand your choices for care. There are some issues, though. The premiums are relatively expensive. Some policies make it difficult to qualify for benefits. And there's no guarantee you'll ever need to use the policy, in which case you get nothing in return for your premiums. Experts recommend you review your options with a financial planner or attorney who can help you make an informed decision.

TAX TIP
Some states offer income tax deductions or credits if you pay long-term care insurance premiums. Your tax advisor can tell you whether you qualify.

LTC INSURANCE BENEFITS

There are two ways that long-term care insurance policies can pay benefits: by reimbursing you after you submit claims, or by **indemnity**, which pays you a fixed daily benefit for every day you need care.

Look for policies that adjust for inflation, either by increasing the benefit by a fixed percentage every year or by a rate determined by an actual measure of inflation, such as the **Consumer Price Index (CPI)**. Otherwise, a benefit that seems sufficient today could fall far short of what you need years later.

COST OF LTC INSURANCE

Since long-term care insurance policies are customized for individual buyers, what you pay for coverage depends on some fixed factors, such as your age and health, and on the specific features you choose. In general, the longer your coverage lasts, the larger your potential benefit, and the less time you have to wait to receive benefits, the more expensive your policy will be.

Age: The older you are, the higher the premium.

Health: You'll need to answer questions about your medical history.

Length of time you'll receive benefits: Some policies pay benefits for two to five years, and some pay benefits for your lifetime.

Elimination period: You probably have to pay for care on your own for a set time before benefits kick in.

Type of care: The policy may cover nursing home care, home healthcare, or both.

Daily benefit: Most policies pay $50 to $250 per day, either by claims reimbursement or by indemnity.

Maximum benefit: Most policies set a limit, or cap, on the total benefits you can receive.

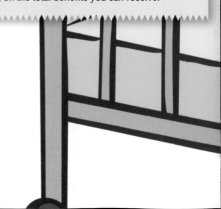

QUALIFYING FOR BENEFITS

Some policies pay benefits if your doctor deems it necessary. Other policies pay benefits only if the insurance company's medical examiner agrees.

Many policies pay benefits based on a list of **activities of daily living (ADLs)**. These include getting out of bed, moving around the house, eating, bathing, dressing, and using the toilet. The policy will pay benefits if you need assistance performing a specific number of ADLs. Experts recommend you look for a policy that requires help with no more than two ADLs.

Think twice about buying a policy that requires prior hospitalization to qualify for benefits, since many people who need long-term care have chronic, deteriorating conditions that don't result in hospitalization. You may also want to check if the policy covers care that results from a loss of mental faculties, such as occurs with Alzheimer's.

Furthermore, consider the policy's restrictions on care providers. Some policies pay only for care from certified healthcare professionals or nursing homes certified by Medicare. Yet, some high-quality nursing homes and care providers aren't certified. Certain nursing homes even refuse Medicare patients entirely. If you want more choices, you might want to pay more for a flexible policy.

WHEN TO BUY

The average age for a long-term care insurance claim is 78. However, if you wait until you're retired to buy a long-term care policy, your premiums may be too high for you to manage on your retirement income. But if you buy a policy too early, you may end up paying more in premiums.

Most experts suggest that you consider buying long-term care insurance in your 50s or early 60s. By then you may need less life insurance, which could free up money for long-term care insurance premiums. You may also be able to find a policy that offers 10- or 20-year payment options, which allow you to finish paying for coverage by the time you're 65 or when you retire.

LINKED BENEFIT POLICIES

As an alternative to traditional long-term care insurance, you can buy a life insurance policy that accelerates or prepays the death benefit if you need long-term care. This type of plan may be especially attractive if you're financially secure, prefer to pay a single premium, and like the idea that if you use only a portion of the death benefit paying for long-term care, your heirs will receive the balance.

You'll want to check the ratings of the companies whose policies you're considering. If a policy issuer has a long tradition and sufficient assets, you can be more confident your coverage will be in place when you need it.

CARING FOR PARENTS

You might consider long-term care insurance as a way to provide care for your elderly parents without having to dip into your own savings or retirement accounts.

50% OF WOMEN WILL NEED LONG-TERM CARE

WOMEN AND LONG-TERM CARE

- On average, women live five and a half years longer than men
- Older women are more likely than men to live alone
- Women over 65 are more likely than men over 65 to need help with daily living
- Women are more likely to take care of others, using their own assets to do so
- The average woman over age 65 has an income of about $13,000 per year

Source: Women's Institute for a Secure Retirement, 2000

Moving Ahead Toward Your Goals

If you know where you want to be, you can plan the route and set the pace.

Staying focused on the financial goals that are really important to you can inspire you to increase the amount you're adding to your saving and investing accounts each pay period. And it can provide the motivation you need to keep on top of the progress you're making toward those goals.

Some of your aspirations may be ones that other women share. You may want to buy your first home or trade up to one that better meets your needs. If you have children, one of your primary goals may be ensuring that you'll be able to afford tuition at the colleges or universities where they really want to go. And, if you're thinking about retirement at all, you probably know that you want to be financially secure enough to be able to live comfortably and to do the things that are important to you.

One of the challenges in trying to balance these potentially competing goals—and others that may be more uniquely your own—is figuring out how you can shift the emphasis to focus on one or the other at a certain time without losing sight of your big financial picture.

10% HERE AND 10% THERE

You think you can't afford to invest 10% of your income? Try calculating it this way:

1. **Multiply your annual income by 10% (0.10)**
2. **Divide the answer by 52**
3. **Divide the answer by 7**

That's the amount you need to set aside each day to invest 10%.

If you wrote your investment account a check for the weekly amount every Monday morning, or better yet had it debited directly from your checking account, you'd probably never miss the money. And, at the end of the year, you'd have something to show for your efforts.

MAKING DREAMS A REALITY

Your financial goals don't have to be limited to big-ticket items or meeting family responsibilities. If your dream is taking a year off to travel around the world, there's no reason not to pursue it. If what you want to do most of all is get an advanced degree and switch careers, saving enough to cover tuition may take center stage. Or if you want to be able to plan your daughter's wedding or your parents' 50th wedding anniversary without having to count every penny, your focus may be on short-term investing.

SPECIALIZED INVESTMENTS

Because the income taxes you're responsible for paying require a significant percentage of your income—perhaps some that you would otherwise invest—the federal government offers some tax benefits as an investment incentive.

Taxes on earnings in certain retirement savings plans are deferred until you withdraw the money. In other retirement plans, earnings are totally tax free if you follow the withdrawal rules and satisfy other requirements.

Earnings in designated education investments, including 529 plans, Coverdell education savings accounts (ESAs), and, in some cases, US savings bonds, are also tax free if you use the money to pay for qualified education expenses and meet the other requirements.

And while investments you make to accumulate money for a down payment on a home don't get special treatment, you may be entitled to deduct some or all of your mortgage interest and local real estate taxes on your federal tax return, reducing what you owe.

While these breaks may not make you feel any better about paying taxes, they may encourage you to invest more.

MAJOR FINANCIAL GOALS

 Buying a Home

 Paying for College

 Planning Retirement

To Buy or Not to Buy?

That may be the question. The answer is both personal and financial.

If you're planning to buy a home, you probably have good reasons for your decision. It may be that you share the feeling that owning your own home is a key part of the American dream. But there are also financial issues involved in buying real estate that you need to consider as well.

From one perspective, a home is an investment, maybe the single largest one you'll ever make.

Like certain other investments, real estate has the potential to increase in value over the years, so that you can sell it for more than you paid.

But unlike investing in equities such as stock or mutual funds, which you buy as a way to achieve your financial goals, most people consider owning a home as an end in itself.

FOR SALE

REASONS TO BUY

There are strong emotional reasons for buying a home—and potentially stronger financial reasons.

Owning can help you feel grounded, and part of a community. It can provide a sense of accomplishment and a place to build family traditions. Often, you have more space than you would in a rental unit that costs the same amount of money. And owning can save you money.

That's because you can deduct mortgage interest you pay on your primary home and a second home when you file your federal income tax return. You can also deduct real estate taxes you pay to local governments. Those deductions have the potential to reduce your taxes significantly, especially in the first few years after you buy when the bulk of your mortgage payments goes to pay interest.

REASONS TO RENT

On the other hand, you might decide to rent rather than buy a home for practical and financial reasons.

If you're on your own, for example, getting together a down payment and managing the expense of a mortgage, taxes, insurance, and upkeep may put too great a strain on your budget. And having all your assets tied up in your home has serious drawbacks. Among other things, it limits your ability to invest enough to meet the other goals that are important to you.

Another reason to rent is a job that keeps you on the move or requires you

LACK OF LIQUIDITY IS ONE OF THE MAJOR PROBLEMS WITH INVESTING IN REAL ESTATE

to relocate periodically. It's not always easy to sell when you're transferred or change jobs. While your employer may help out with the cost of selling one home and buying another, you can't count on it. And the most expensive part of buying is the one-time, up-front costs.

122

FAMILY GIFTS

If your parents or grandparents are willing to help you out with buying a home, each of them can give you a tax-free gift of up to $11,000 a year. It's a case where a timely gift may make a lot more sense than an inheritance.

Be careful, though. Gifts over the limit may be taxable for the giver. And loans from family members earn **imputed interest** if the lender doesn't charge you any—or enough—interest. That means he or she has to pay income tax on the interest that normally would be paid. One exception occurs when a parent's loan enables a child with no investment income to buy a home.

HOW BUYING WORKS

There are usually three distinct phases in buying a home: accumulating the down payment, finding a mortgage, and building your equity.

1 Generally you need a **down payment** of at least 10% and sometimes as much as 20% of the purchase price available in cash in order to buy. You can also investigate some federal and state programs, like those run by the Federal Housing Administration (FHA), which require a smaller amount up front. Your attorney or real estate agent should be able to tell you about special programs.

2 When you have enough for a down payment, you can begin looking for a home and a mortgage. A **mortgage** is a long-term loan that provides the money you need to buy the home. You pay the loan back, usually in monthly installments over a 10- to 30-year period.

3 When you've arranged your mortgage and bought your home, you gradually build your **equity**, or ownership, by paying off the mortgage. In most cases your monthly payment will also include enough to cover the real estate taxes and insurance on the property.

INVESTING FOR A DOWN PAYMENT

If you're planning to buy your first home, you'll have to decide how to invest the money you're using for a down payment.

Timing is a major consideration. The sooner you plan to buy, the fewer risks you may want to take. You probably don't want to be in a position to have to sell investments if their price drops suddenly, or risk having to postpone your plans. On the other hand, the more price-stable an investment is, the less you'll earn on it.

One technique advisors suggest is to split up the money you are accumulating, putting part in mutual funds and stocks, and the balance in interest-bearing investments that will mature when you plan to buy.

You could also set goals for equity investments, in either price gain or total return, and sell if an investment reaches that level. That's a different approach from buy-and-hold investing, but it could help you to build your down payment.

GENDER ISSUES

If you're single, it may be harder to get a mortgage than if you're married, and harder than if you were a single man. While it's illegal to discriminate based on age, race, or gender, a lender can always turn you down.

Sometimes you can make out better applying to a bank or credit union you already have a relationship with, or using a mortgage broker who specializes in finding interested lenders. You might also consider a private arrangement with sellers who would be willing to finance the purchase—although you don't want to do that without the advice of a real estate lawyer you trust.

Qualifying for a Mortgage

The path to a mortgage isn't always a straight line, even when you have good directions.

You can take a mortgage from commercial banks, savings banks, credit unions, mortgage banks (also called mortgage loan companies), and other financial services companies. If you already have an account with a lender, you may want to check there first to see if you qualify for a preferred rate. However, it usually pays to shop around before you apply to get the best rate and the lowest closing costs.

You probably won't know the exact interest rate you'll pay on your mortgage before you sign the final papers, though you may be able to lock in the rate that's available when you apply. That assurance may be a deciding factor in selecting the lender.

If your initial application is rejected, or if you aren't sure how to find a lender, you might decide to work with a **mortgage broker**, a person whose job is to match you with a lender.

APPLY HERE

① Package your financial information, putting your assets and liabilities in the best possible light. Regular employment, little debt, good credit, and investment assets can help.

As a general rule, you can afford to buy a house that costs up to 2½ times your annual income.

WHAT LENDERS WANT TO SEE

Lenders evaluate your application to decide if you're a good investment risk. In most cases, they use criteria set by Fannie Mae and Freddie Mac, companies that buy mortgages from lenders. Here's an overview of those standards:

- No more than 28% of your total income needed to pay mortgage, insurance, and taxes
- A good credit record, as loan defaults and a history of late payments are a problem

- No more than 36% of your total income needed to pay your mortgage plus debts, as large credit card balances can be a problem
- A history of regular employment at a full-time job

② Look for the lowest rate mortgage you qualify for to reduce the interest you'll owe.

MORTGAGE RATES

The interest rate you're able to arrange on your mortgage is determined primarily by the general interest rates at the time you borrow and your credit rating. When rates are low, you pay less. And if they're high, you pay more. Both the rate you pay, and the **term**, or length, of your loan make a big difference in what it will cost you to buy.

This chart gives you a quick sense of the difference the rate makes on the monthly payment of a 30-year fixed-rate $125,000 mortgage:

Interest rate	6%	8%	10%	12%
Monthly payment	$749	$917	$1,097	$1,285

3 Decide which is more important: fixed payments or a lower initial rate. That will help you choose the type of mortgage.

MORTGAGE TYPES

Most lenders offer both fixed-rate and adjustable-rate mortgages. With a **fixed-rate mortgage**, the amount of interest you owe is set when you borrow because the rate stays the same over the length of the loan.

With an **adjustable-rate mortgage**, the interest rate, and amount of interest you pay, rises or falls as interest rates in general move up or down.

The appeal of a fixed-rate loan is that you know what your housing expenses will be, so you can plan your budget more easily. But an adjustable-rate loan is usually cheaper initially, so it may be easier to qualify for.

You can sometimes find a hybrid mortgage at a lower rate than a regular fixed-rate loan, which lets you plan your costs for the first few years. The most appealing have fixed rates for three, seven, or ten years, and then adjust every year.

You'll also need 5% to 10% of your new home's cost in cash to close the deal.

FIXED
ADJUSTABLE
PRIME

You'll want to discuss your choices with your lender or financial advisor to select the one that's best for you.

4 Don't focus only on getting things done easily. Focus on getting a good deal on your mortgage.

MORTGAGE SHORTCUTS

The usual approach is to find the property you want and then go looking for a mortgage. But sometimes, when lenders have mortgage money available, they may offer you a chance to **prequalify**. That means you apply for a mortgage before you have chosen a home to buy. The lender will let you know how much you can borrow and confirm that the money is available.

Prequalifying is probably worth doing if you're serious about buying, since you can shop with more confidence if you know how much you can afford. But there is a charge, so it's not something you want to do lightly.

Another way to simplify buying is to look at new construction rather than buy from a previous owner. Sometimes a builder is able to negotiate with a lender for lower rates or quicker approval than you could get on your own. But always check first to be sure it is the best deal you can get.

5 Work with a real estate lawyer to be sure you don't miss any important details about what you owe, the terms of repayment, and any fees or penalties.

6 If you're turned down for a mortgage, insist on an explanation of the reasons.

EXTRA HELP

Mortgage research firms, like HSH Associates, provide a list of lenders and current rates in your area for a small fee. You can reach them at 800-873-2837 or www.hsh.com. If you know what the going rates are, you'll be able to make better-informed choices.

APPROVED

Building Equity

As you gradually pay off your mortgage, you own a bigger share of your home.

When you buy a home and make a down payment, you have **equity**, or a percentage of ownership, in the property. However, your equity changes as you pay off your mortgage loan and the value of the home changes with market conditions.

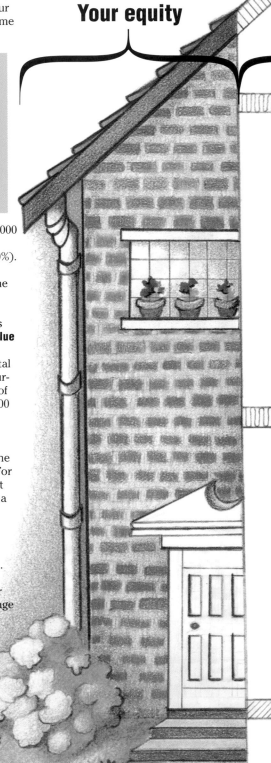

Your equity

VALUE OF HOME
− OUTSTANDING LOANS
= YOUR EQUITY

for example	
$ 200,000	Value of home
− $160,000	Outstanding loans
= $ 40,000	Total equity

For example, when you buy a $200,000 home with a $160,000 mortgage, your equity is 20% ($40,000 of $200,000 = 20%).

In other words, your initial equity equals your down payment. At the time you've repaid the mortgage principal plus interest, your equity is 100%.

From a lender's perspective, what's important is the mortgage's **loan to value ratio**, or **LTV**. That's the relationship between the loan principal and the total value of the property—initially, the purchase price. Using the same example of buying a $200,000 home with a $160,000 mortgage, the LTV would be 80%.

CHANGING PROPERTY VALUES

The value of your equity changes as the market value of your home changes. For example, suppose a house you bought for $200,000—with $40,000 down and a $160,000 mortgage—is immediately revalued at $300,000. Your equity is $140,000, or 46.7%, based on the increase in value because the amount you owe the lender ($160,000) is fixed.

However, the reverse could be true, though it happens less often. For example, if you had a $160,000 mortgage on a home you bought for $200,000 but resold for $160,000, you would owe it all to the lender because your equity would be $0.

As you pay your mortgage, you build your equity

LOOK BEFORE YOU LEAP

You should consider the potential drawbacks as well as the advantages of home equity loans:

- **You reduce your equity by borrowing against the value of your home**

- **If you fall behind on repayment of your home equity loan, you risk losing your home even if you make your regular mortgage payments on time**

- **Since most home equity loans have adjustable interest rates, the cost of borrowing could increase**

HOME EQUITY LOANS

Having equity in your home means you may be eligible for a **home equity loan**, one of the easiest and most economical ways to borrow money. The application is similar to a mortgage application because your home serves as **collateral**, or security, for the loan.

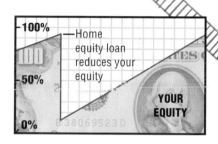

The amount you can borrow is influenced by a number of factors, including how much you owe on your mortgage and the lender's appraisal of your home's current value. Generally speaking, you can borrow up to 80% of your equity although some home equity loans have a **ceiling**, or upper limit, of $50,000.

Home equity loans have an advantage over personal loans, too, because the interest you pay is often tax deductible. However, if the outstanding balance on your home equity loan is more than $100,000 (or $50,000 if you're married but file a separate tax return), you have to calculate how much of the interest qualifies as a deduction using IRS Publication 936.

TRADING UP

Once you've bought your first home, it's generally easier to buy another one, for two reasons: a credit history and more money to invest. If you've made regular mortgage payments, you've established a good credit record. And if you make a profit when you sell, you'll have more money for a new down payment. That will let you buy a more expensive home, or borrow less money—or both.

You may plan to trade up by starting with a modest home, perhaps improving it, and selling when you can make a profit.

This can be risky—prices can drop, mortgage rates can rise, people can hate the paint you picked out. But often it works just fine.

The tax code also works in your favor when you sell one home and buy another. That's because you don't have to pay any tax on your **capital gains**, or profit on the sale, of up to $500,000 if you're married and $250,000 if you're single. The only conditions are that you have lived in the home for at least two of the previous five years, and that at least two years pass before you use the exemption again.

Refinancing

You may be able to take advantage of dropping interest rates.

The interest rate you pay on your mortgage makes a major difference in the cost of borrowing. A rate that varies by as little as 50 **basis points**—which translates to 0.5%, or half a percent—can mean thousands of dollars difference in the total cost of buying a home. That's one reason that seeking the lowest rate is an important part of your initial search for a mortgage. But dropping interest rates may also be good reason to investigate **refinancing** your mortgage.

When you refinance, you arrange a new mortgage at a lower rate than the rate you're currently paying. You use the money you borrow with the new mortgage to pay off the remaining balance on your existing mortgage. In some cases, you may actually borrow more than you owe so that you'll have extra cash to make improvements to your property, pay college tuitions, or consolidate your consumer debt. While that will increase the amount you must pay back, you may discover that it's the least expensive way to borrow.

WEIGH THE COST

Refinancing has a price tag. The lender will usually charge origination and application fees, credit check fees, and the same types of closing costs you paid with your existing mortgage. You'll want to have an attorney review the agreement, and you'll have to pay for the services of the lender's attorney as well.

Because of the cost, you'll want to be sure refinancing actually makes sense for you. Here's how you do the calculation:

1 Itemize the cost of refinancing. To come up with those numbers, ask your potential lender for an estimate of the fees you should expect to pay, including any prepaid interest, called **points**. You can also review what you paid to arrange your existing mortgage, as the cost is likely to be similar.

2 Add in any prepayment penalty for paying off your existing mortgage.

3 Total the figures in steps 1 and 2 to find the cost of refinancing.

4 Subtract the principal and interest of your new monthly mortgage payment from the principal and interest of your existing mortgage.

5 Divide the total cost in step 3 by the difference between the payments in step 4. That's the time, in months, it will take to **amortize**, or pay off, the expense and begin saving money.

FINDING INFORMATION YOU NEED

Your best source of information about refinancing costs is often the new lender you're considering. You'll need to provide the details of what you paid for your home, what you still owe on your existing mortgage, and how much you're paying each month. If you want to increase the amount you're borrowing, you should make that clear as well.

The lender can itemize all the costs involved in the refinance and estimate your new monthly payment. What won't change is the portion of your monthly payment that goes toward insurance and local real estate taxes, which are linked to the value of your property rather than the size of your mortgage.

Ask the lender to evaluate your costs, too, if you've had your present mortgage for a number of years. You'll want to compare the total combined interest you'll owe on the old and new mortgages with the interest left to pay on your existing mortgage.

REVERSE MORTGAGES

If you're 62 or older and living on a fixed income, you may consider a **reverse mortgage**. This arrangement allows you to convert your home equity to a loan, which you take as a lump sum, a series of regular payments, or a line of credit. But it's something you want to do with extreme caution.

As the lender pays each loan advance, or as you write a check against your credit line, your equity is reduced and your debt to the lender grows. That amount must be repaid when you die or move out of the home, usually by selling the property. The total amount that's owed can't be more than the value of the property.

The amount you can borrow depends on your age, the equity you have in your home, and the interest rate the lender is charging. That rate, the fees, and the closing costs are usually significantly higher than with a regular mortgage. Some reverse mortgages are insured, which adds to the cost of borrowing but guarantees you'll receive your payments.

If you anticipate that you'll be moving from your home before that amount of time is up, refinancing probably doesn't make financial sense. But if you plan to stay put, you may want to go ahead with the arrangements.

Some lenders offer refinancing with no closing costs and no points at certain times. You'll want to read the terms of the offer carefully, so you're clear about what you're committing yourself to. Generally these loans impose a penalty if you pay off the mortgage within the first three years of the term. If you aren't planning to move, this kind of refinancing could be the best deal.

WHY REFINANCE?

You may refinance for one or more of the following reasons:

- **Secure a lower interest rate, which will reduce your monthly payment and the overall cost of your home**
- **Consolidate outstanding debt into a single payment at a lower rate**
- **Reduce the term of your loan, which may increase your monthly payment but is likely to reduce the total cost dramatically**
- **Switch from an adjustable-rate loan to a fixed-rate loan or from a fixed-rate to a hybrid loan**

The Cost of College

Whether you think of it as a goal, or as an investment in your child's future, a college education is expensive.

If you have children who'll be heading to college, it's important to have a sense of what four years are likely to cost you. By 2020, it could be as much as $287,000 at a private institution and $133,000 at a public one, based on College Board estimates. So what you need is an effective, highly focused investment strategy. Its dual goals are building your college savings accounts while allowing you to take advantage of the various tax breaks the government provides for higher education expenses.

THE POWER OF COMPOUNDING

The money you start saving today has the potential to grow over time, helping to provide the money you'll need to pay for your children's college expenses. The more you can add each month, and the longer your time frame, the greater your opportunity for growth.

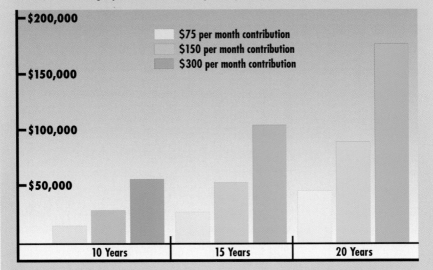

- $75 per month contribution
- $150 per month contribution
- $300 per month contribution

| | 10 Years | 15 Years | 20 Years |

$200,000 / $150,000 / $100,000 / $50,000

This hypothetical example illustrates the future value of different regular monthly investments over three long-term periods. It assumes an annual effective investment return of 8%. This illustration does not represent the performance of any specific investment and does not reflect the impact of any taxes, fees, or sales charges that may apply. Returns will vary and different investments may perform better or worse than this example. Automatic or periodic investment plans do not guarantee a profit and do not protect against loss in a declining market.

Source: OppenheimerFunds, Inc.

MONEY WELL SPENT

When you're facing the expense of paying for a college education, you may wonder about the return on your investment. It's actually a pretty impressive figure. The US Bureau of the Census reports that people with a bachelor's degree earn over 80% more, on average, than someone with only a high school diploma. The difference in lifetime earning potential is more than $1,000,000.

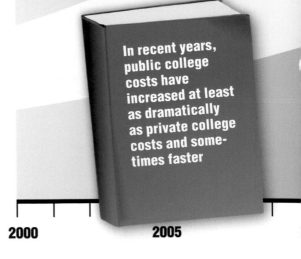

In recent years, public college costs have increased at least as dramatically as private college costs and sometimes faster

YEAR   2000   2005

A REAL CRUNCH

You'll probably need more money in a shorter period of time to pay for college than you will for anything else—with the possible exception of setting up a new business. And, if the past is any indicator, college costs will continue to go up.

In the last few years, tuition increases have averaged more than 8% a year, more than double the rate of inflation. Many public colleges have raised tuition and fees even more dramatically, as the cost of providing education has increased faster than the level of state support.

But there's good news, too. The amount of financial aid has increased, providing some level of assistance to more than 75% of all students at four-year private colleges and universities and to more than 60% of those enrolled in public institutions, according to the College Board.

COST OF 4 YEARS OF COLLEGE

TOP PRIVATE COLLEGES are the most expensive but may offer the most financial aid

PRIVATE COLLEGES try to attract outstanding students from all financial backgrounds

PUBLIC COLLEGES are usually the least expensive but may offer less financial aid

- $275,000
- $250,000
- $225,000
- $200,000
- $175,000
- $150,000
- $125,000
- $100,000
- $75,000
- $50,000
- $25,000
- $0

LOAN NOTES

While some students receive scholarships, which don't have to be repaid, most financial aid is interest-bearing loans. Your child will be responsible for paying back any money she borrows, with the first payment due no later than six or nine months after finishing her degree or withdrawing from school.

2010   2015   2020

College Investing Primer

Learning the ABC's of investing can move you to the head of the class.

If there's college tuition in your future, you already know you need to create an investment strategy and put it into operation. The longer you delay, the greater the likelihood you'll face the prospect of having to borrow large sums or limit your child's college choices, or both.

AN INVESTMENT PRIMER

They're not quite as simple as ABC, but here are some frequently suggested ways to approach investing for college.

1 Establish education accounts, separate from any other investment accounts

2 Add money regularly, such as every month

3 Choose investments based on your children's ages, stressing growth in the early years and safety as they get closer to 18

INVESTMENTS TO AVOID

There are a number of investments that don't usually work very well as ways to invest for college savings, either because they're too aggressive or not aggressive enough. Or they may be hard to turn into cash when you most need them. They include:

- Any investment that doesn't pay enough interest to beat the rate of inflation, including savings accounts, short-term bond funds, money market funds, and similar investments

- Bonds you'll have to sell before they mature because the price fluctuates, so you could lose money

- Any investment that's not easily liquidated, such as real estate, unit investment trusts, and limited partnerships

- Derivatives, which are investments whose value depends entirely on the way some other investment performs, usually within a specific period of time

- Any investment that would cost you penalties and taxes if you liquidated it, including annuities or IRAs

When your children are young, most financial advisors would urge investing primarily in equities, such as stocks and stock mutual funds. If you reinvest all the earnings or use them to make similar investments, your portfolio has the potential to grow.

THE VALUE OF EQUITIES

Most experts agree that investments with the potential to increase in value—such as stock and mutual funds—are appropriate choices for college expenses that are also likely to increase over time. On the other hand, because they're not insured, equity investments can lose value as well as gain it. And those losses—as well as potential gains—can occur quickly. That's a reason to reduce your equity holdings as your child moves closer to enrolling.

A BIG CHOICE

There are more than 3,800 degree-granting institutions in the US—including universities, four-year colleges, and two-year colleges. About half are public, which means they're supported by state or local governments, and the rest are private.

THE NAME ON THE ACCOUNT

Should you put investments earmarked for college in your child's name instead of your own? There are two arguments in favor of this—that you'll be less apt to spend the money for something else, and that your child may owe less tax on any money the investments earn. But there are also several strong arguments against this practice:

- Children under 14 pay tax at their parent's rate on interest and dividend income over $1,500, so there is little tax advantage

- Once you put money in a child's name, you give up the right to use it, and at 18

(21 in some states) the child can spend it as he or she wishes

- If you are planning to apply for financial aid, a child is expected to contribute a higher percentage of his or her assets than you are of yours (35% vs. 5.65%)

As they get older you may want to begin switching some of your portfolio into less volatile investments, including equity income funds and medium-term Treasury notes. If prices increase sharply, you might also sell some of your investments to protect your gains. But you'll still want to invest for growth.

TIMING IT RIGHT

There are some investments you can time, like the dates your CDs and Treasury bills come due. Since you'll need a cash transfusion, usually in August and January when the new semesters start, you can plan to have the money available then. Colleges usually require payment in full when students register.

When you're buying zero-coupon bonds, it's especially important to buy those that mature during the four- or five-year period that you'll need the cash. If you have to sell them before they're due, you may take a real beating on the price. And if you're buying US Series EE or I Savings Bonds, remember that you have to keep them at least five years or you'll lose three months' interest.

As your children are closer to college age and actually enroll, you may want to include more income-producing investments and continue to transfer part of your equity assets into more conservative investments each year. The schedule should be dictated by when your tuition bills come due, not by what you think the market's going to do. But, if the stock market goes way up at any point in this period, you may want to take advantage of selling when the prices are high. In other words, you may want to speed up—but just a bit—the shift from stocks and mutual funds to more stable investments.

CATCHING THE LOWER RATE

One way to take advantage of your child's potentially lower capital gains tax rate is to make a gift of stocks or stock mutual funds to the child before they're sold to pay college tuition. Since your child, not you, is selling the investment, the tax rate on any long-term gain may be 5% rather then 15%. And you won't owe any gift tax if the value of the assets is $11,000 or less ($22,000 if two givers are involved) at the time of the gift.

Education Investments

The earlier you start planning for college, the easier it will be to pay those tuition bills.

The best time to start saving for college—for your children, nieces, nephews, or other family and friends—is as soon as they're born. But if you didn't get off to a quick start, don't despair. You can start now by choosing among a number of different investment plans that not only provide the opportunity for your savings to compound tax deferred but offer the possibility of tax-free withdrawals for qualified expenses when the student enrolls.

In fact, some of these plans weren't introduced until 1995, and the tax-free withdrawal provision wasn't added until 2002. There is one caution, though. You should keep in the back of your mind that Congress must act to make tax-free withdrawals permanent or that benefit will expire in 2011.

529 PLANS

The college savings plans known as 529 plans are among the newer ways to invest for college. These plans are sponsored by individual states and managed by financial institutions, such as brokerage firms, insurance companies, and mutual fund companies. When you set up the account, you designate a beneficiary for whom you'll use the money to pay qualified higher education expenses, including the cost of technical or trade school, college, or graduate school. The beneficiary can be anyone, including yourself.

Since every state offers a 529 plan, you have the flexibility to choose the one that best meets the criteria you set. In fact, you can open more than one 529 plan for the same beneficiary if you choose, since in most cases neither you nor the plan beneficiary have to live in the sponsoring state to participate in its plan.

Among the things you'll want to consider in choosing a 529 plan are:

- The investment options and their historical returns
- The fees, expenses, and state tax treatment of different plans
- Beneficiary rules
- Contribution limits

You may want to begin your search by investigating the plan sponsored by the state where you live, as many states offer extra incentives to residents enrolling in their plan. Your withdrawals may be free of state as well as federal income tax, for example. Or you may be entitled to deduct your contribution on your state tax return. But you may lose those advantages by choosing another state's plan. For more information, you can check www.collegesavings.org, a website sponsored by the College Savings Plan Network.

Remember, though, that as with any uninsured investment, returns on 529 accounts are not guaranteed and you could lose money, especially in the short term.

PREPAID PLANS

You may also consider a prepaid tuition plan, another type of 529 plan. With a prepaid plan, you pay for future college costs by buying tuition credits at today's rates. The catch is, many of these plans don't guarantee that your prepayment will cover the full cost when your child enrolls.

ON THE RIGHT TRACK

Most 529 college savings plans offer either age-based or fixed tracks, or both. An age-based track allocates your investment across different asset classes based on the beneficiary's age when you open the account, and then reallocates to create a more conservative portfolio as the child gets closer to college age.

With a fixed track, you choose whether to invest in equities, fixed income, balanced, or stable value funds. The portfolio's exposure to risk doesn't change over time, and the results are based on how the underlying investments perform.

COVERDELL EDUCATION SAVINGS ACCOUNTS

Like 529 plans, **Coverdell education savings accounts (ESAs)** offer tax-deferred growth and tax-free withdrawals when you use the money to pay for qualified education expenses. With ESAs, that includes expenses incurred in grades K through 12, as well as college and graduate school.

With an ESA, you choose the investments for your account, which gives you more control over how your money is allocated than you have with most 529 plans. There are limitations, though. Instead of investment ceilings that can be as high as $275,000 for some 529 plans, annual ESA contributions per beneficiary are capped at $3,000. There are income limits governing who can contribute to an ESA. And the beneficiary must be younger than 18 when the account is opened, and must use the money before turning 30, although you can change beneficiaries to another member of the same family.

US SAVINGS BONDS

When you redeem certain US savings bonds to pay for qualified education expenses, you may qualify for a tax break. There are two types of bonds that are frequently used for education expenses, Series I and Series EE. Series I bonds are sold at face value and indexed for inflation, while EE bonds are sold at half their face value, and earn interest at 90% of the market yield on five-year Treasurys.

There's a small catch to the tax break for education expenses on US Savings bonds: Your adjusted gross income must be less than the limit set by Congress in the year you withdraw to qualify for the tax-free benefit.

In 2003, those amounts were $58,500, phased out at $73,500, for single taxpayers and $87,750, phased out at $117,750, for joint filers.

---

1 Compare the investment alternatives of different college investment plans, and narrow the list to those that are best for you. You may decide to use a combination of plans.

2 Evaluate 529 college savings plans to find the ones with the most attractive investment alternatives at the lowest cost. You may want to start by investigating your home state's plan.

3 Combine making contributions to a 529 plan with putting money into some other college saving opportunities such as an ESA or savings bonds, to diversify your investments.

4 Don't plan on raiding your retirement plan to pay for college expenses—your beneficiary could receive grants or scholarships, but you alone are responsible for your retirement.

Strategies for Paying

Persistence comes in handy when you're looking for ways to meet college costs.

There's little question that **529 plans** and **Coverdell education savings accounts (ESAs)** deserve the positive attention they receive. But they're not the only way to pay for college. Parents were successful in finding ways to foot tuition bills long before these plans were introduced, and some of those methods still merit investigation. Several of these approaches, like taking a home equity loan, involve long-term commitments and a level of risk you'll have to consider carefully. But it pays to know about the choices you have, since one of them may just be the solution you're looking for.

TUITION BULLETINS

GIVING GIFTS TO MINORS

If you want to give your child—or any minor—substantial financial gifts, you can set up a **custodial account**. You or a person you select controls the account until the child reaches majority, which can be 18, 21, or 25 depending on the state where the account is set up and the type of account it is. It doesn't cost anything to set up an account and the only fees are trading costs when you buy or sell securities and the fees attached to mutual funds you own.

Custodial accounts fall under either the **Uniform Gifts to Minors Act (UGMA)** or the **Uniform Transfer to Minors Act (UTMA)** and are generally known by those acronyms. The major difference is that UTMA contribution rules are more flexible, permitting assets, such as real estate and fine art, that don't produce regular earnings.

You can contribute as much or as little as you like to an UGMA or UTMA account, though annual gifts over $11,000 (or $22,000 if you and your husband make a joint gift) are potentially taxable to the giver. You can invest the assets as you see fit, and pay any income or capital gains tax that may be due each year at the beneficiary's rate once she's 14 or older. If she's younger, tax on investment earnings over $1,500 is figured at her parents' rate.

TAKE A SECOND LOOK

Custodial accounts may work well as college savings plans because you have enormous discretion over how to invest the assets. The more confident you are about choosing a diversified portfolio, the more attractive this approach may seem. However, UGMAs and UTMAs also have some potential drawbacks.

- If the beneficiary applies for financial aid, she or he will be expected to contribute up to 35% of the balance each year in keeping with the standard formula
- When the beneficiary reaches majority, she or he has the right to assume control of the account
- Any earnings are taxable, unlike earnings in a 529 or ESA

COLLEGE? SURE

You can buy special certificates of deposit, called CollegeSure® CDs, which let you prepay future college costs at today's rates, plus a premium based on the child's age and the amount you invest. The CDs, issued by the College Savings Bank of Princeton (NJ), pay annual interest rates linked to increases in an index of average college costs and never less than 2%. Your CDs are insured up to a total of $100,000, and at maturity you're free to use the money as you choose.

You may be able to earn more in a diversified portfolio you put together yourself. And interest on the CDs is taxable, unless you own them within a Coverdell education savings account or participating state 529 plan. For more information, go to www.collegesavings.com.

WHAT'S NOT SMART

One of the conflicts you may wrestle with is whether to use the money you've invested for retirement to pay for your child's education. Most financial advisors think it's a bad idea because it may leave you short of income later on. But if it makes the difference between your child's going to school or not, you may consider a loan from your employer's plan—if the plan allows loans—or a withdrawal from your IRA.

The loan isn't income, so there's no tax. But if you leave your job before repaying the full amount, the balance will be considered an early withdrawal, subject to tax and penalty if you're younger than 59½.

If you take money from your traditional IRA, you'll owe income tax on the amount you withdraw, though not a prepayment penalty. That's because paying college expenses is considered one of the legitimate reasons for early withdrawal.

WHERE THERE'S HOPE

Once you actually start paying tuition, you may qualify for a $1,500 Hope Scholarship or $2,000 Lifetime Learning tax credit. Get more information from IRS Publication 970.

HOME EQUITY LOANS

Your biggest ace in the hole when it comes to paying for college may be the equity you've built up in your home. That's because you can usually borrow more cheaply with a **home equity loan** than with any personal loan, and the interest you pay may be tax deductible in most circumstances, lowering the cost of the loan even more.

If you bought your home when your child was small, the original mortgage may be nearly paid off.

That makes it easier to arrange an equity loan. And writing a check to the lender every month won't come as such a financial shock since you've been making mortgage payments all along.

Home equity loans are not a perfect solution, though. First, the money has to be paid back, usually starting immediately. And, if for some reason you **default**, or fail to pay back your loan, you run the very real risk of losing your home.

DEGREES FOR LESS

If you're looking for other ways to save money on college costs, you might consider encouraging your child to consider an accelerated program:

- Some colleges offer credit for high school advanced placement courses, which could mean finishing a degree a semester, or even two, early

- Some colleges offer three-year programs that move students through their required courses more quickly

- Credits earned at local colleges during summer school may count toward graduation and can reduce the number of semesters required

- Two years at a community or junior college before transferring to a four-year college or university will help lower the total cost of a degree

A BOND DEAL

Baccalaureate bonds are something else to keep an eye out for. Some states issue special tax-exempt zero-coupon bonds, usually sold in small denominations so you can build up a portfolio of them on your own investment schedule.

Because the bonds mature on a specific date, you can time them so you'll have cash on hand every semester or every year. Some of them provide an extra bonus if you use the money to pay tuition at an in-state school. But if you sell these bonds before they mature, you stand a good chance of losing money, as well as depleting funds you'll need for college.

Applying for Aid

You've got to be prepared to put in some time and effort.

To apply for financial aid, your child must fill out a Free Application for Federal Student Aid (FAFSA) either on paper or online. In addition, some colleges require a separate financial aid profile. Chances are you'll have to provide most of the information for these applications, though, as most of the questions are about your family's financial situation, including your tax records, investment accounts, and other assets and liabilities.

Both forms can be submitted as of January 1 of the year for which you're requesting aid—generally the January of your child's senior year in high school and each following January until the senior year of college.

The catch is—as anyone who's been through this can tell you—the forms are complicated and extremely probing. (Some people would even describe them as intrusive.) But there's virtually no way around filling them out if you want financial aid.

FAFSA

Step One: For questions 1-34, leave blank a[...]
(as it appears on your Social Security card)

1-3. Your full name (as it appears on your Social Security card)
1. LAST NAME: SHORTFALL

4-7. Your permanent mailing address
4. NUMBER AND STREET (INCLUDE APT. NUMBER): 987 MAIN STRE[...]
5. CITY (AND COUNTRY IF NOT U.S.): MYTOWN
9. Your da[...] 05

8. Your Social Security Number: 987-65-4321

11-12. Your driver's license number and state (if any)
11. LICENSE NUMBER

13. Are you a U.S. citizen? Pick one. See page 2.
a. Yes, I am a U.S. citizen
b. No, but I am an eligible
c. No, I am not a citizen o[...]

15. What is your marital status as of today?
I am single, divorced, or w[...]
I am married/remarried .
I am separated ....

FINANCIAL AID FORMULAS

There are standard formulas, known as federal need analysis methodology, for figuring how much you're able to contribute to your child's education, and whether your family qualifies for federal financial aid. The Department of Education sends you a student aid report (SAR) within a month of your application, stating your expected family contribution (EFC). Colleges use that figure to determine the aid you are eligible for.

The amount your family is expected to contribute remains constant, regardless of the cost of the school. For example, if your contribution for the school year is set at $8,000, that could pay the entire cost at some public colleges. But it covers barely a quarter of the tuition at the most expensive private schools.

The computation takes a number of factors into account:

- **Your family's income, including nontaxable income**

- **Your family's assets, if your taxable income is more than $50,000, though the value of your family's home isn't included, nor is money in employer sponsored retirement accounts or annuities**

- **Your child's earnings, investments, and savings**

- **Your family's size and the number of children in college at the same time**

WHOSE INCOME COUNTS?

Parents are considered responsible for their children's education. If you and your child's father are separated or divorced, the FAFSA asks for financial information either for the parent with whom the child lived for most of the year or the one who provided the most financial support. If you're the parent and you've remarried, you have to provide your new husband's financial information. The same is true with your former husband, if he has remarried. But only one family's income is required, not both.

FAMILY HELP

In figuring the aid you're eligible for, colleges don't count gifts from family or friends. But if your child's grandparents create a trust to pay for college, the Internal Revenue Service considers the income from the trust as income to you as a parent—since education is your responsibility.

However, grandparents—or anyone else—can make a direct gift to the college your child attends to offset the cost of tuition. That's not considered income to you, or a gift to your child.

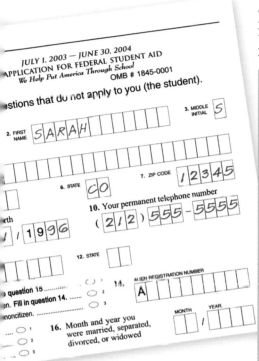

WHAT IF YOU'RE THE STUDENT?

If the tuition you're concerned about is your own, most of the same rules apply. Your income will still determine the kind of aid you qualify for, but you may catch some breaks.

If you're older than 24, your parents' income doesn't count in figuring how much you can afford. That's true even if you live in your parents' home.

You also qualify for all the same federal grants and loans that a dependent student does. And if you're going back to school because you've lost your job or your marriage has dissolved, you may be eligible for a Pell grant even if you don't strictly meet the financial guidelines.

If you're planning a specific career, like teaching or certain kinds of medical work, or you're willing to commit yourself to a period of public service, you can sometimes get better loan terms.

Graduate schools often provide fellowships or other financial incentives for choosing their program. While you might owe taxes on money you get for teaching or other degree-related jobs, the institution will often help you find enough money to complete your degree.

10 THINGS TO KNOW ABOUT FINANCIAL AID

1 Colleges with aid-blind admissions policies admit students regardless of their need for aid. Some colleges guarantee enough aid to allow everyone admitted to attend.

2 Your income during the calendar year before your child applies for aid establishes your eligibility.

3 Colleges are responding to increasing demand for aid by providing more of it—for the first year. But students may have to pay a larger share in the next three years, unless the college agrees to lock in the initial aid level.

4 It rarely works to claim that your children support themselves, since most colleges won't consider them independent and therefore eligible for aid in their own right until they turn 24.

5 Some colleges are willing to negotiate their initial aid offer, and others will reconsider, if you ask.

6 If your child qualifies for federally subsidized student aid, the government pays the interest on loans while she is enrolled in school.

7 Most financial aid loans are made to students, not parents. It is your child's responsibility to repay them.

8 As a parent, you can apply for a federal PLUS loan, which has capped interest rates, and lets you borrow up to the full cost of attending college minus any financial aid.

9 About 70% of college graduates borrow money to pay for their educations, according to student loan source Nellie Mae.

10 Scholarships or grants to cover expenses other than tuition are considered taxable income.

Investing for Retirement

Whether retirement is down the road or just around the corner, planning for it is a must.

Retiring may be the last thing you want to do. Or it may be the goal that keeps you going. Whether or not you're planning *on* it, you should be planning *for* it. The reason is simple: You're going to need the money.

Unlike mortgages and educational expenses, which eventually get paid off,

retirement means a permanent change—and usually a reduction—in the income you'll have to live on for the rest of your life. So when you cash your last paycheck, you'll need a substantial source of other income ready to fill the void.

How much of your current income you'll need

Since the income you'll need to live comfortably in retirement depends on your personal lifestyle, there's no fixed amount that applies to everyone. But most retirement experts recommend that you plan to replace at least 80% of your preretirement income with pensions, Social Security, and investments.

Many financial advisors who work with women urge them to plan to replace all of their preretirement earnings, adjusted for inflation, because they earn less.

Where you'll get it

SOCIAL SECURITY **+** **PENSION**

Women earn only approximately 76% of what men earn, so they receive less from these two standard resources, according to US Bureau of the Census, 2002.

ESPECIALLY FOR WOMEN

Lining up retirement income is especially critical for women, since two of the standard resources—pensions and Social Security—are linked to a lifetime of earned income. Since women earn, on average, 24% less than men, and often work fewer years, they can expect to receive less from those sources when they retire. For example, there has typically been a gap of about $200 a month in the Social Security benefits paid to men and women based on their own earnings.

What's more, since women as a group live longer than men, they need income over a longer period of time. For example, women make up a large proportion of the fastest growing segment of the population: people over 80. That means living for many years on retirement income.

A KEY QUESTION
When you take a job, remember to ask about the retirement plan. You'll want to know the kind of plan it is, when you can join, and whether there's an employer match. You might also ask if you can move retirement savings from an earlier plan into the new one.

A FIRM LEG TO STAND ON

Retirement income is generally described as a three-legged stool—balancing on pensions, Social Security, and investment income. So as fewer and fewer employers offer traditional pensions, and more debate surfaces about how Social Security will survive the gradually growing number of beneficiaries and the decreasing number of workers, investments must carry more and more of the weight.

That's why it is so critical to focus on investment strategy as a key part of your retirement planning. You control how much you invest, and what you invest in. As an added incentive to build your investments, you can put money in special tax-deferred retirement accounts that let you postpone taxes on your earnings until you start to take the money out—usually after you retire or by age 70½. That means you can buy and sell the investments in those accounts, as well as reinvesting any interest and dividends without having to worry about paying income taxes or capital gains tax on any profits.

TARGETED INVESTMENTS

There are three primary ways to invest for retirement. Each has distinctive advantages and some potential limitations.

TAX-DEFERRED RETIREMENT PLANS

Employer sponsored retirement plans are tax deferred, whether the employer makes the contribution, you contribute, or both you and your employer do. Neither the amounts that are added nor any earnings are taxed until you withdraw. In addition, when you contribute, your salary is reduced by the amount you put in, so you owe less current income tax as well.

You can also invest in a personal tax-deferred plan, such as an individual retirement account (IRA) or a deferred annuity to supplement or substitute for an employer's plan.

As an added bonus, when you start withdrawing after you retire, you may find you're paying tax at a lower rate than you would have paid when you put the money in. (You can't count on that, though, since there's no way to predict tax rates or your income even a few years ahead.)

Tax-deferred retirement plans do have some limitations, though:

- There's a cap on the amount you can invest through most plans each year
- You usually can't use the money before you reach age 59½ without having to pay a 10% penalty on amounts you withdraw
- You usually must begin withdrawing after you turn 70½

+ INVESTMENTS

Growth & Income Fund

Investments produce the same results whether they're owned by men or women.

TAX-FREE RETIREMENT PLANS

If you're eligible to contribute earned income to a Roth IRA because your adjusted gross income (AGI) is less than $110,000 if you're single or $160,000 if you're married and file a joint return, you can withdraw tax-free income after you turn 59½ provided your account has been open at least five years.

The higher the rate at which your retirement income is taxed, the greater the savings that tax-free income provides. The only drawbacks are that the contributions you make aren't tax deductible when they go into your account, and there's a cap on what you can add each year.

TAXABLE INVESTMENTS

The most flexible way to build retirement savings is in a regular investment account. There's no limit on the amount you can put into the account each year, and no restrictions on when you can withdraw—or when you must start.

Another advantage of regular over tax-deferred investing is that the profit on any investment that has increased in value when you sell it is taxed at the lower long-term capital gains rate, provided you have owned the investment more than a year. That rate is 15% or 5% depending on your income tax bracket.

In contrast, earnings you withdraw from a tax-deferred plan are taxed as regular income even if the money you're withdrawing represents the profit on an investment you've owned 20 years or more.

The downside of regular investments is that you've already paid tax on the money you invest, and you pay taxes every year on most investment earnings.

It Pays to Give at the Office

By reducing your paycheck a little, you can build your retirement savings.

When you participate in a salary reduction plan, you agree to have a percentage of your salary deducted from your gross income and deposited in a retirement investment account. The amount that's deducted is considered **deferred income**, so you don't pay tax on it in the year you earn it.

Investing this way has a double advantage: Your tax bill is smaller each year you contribute, and your retirement investments get a regular infusion of cash. Remember, though, that investing has risks, and there's no guarantee what your account will be worth at any given time.

WHAT'S A PRETAX DOLLAR?

Pretax dollars are what you earn before the amount you owe in federal, state, and local income taxes is subtracted. You invest pretax dollars in salary reduction plans, but after-tax dollars in most other investments. Whatever your earn, you reduce what you owe in taxes when you take advantage of pretax investing.

IT'S YOUR CALL

Unlike Social Security taxes, which are automatically deducted from your earned income, a salary reduction plan usually lets you decide:

- **Whether to participate**
- **How much to contribute**

But sometimes having the choice may not be such a good thing—especially if you postpone signing up. The reality is, if you don't put in as much as you can each year, you increase the risk of not having enough saved when you're ready to retire.

WHAT YOUR CHOICES ARE

	THRIFT OR SAVINGS PLAN
Funding	Employee and employer
Method	Employer matches some or all of the amount employee defers from pretax salary into the plan
Eligibility	Federal employees and employees of companies offering plans
Limits	Up to $12,000 of earnings in 2003, rising to $15,000 in 2006

MATCHING CONTRIBUTIONS

A potential benefit of participating in a salary reduction plan is that your employer may match part of your contribution, providing what amounts to a tax-deferred bonus. That's another reason for joining the plan, as, you usually must contribute yourself to qualify for matching.

One way matching typically works is that your employer contributes 50% of what you add, to a limit of 5% or 6% of your income—though some add more and some less. If your employer does match, you may want to consider contributing at least enough to qualify for the maximum.

YOUR CONTRIBUTION			EMPLOYER CONTRIBUTION			TOTAL
6%	of a $30,000 salary	$1,800	50%	of employee contribution	$900	$2,700
6%	of a $60,000 salary	$3,600	50%	of employee contribution	$1,800	$5,400
10%	of a $60,000 salary	$6,000	50%	of 6% of employee salary (cap applies)	$1,800	$7,800

CATCH-UP CONTRIBUTIONS

If you're 50 or older, you can make catch-up contributions to your employer sponsored retirement savings plan if the plan permits those contributions. You can also make catch-up contributions to your individual retirement account (IRA) whether or not you add the extra money to your plan at work.

You can participate even if you've contributed the maximum amount to your plans in previous years. In 2003, you can put an additional $2,000 into your employer plan and an extra $500 in your IRA. Those amounts are scheduled to increase to $5,000 a year for employer plans and $1,000 a year for IRAs.

Your choice in tax-deferred salary reduction plans depends on where you work. That's because specific plans have been authorized for different types of employers by different sections of the Internal Revenue Code (IRC).

401(k) PLAN	403(b) PLAN	457 PLAN	SIMPLE PLAN
Employee and employer	Employee and employer	Employee	Employer and employee
Employee contributes pretax salary to the plan and employer may make matching contribution	Employee contributes pretax salary into the plan and employer may match part of the amount	Employee contributes pretax salary to the plan	Employee may contribute pretax salary and employer must contribute based on one of two formulas
All employees of businesses that sponsor plans	Employees of nonprofit, tax-exempt organizations	State and municipal workers and employees of non-government tax-exempt organizations	Available to companies with 100 or fewer employees
Up to $12,000 of earnings in 2003, rising to $15,000 in 2006	Up to $12,000 of earnings in 2003, rising to $15,000 in 2006	Up to $12,000 of earnings in 2003, rising to $15,000 in 2006	Up to $8,000 of earnings in 2003, rising to $10,000 in 2005

You're in the Driver's Seat

When you're making decisions, you can choose the route that's best for you.

Saying "yes" to a salary reduction plan moves you straight to the next set of decisions: What are your investment alternatives and which ones should you choose?

INVESTING THE MONEY

Salary reduction plans are usually **self-directed**. You must choose how to invest your contribution, usually from a minimum of three to seven alternatives that your employer offers. The list generally includes equity, fixed income, and money market mutual funds, as well as other investments.

Your initial choices don't have to be binding, since you can shift the money in your account from one investment to another. For example, you may want to transfer a part of a fixed income account into a fund that invests in stocks. Or you may want to put some of the money you've allocated to stocks into a growth and income fund.

You owe no capital gains or income tax if you move assets within your account, though there may be transaction fees. You may also pay a penalty if you move money out of some fixed-income accounts.

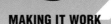

MAKING IT WORK

If you decide to participate in a salary reduction retirement plan, experts suggest two ways to make the most of it:

- **Contribute as much as you can every year that you're eligible**
- **Put your contributions into investments that you expect will increase the most in value over the long term**

SMOOTHING THE RIDE

There are two ways to strengthen performance in a salary reduction plan:

- **Monitor the performance of your plan's mutual funds against other funds with similar investment objectives.**

    To improve your investment's potential for long-term performance, you could request an expanded list of investment options. One thing working in your favor: Executives have the same choices and pay the same fees as other employees, so there may be high-level support for changes.

- **Check to see how much you're paying in management fees.** Company pension funds typically pay 0.5% of their assets in fees, while the average 401(k) participant pays 1.4%.

    To reduce the fee, you and other employees may be able to persuade your employer to negotiate a group, rather than individual, fee structure. Since 401(k) accounts are a huge percentage of a mutual fund company's total investments, a fund might be willing to take a smaller fee to keep a client happy.

INVEST AS MUCH AS YOU CAN EVERY YEAR YOU'RE ELIGIBLE

15% LIMIT

CHOOSE A DIVERSIFIED PORTFOLIO OF INVESTMENTS TO HELP REDUCE RISK AND INCREASE LONG-TERM RETURN

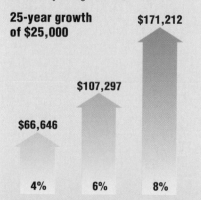

SOME THINGS NEVER CHANGE

The same principles of sound investing that apply to your regular investments apply to salary reduction plans as well. But you may want to place an even greater emphasis on long-term growth historically provided by equity investments. Retirement, after all, is a long-term proposition, especially since women tend to live longer than men. You may also decide to allocate some of your portfolio to income investments, including bond funds and dividend-paying stock funds, since you can postpone taxes on your earnings. But you want to be sure that any interest-bearing investments pay more than the rate of inflation. That means you should probably resist the temptation to choose investments like savings accounts, since they probably will not earn enough to cover your expenses later on.

BY BEING TOO SAFE YOU RISK SORRY RESULTS

When you're choosing the investments for your retirement plans, you should consider those with a history of greater growth potential. Although you benefit from compounding with many types of investments, those with higher returns over the long term accumulate more earnings. For example, a 25-year investment with an annual compound return of 8% would produce a nest egg more then 2½ times larger than an investment yielding 4%.*

25-year growth of $25,000

$171,212

$107,297

$66,646

4%   6%   8%

Source: OppenheimerFunds, Inc.

*This hypothetical example is for illustrative purposes only and does not represent the return on any specific investment or predict future performance.

A LIFELONG COMPANION

If you change jobs—eleven times in a career is average—there's an added advantage to having a salary reduction plan. You can take it with you.

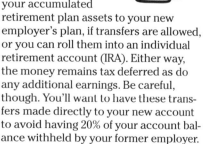

The reason is that contributory plans are **portable**. When you change jobs, you can transfer your accumulated retirement plan assets to your new employer's plan, if transfers are allowed, or you can roll them into an individual retirement account (IRA). Either way, the money remains tax deferred as do any additional earnings. Be careful, though. You'll want to have these transfers made directly to your new account to avoid having 20% of your account balance withheld by your former employer.

With a contributory plan, the money you put in is always yours. You don't have to wait to be **vested**—which in this case means staying at a job long enough to qualify to keep any matching contributions—to authorize a transfer. And if you are vested, usually after no longer than six years in this type of plan, you may also move what your employer has added.

IRAs

An IRA may be your first line of defense in protecting your future.

No retirement plan? You're not alone. While 75% of American women work, only about half of them are currently covered by a retirement plan. But an **individual retirement account (IRA)**, or personal retirement savings plan, is available to anyone who earns income or is married to someone who does.

With an IRA you can invest up to the annual limit and defer income taxes on any earnings, which are reinvested. You have the potential for faster growth than if you were paying taxes on an account earning the same rate of return. And depending on your income, you may qualify for the additional tax advantages of being able to lower your current taxes by deducting your contribution or of selecting a Roth IRA with its promise of eventual tax-free income.

GOOD REASONS TO OPEN AN IRA

- **Have a personal savings plan**

- **Defer or eliminate tax on earnings**

- **Add to your retirement account**

- **Choose among a variety of investments**

A TAX BREAK FOR TRADITIONAL IRAs

If you meet either one of the qualifying tests, you can deduct your traditional IRA contribution on your income tax return. However, remember that contributions to Roth IRAs are never deductible, whether or not you have a retirement plan or meet the income test.

TEST #1
RETIREMENT PLAN COVERAGE

If you're not eligible for a pension or salary reduction plan where you work, you can deduct your full IRA contribution, whatever your income. You're eligible whether you're single or married. Even if your husband is part of a pension plan or is contributing to a salary reduction plan, it doesn't affect your eligibility provided your combined AGI is less than $150,000. You can take a decreasing deduction until your AGI reaches $160,000.

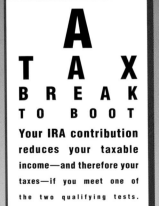

Your IRA contribution reduces your taxable income—and therefore your taxes—if you meet one of the two qualifying tests.

TEST #2
LEVEL OF INCOME

If you are eligible for a pension or salary reduction plan where you work, you can only deduct your full IRA contribution, up to $3,000 in 2003, if your income is either less than $40,000 if you're single or less than $60,000 if you're married and file a joint return. For each additional $1,000 you earn, you can deduct less, until the deduction is phased out entirely at $50,000 (single) and $70,000 (married). Those contribution amounts are scheduled to increase gradually through 2005 (single taxpayers) or 2007 (married filing joint return).

JUST SAY IT'S SO

You can establish an IRA with a bank, brokerage firm, mutual fund company, or an insurance company. When you fill out the paperwork and deposit your money, the IRA exists. It's as simple as that.

The institution acts as custodian and invests the money as you direct in stocks, bonds, mutual funds, CDs—the same kinds of investments that are available outside an IRA except art, jewelry, real estate, and collectibles. But you can't use your IRA to buy life insurance.

You usually pay an annual fee $10 to $50—for maintaining the account. Some custodians waive fees, though, if your account is large enough. That can be a persuasive argument for consolidating your IRA investments with a single custodian.

DON'T STOP NOW

To get tax-deferred growth, you agree that if you withdraw from your account before you reach age 59½, you'll owe a 10% penalty plus the tax that's due on the withdrawal amount, in most cases. But you can still put money into your IRA after you reach age 59½. And you can make extra annual catch-up contributions once you turn 50. In 2003, you can add up to $500 more, for a total of $3,500.

After you turn 59½, you can tap it anytime you need the money without paying the early withdrawal penalty. You must begin taking money out of your traditional IRA in the year after you turn 70½, and must withdraw at least the required amount each year. The way you figure that amount is spelled out in IRS Publication 590. You can work with your financial or tax advisor to be sure you get it right.

HOW NOT TO DO IT

Sometimes it's easier to decide how to make an investment decision—in this case, where to put your IRA money—by being clear on what you should *not* do. Here is what many financial experts warn against:

⊘ Buying tax-free investments, like municipal bonds or municipal bond funds, for a traditional IRA because all earnings are ultimately taxable.

⊘ Investing primarily in low-interest savings and money market accounts because you won't earn enough to offset inflation.

⊘ Sticking with an investment that isn't living up to expectations. You can move IRA money easily from one investment to another without owing tax on earnings.

⊘ Opening a different IRA account every year. You'll pay more in fees, and you'll have more records to keep track of.

⊘ Misplacing your tax records of non-deductible IRA investments. If you can't prove the tax was paid, you may pay tax twice on the same money.

ROTH OR TRADITIONAL?

Because there are choices in IRAs, between the traditional tax-deferred IRA and the newer tax-free Roth IRA, you need to know how they compare in order to select between them.

The appeal of the Roth is that you get the added benefit of tax-free income on your tax-deferred earnings when you take money out, provided you're older than 59½ and your account has been open at least five years.

But to be eligible to contribute the full $3,000 to a Roth, your income must be less than $95,000 (with partial contributions phased out at $110,000) if you're single, and your joint income less than $150,000 (phased out at $160,000) if you're married. The contributions are never deductible.

In contrast, everyone qualifies for a traditional IRA, and, as the tests opposite show, in some cases you may be eligible to deduct your contribution, reducing current income tax.

Many experts advise choosing a Roth if you qualify, and add that it may pay to transfer your existing IRA to a Roth. Although you may owe current tax, you'll avoid future taxes. But they all agree that before you make a decision it's smart to talk to your own advisor or someone at the financial institution where you have your existing account or plan to open a new one.

EARLY WITHDRAWALS

Though IRAs are intended as long-term retirement investments, you may be able to withdraw your accumulated assets without the 10% federal tax penalty in some very specific situations.

For example, you can use IRA money to pay college tuition, spend up to $10,000 of it to buy a first home for yourself or a family member, or use it for medical expenses. While you will usually owe the income tax that applies to the withdrawal amounts, you won't owe the extra 10%.

The best approach, if you need to withdraw your IRA money early, is to confirm that your plans meet the tax requirements before taking out the money.

More Tax-Deferred Alternatives

You can seed and cultivate tax-deferred investments in different ways.

The rewards of tax-deferred investing—the potential for compounded growth and reduced taxes—are ideal reasons to seize every opportunity to salt away money for retirement. And you don't have to work for someone else to take advantage of tax deferral. You can set up your own plan if you're self-employed. You can inherit tax-deferred investments. Or you can invest through a spousal IRA.

Spousal IRAs

If you don't earn income, you can't contribute to your own IRA. But, your husband can establish a spousal IRA in your name, setting aside double the normal annual contribution split between the two accounts. For example, he could put $3,000 in his own account and $3,000 in yours in both 2003 and 2004. (That amount is scheduled to increase to $4,000 in 2005 and $5,000 in 2008.) The only restriction is that the annual cap applies to each account.

You can invest the money as you see fit, eventually withdraw it, and spend it as you wish. A spousal IRA can be a good way to get a head start on building a retirement fund. And having a spousal IRA now won't keep you from contributing to your own IRA sometime in the future or making catch-up contributions after you turn 50.

BOTH WORKING

HER IRA $3,000 + HIS IRA $3,000 = **$6,000** Maximum contribution $3,000 each

ONE WORKING

HIS IRA $3,000 + HER SPOUSAL IRA $3,000 = **$6,000** Maximum contribution, $3,000 each

Keoghs and SEPs

There are lots of good reasons to run your own business, most of them unrelated to retirement investing. But as a business owner, you can establish a tax-deferred, tax-deductible plan that lets you and your employees invest for the future at the same time as you're earning a living.

Like other qualified retirement plans, Simplified Employee Pensions (SEPs) and Keoghs enjoy the benefits of tax deferral, both on the investment amount and any earnings. As with other plans, you can put the money to work in a broad range of investments.

What gives Keoghs and SEPs their added appeal is their higher contribution limit—up to 25% of your earnings, with a cap of $40,000 in 2003. That amount will increase over time to keep pace with inflation.

But since there are tax implications to setting up these plans, you should always consult your accountant or other tax advisor. That will save you headaches, and probably money.

HOW THEY WORK

While both Keoghs and SEPs are qualified retirement plans that limit access to your funds until age 59½ and require you to start withdrawing when you reach age 70½, there are some important differences between them, as the chart on the following page shows.

Rollovers

If you have money in an employer's retirement savings plan or your own Keogh plan, you can usually transfer it to an IRA if:

- **You leave your job or retire**
- **Your husband dies and you get a payout from his employer**
- **You receive payment from an eligible plan that has ended**
- **You get money from your ex-husband's plan as part of a divorce settlement**

Rolling over your retirement funds into an IRA—rather than spending them or using them to cover anything short of an outright emergency—is essential if you want to keep up the investment momentum you've established. What's more, you may be able to roll the money back into a new employer's retirement plan if the plan allows this type of transfer.

IRA TO IRA

Moving money from one IRA directly to another—for example, from a bank to a mutual fund—is a tax-free transaction, even if you transfer an account that has earned thousands of dollars in dividends and interest.

However, you have to put the entire withdrawal into the new IRA within 60 days after taking it out of the old one. If you miss the cut-off, you'll owe taxes and, potentially, a penalty. An easier approach may be to have the custodian make a direct transfer.

INTO A ROTH?

If your annual income is less than $100,000, you qualify to roll over your existing IRAs into a tax-free Roth IRA. In the year you transfer, you will have to pay tax on your accumulated earnings and on any contributions you deducted, but there'll be no tax when you eventually withdraw if you're over 59½ and the account has been open five years. It can be a smart move, but you ought to consult a financial expert before you decide.

KEEPING AHEAD OF THE TAXMAN

If you roll over retirement money directly to the custodian or trustee of your IRA, it's a tax-free transaction, and the entire amount goes on growing tax deferred. But if the payout goes to you first, 20% is automatically withheld even if you deposit the check immediately in the rollover account.

You'll eventually get the 20% back—provided you've deposited the entire amount of the payout within 60 days. But you'll have to wait for the refund until you've filed your income tax return.

The real rub is coming up with the missing 20% out of your pocket in order to make the full deposit. If you don't, the IRS treats that amount as a withdrawal and you'll owe tax (and maybe a penalty on it).

The solution: Always do a direct rollover.

ADVANTAGES

KEOGHS

- Offer several ways to structure a plan
- May let you shelter more money than some other plans
- Allow employers to set criteria for employees to qualify for participation

SEPS

- Simpler and cheaper to set up
- Easier to administer, both internally and for the IRS
- Don't commit you to annual contributions

LIMITATIONS

KEOGHS

- May commit you to contributions even in poor years
- Expensive to set up and administer
- Complex tax-reporting requirements

SEPS

- Employers must cover all employees, but may set eligibility requirements based on years of service

Deferred Annuities

Certain annuities are tax-deferred savings plans that may or may not be right for you.

Fixed and variable deferred annuities are another way to save for retirement. According to the terms of the contract you sign when you purchase an annuity, at maturity you have the right to convert your account balance to a stream of lifetime income, to take a lump-sum payment, or use your balance to buy another annuity.

SPELLING IT OUT

When you buy an annuity as a **personal retirement plan**, the earnings on your contribution—known as the inside buildup—accumulate tax deferred. But the money you put into an annuity is not tax deductible.

Annuity CONTRACT

1. I agree to invest my money now.

2. You'll pay me back, plus earnings, when the annuity matures.

☐ FIXED ANNUITY

A **fixed annuity** guarantees you'll earn at least a specific rate of interest over the life of the annuity, although what you actually earn in any given period may fluctuate in response to changes in the general interest rate or some other benchmark. These annuities are insurance company products, though they're sold by financial advisors and bank reps as well as insurance agents.

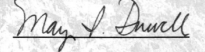

☐ VARIABLE ANNUITY

A **variable annuity** lets you select various mutual fund investment portfolios, also called subaccounts, from a specific list of choices. What you earn depends on how well the subaccounts you've selected perform. Variable annuities are insurance company products that are securities sold through a variety of licensed and registered financial advisors.

INSURANCE PROTECTION

One of the most distinctive features of variable annuities is the guaranteed death benefit they may offer. What that benefit means is that if you die before you begin collecting income from the annuity, the issuing company will pay your beneficiary (or beneficiaries) at least the amount of money you put into the annuity.

Some annuity contracts are more generous, locking in any gains on a regular schedule so that your beneficiaries would receive more than your principal even if the account balance later dropped back below the principal amount.

But you should investigate the financial strength of the insurance company offering the annuity by checking its ratings before you buy. The value of its guarantees depends on its ability to pay its claims.

ANNUITIES—PROS AND CONS

You may be asking yourself why, if annuities seem to have so many advantages, they are sometimes so controversial. Here's a summary of the debate:

THE ADVOCATES

- Your investment grows tax deferred and a portion of your income may be tax free

- Variable annuities make your investment decisions easier by narrowing your choices to a preselected group of investment portfolios

- Variable annuities offer potential for growth and inflation protection

- Variable annuities protect your principal and, in some contracts, your earnings

- There are generally no caps on the amount you can invest each year

- You frequently have your choice of payout—lump sum, lifetime, or periodic income

THE CRITICS

- As a woman, you'll generally get a smaller lifetime payout than a man of the same age with the same investment because, statistically, you'll live longer

- Annual fees on variable annuities may be higher than the fees on comparable mutual funds, which means you must earn more to make out as well

- Most annuities have surrender fees—typically 7% or more of the amount you invest—if you decide to end the contract during the surrender-charge period, typically seven to ten years

- With fixed annuities, the safety of your investment depends on the financial strength of the insurance company selling you the annuity, so make sure you check the company's ratings

FLEXIBLE WITHDRAWALS

As with all tax-deferred retirement plans, you may face tax penalties if you withdraw from your annuities before you turn 59½. If you take your money out before then, you may owe a 10% penalty as well as the tax that's due on your earnings. So while there are some exceptions to the penalty rule, it's wise to think of annuities as long-term savings.

On the other hand, you have more flexibility in timing your withdrawals after 59½ than you do with IRAs or employer sponsored plans. You can access your money at any time. Or, with most annuities, you can defer taking income until you reach 85 or 90, depending on the state where you live. That allows you to continue to accumulate tax-deferred earnings and postpone adding income until you're paying income tax at a lower rate.

INVESTMENT VS. PENSION PAYOUT

Don't confuse a deferred annuity with a **pension**. A pension, sometimes called a life-stream payment, is the standard method of collecting the retirement income your employer pays you. It means getting a check each month for the remainder of your life.

If you're eligible for a pension, taking it as an annuity may make lots of sense. By law, employers must use the same life expectancy table for women as for men in calculating the amount of your monthly payment. But, as a woman, you are likely to live longer—and so collect more overall—than a man the same age.

Immediate Annuities

The name says it all: Immediate means right away.

The big difference between an immediate annuity and a deferred annuity is that when you buy an immediate annuity, the purchase price is converted into a series of income payments, which you begin to receive right away.

You choose the way you want the income paid from the alternatives the annuity provider offers. The payout might be over your lifetime—known as a **life annuity**—or your lifetime and that of another person—known as a **joint and survivor annuity**. You can also arrange for a guarantee period as part of either lifetime payment option so that your beneficiary will receive the payments for a specific number of years if you should die before that time is up.

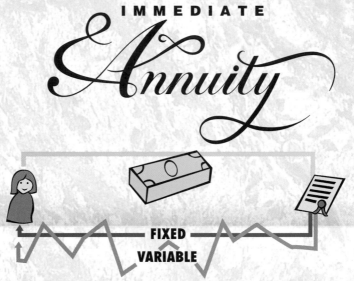

FIXED OR VARIABLE?

The bottom line difference between fixed and variable immediate annuities is the way your income payment is calculated.

A fixed contract pays you the same amount of income, month in and month out, for as long as you live. If you buy a joint and survivor annuity, the survivor continues to receive a fixed income for life.

With a variable annuity, you can receive payments for your lifetime, or two lifetimes with a joint and survivor contract, but the amount is not guaranteed. The payment fluctuates to reflect the market performance of the underlying investments in your annuity subaccounts.

The advantage of a fixed annuity is that you know exactly what will be coming in every month. That makes it easier to budget. The downside is that the amount won't increase to keep pace with inflation. The longer you live, the smaller the percentage of your financial needs the annuity is likely to cover.

There are two sides to variable annuities as well. It is possible that your income will increase over time, especially when the financial markets are strong. That means inflation is less of a problem and you'll have more disposable income. But if markets are flat or falling, your income could drop, perhaps significantly, and reduce your standard of living.

PERSONALIZED PLANS

To take advantage of the strengths of both types of annuities, you might ask your annuity provider to design a personalized contract or purchase two contracts. For example, you might use part of your principal to buy a fixed annuity and the balance to buy a variable contract.

Then you'd always have a regular sum coming in, and you might use the fluctuating amount for extras, travel, or whatever is important to you.

Another strategy may be to split your variable annuity payout in two. One could be a lifetime contract and the other time-specific. You might allocate income from the shorter payout for the things you plan to do in early retirement, yet you'd still be guaranteed income for life.

Alternatively, you may be able to choose either time-specific or amount-specific payment terms. Whatever decision you make is included in the contract you sign. If the contract is **commutable**, you can change your mind. But usually your income decision is final.

THE MONEY TO BUY

Since you buy an immediate annuity with a lump-sum payment, you do need cash on hand. But, in fact, suddenly having a lump sum may be the reason you consider an immediate annuity in the first place.

Suppose, for example, that you've just received a large inheritance, have realized a substantial profit from selling your business, or have the opportunity to take a lump-sum payout from your retirement savings plan. If you're uncertain about creating and managing a diversified investment portfolio or you recognize that you'd be more comfortable knowing you'll have a steady stream of income that you can't outlive, an annuity may be the answer.

You may also be able to convert a cash value life insurance policy that you no longer need to an immediate annuity and continue to defer income taxes. But you should consult a qualified estate planner to be sure the policy qualifies for conversion.

ESTIMATING YOUR INCOME

The annuity provider determines the amount of monthly income you receive. It depends on

- The **annuity principal**, which is the lump sum you use to purchase the annuity contract

- The payment method you choose

- Your age, and the age of the other annuitant if it's a joint and survivor annuity

- Whether the annuity is fixed or variable

However, it pays to comparison shop, as different providers are likely to offer varying amounts of money even though the purchase price and payout terms are the same.

CHOOSING A PAYOUT

One of the biggest decisions you make with an immediate annuity is choosing between a single life payout and a joint and survivor payout. If you're single and have no dependents, it's probably an easy decision. But in other cases, it may be harder.

The issue is that joint and survivor payments are always smaller than single payments when the principal you invest is the same. But the total paid out over two lifetimes can be higher.

The primary reason for selecting joint and survivor is to provide a lifetime income for your husband or partner should you die first and vice versa. If the survivor will need the money, the choice will probably be clear.

But there may be cases when having the larger income a single life annuity would provide makes more sense. That includes situations when your husband or partner

- Has a guaranteed lifetime income from another source

- Is ill and unlikely to survive you

- Is much older than you are

TAXING MATTERS
One of the benefits of regular annuity income is that part of each monthly payment is nontaxable because it represents return of your **cost basis**, or principal, rather than earnings. You paid tax on that amount before you used it to purchase the annuity and you're not taxed twice.

Coping with the Unexpected

You have to be prepared for the things you can't predict.

However carefully you plan for the future, unexpected events can interrupt the progress you've been making toward your financial goals or, in the worst circumstances, threaten to derail your expectations.

While there's no foolproof way to predict or prevent what might happen, whether tomorrow or years down the road, there are things you can do now to help protect yourself and your loved ones financially whatever the future brings. One of the most important is having good records.

THE FIRST STEP

If you've already got a record-keeping system in place, or your husband or partner has set one up, review the way it's organized. If some of the information is online and the rest is on paper, you'll want to be sure they work together and back each other up.

You should have the passwords to all accounts and other records stored in a secure place. If you're not completely comfortable using online records, you may want to have back-up toll-free phone numbers on hand. You'll want to keep keys to safe deposit boxes in a secure place. And you may want to prepare a summary letter of the accounts and other records you have and where they are for a family member or friend. Then they'd know whom to contact in an emergency.

You'll also want to be sure there's an up-to-date record of any debts you'll be responsible for. That includes income taxes, all loans, and personal debts.

TAX MATTERS

Though it doesn't happen often, you have to be prepared for the possibility that the IRS will have questions about your tax return. If that happens, detailed and accurate records about your income, deductions, and credits, are essential.

JUST THE FACTS

When you put together your financial records, here's some of what you'll want to know:

- What investments do you have, and where are they held or recorded?

- What pension and other retirement plans exist and who administers them?

- What are your family's life, disability, liability, and health insurance arrangements? How would you make a claim?

- Does your husband or partner have a will? Do you? Where are the wills kept? Are they up to date?

- Have the wills been reviewed since the estate tax provisions changed?

GETTING ADVICE

If you divorce or are widowed, are faced with mandatory early retirement, or fear a major strain on your budget, you'll want professional advice.

Many of the financial decisions you make when you're under emotional pressure, such as which marital assets you want in divorce or which pension payout to take, can't be changed even if you later realize that you've made a bad decision. The same is often true when you're dividing property and settling estates, since it can be easy to overlook critical details, and you may be pressured to act by someone who has a vested interest in the outcome.

It's important to hire someone with expertise that matches your need, since both the law and your emotions can trip you up if you aren't receiving the best advice. You may want to start the search by asking your current financial advisor, accountant, or lawyer for a reference. Just remember that the final choice of advisors is yours, and you have to be satisfied that your interests will get the attention they deserve.

carefully financial security, events which... life into turmoil.

If you're not sure what to keep, start with the IRS publications on record-keeping requirements. Take a look at Publication 17 or Publication 552, "Recordkeeping for Individuals." You can download them at the IRS website at www.irs.gov.

The IRS typically acts on its questions within a year, but has a period of limitations—typically three years from the filing date—in which it can audit your return. If you hear from the IRS, it's smart to talk to your attorney or tax advisor before you do anything. He or she can help you make the appropriate response.

MAKE COPIES

When you are asked to send documents to the IRS, your insurance company, or anyone else, never send originals. Instead, make copies, and, if necessary, have the copies notarized. That way, essential documents won't disappear.

FAMILY RECORDS

You should have detailed and up-to-date records that describe your family assets. And you should know how to contact the personnel office or benefits department where you work and also where your husband or partner works. Here's a list of key items:

 Checking and savings account statements

 Investment accounts with brokerage firms, banks, mutual fund companies, insurance companies, or other financial institutions

 Pension and other retirement plans administered by current or past employers

 Individual retirement accounts (IRAs) and annuities

 Insurance policies

 Titles to real estate, cars, and other property

 Partnership and prenuptial agreements and divorce papers

 Appraisal documents for collections

 Records of outstanding loans

 Tax records

Out of Work?

Unemployment can throw a curve ball at your financial plans.

While you may worry more about losing your job when the economy is in a slump, people can be laid off any time. When companies merge or are acquired, the work force may be downsized. Or business may just be slow.

If that happens to you, do you know how you'd manage financially? It's smart to think about the bills that would have to be paid and whether you have an emergency fund that could help see you through several months of job searching.

A WORD TO THE WISE

If you're participating in a retirement savings plan, you'll be asked how you want your plan assets handled. You own the current value of your account that comes from your contributions and any earnings on those contributions. Your employer's vesting schedule determines if you own the contributions your employer has made to your plan.

You may be able to leave the assets in the plan, at least for the time being, and you always have the right to move them into an IRA.

The alternative that may make the least sense is taking a distribution in cash rather than rolling it over to an IRA. You'll owe income tax plus a potential 10% of

the total if you're younger than 59½ and don't qualify for an early withdrawal. And, if you spend the money, your retirement savings will be gone.

COLLECTING UNEMPLOYMENT

If you're laid off, you may be eligible to collect unemployment insurance. You apply at the local office of your state's unemployment agency. Rules vary from state to state, as does the income you're eligible for. Your benefit, which is taxable income, lasts until either you find a new job or the insurance expires. The term is usually 26 weeks, though it may be extended in times of large-scale unemployment.

NEGOTIATING A SEVERANCE

Unless you have an employment contract, your employer isn't required to pay **severance**, or termination pay, though some employers do. You may want to check with your human resources department about company policy if your supervisor doesn't raise the issue.

One complicating factor is that there's no uniform standard for what severance should be. Some companies offer one week of pay for each year of service. Others provide a flat four weeks of pay, though some offer more in certain circumstances. Similarly, there's no requirement that all employees be treated equivalently. So you may want to be prepared to negotiate what you think is a fair settlement. It will probably pay to do some research online. One source is state unemployment agency websites that offer severance calculators.

When you accept a severance package, many employers require that you sign a legal document releasing the employer from any claims you may have. You should fully understand the implications of signing the release, so you may want to review it with your legal advisor.

IRA

JOB LOSS

EXIT

MAKING THE TRANSITION

You may also want to request:

- Use of your office space, computer, and phone line for a period of time while you search for another job

- Extension of your health-insurance benefits for as long as possible

- Prorated bonus for the months you've worked

- A faster vesting period for stock options so you can exercise them

- Cash for any unused vacation and sick days

STAYING INSURED

It's essential to ensure that you have health insurance for yourself and your dependents. If you've been insured through your employer's plan, you may be eligible for continuing coverage under the Consolidated Omnibus Budget Reconciliation Act (COBRA) for up to 18 months. It's not cheap. You pay the full premium your employer pays, plus up to 2% in administrative fees. But some states may require more generous coverage.

If you're married or in a long-term relationship, your husband or partner may be able to cover you. Most employers offer family plans and some provide coverage for domestic partners. In all likelihood, this will be the least costly option.

EARLY RETIREMENT

Early retirement may be less traumatic than being laid off, but it will require some immediate decisions. If you're part of a pension plan, you may have to choose how your retirement income will be paid. If you don't need the money, you may ask to postpone income until you reach regular retirement age. That's not always an alternative, though.

If you participate in a 401(k) or other retirement savings plan, you'll want to investigate whether to start taking income or roll over your account balance into an IRA. It's wise to discuss the alternatives with your employer's human resources officer and ask your financial advisor to recommend a retirement specialist.

You also need to investigate health insurance coverage. Your employer may provide benefits until you're eligible for Medicare, or you may be eligible for COBRA under the same terms as people who have been laid off. The one thing you don't want to do is let coverage lapse.

The good news is that retiring doesn't have to be the end of your working life unless you want it to be. Unless you're a state employee who wants to work for another agency covered by the same retirement plan, there are usually no restrictions against earning a salary while you are drawing a pension. A new job may also be the solution to the health insurance dilemma—and it may be the perfect opportunity to try a new career.

Divorce: Financial Self-Defense

Good advice and a cool head can help you protect your finances during a breakup.

The end of a marriage often means major financial changes. The unfortunate reality is that a divorced woman usually ends up losing out economically, especially if she has been dependent on her husband's income. Since nearly half of all marriages end in divorce, many women have cause for concern.

By educating yourself about personal finance and investments now, you'll have the knowledge and the confidence to manage on your own if you ever need to.

Prepare to take defensive action in a divorce

WHAT'S AT STAKE

In legal terms, divorce is about dividing up property and resolving issues of child custody and support. If you have few assets and no children, there may be no controversy. Otherwise, you may have to be prepared for a struggle. Although about 90% of all divorces are settled out of court, the most contentious ones can take a long time to resolve.

Divorces are regulated by state laws, and court settlements generally reflect local custom and judicial preferences rather than any uniform state or national standard. You should get advice from an experienced family law attorney who knows the local judges and can tell you how similar cases have turned out.

One of the most difficult issues is the question of equitable distribution of marital property, the standard in most states. Equitable does not mean equal. It is more apt to mean a two-thirds/one-third split, with the more affluent partner getting the larger share.

In the nine **community property** states (Arizona, California, Idaho, Louisiana, Nevada, New Mexico, Texas, Washington, and Wisconsin), marital property is defined as anything earned or owned jointly during the marriage. It is divided equally, in most cases.

Future income is not property and is not subject to division, equitable or otherwise.

AVOIDING KNOCKOUT PUNCHES

High emotions could lead you to rash, regrettable decisions if you're not careful. Before you take any major actions, get professional advice. You need an experienced divorce lawyer on your side, and you'll probably want to consult your accountant and any other financial advisors as well. They can help you figure out what information and documentation you'll need, and what you can do to protect yourself. Remember that if you make more money or have a higher net worth, you could end up paying alimony to your ex.

QUESTIONS OF DEBT

If your marriage has come apart over financial issues, a divorce may not resolve the problems. That's because any debts either of you incurred while married and any joint agreements you signed will probably be considered your responsibility if your former husband does not pay them. If you refuse to pay or can't afford to, your personal credit history could be affected.

Creditors might also try to collect from you on debts your husband runs up during the time you're legally separated. Escaping these demands may be more difficult than you would think. One of the issues that will affect the outcome is how your state defines legal separation.

One of you could agree to pay off debt in exchange for a larger share of the assets. However, if your former husband declares bankruptcy after the divorce, an IOU he has given you may be worthless.

You are also responsible to the IRS for any unpaid taxes that are due on joint returns you've signed, even if you weren't involved in figuring the tax or filling out the forms. But you shouldn't be held responsible for taxes on income your former husband might have concealed from you—and from the IRS.

KEEPING THE KIDS

Unless you believe that your children are in danger, moving them far away from their father could jeopardize your chances of gaining custody later on. Moving out on your own and leaving the children with their father may also work against you in a custody battle. And although you may be tempted to describe your estranged husband's faults to your children, there's a good reason to hold your tongue: Judges often look unfavorably upon one parent's attempts to undermine their children's relationship with the other parent.

FACING THE REALITY

Whether you initiate the decision to end your marriage or have it imposed on you, there are some things experts suggest you consider to sidestep potential financial problems:

- Establish your own checking, savings, and credit accounts as soon as divorce seems inevitable. If your existing accounts are joint, you can ask your lawyer's advice about withdrawing half the balance to open your own account. Technically, you or your husband can take out every penny. But if you do, you might face a court order to repay it, or prejudice your legal case.

- If you are able to work together amicably, consider an escrow account or joint account requiring both signatures to pay family expenses in the time between separation and divorce.

- Make a new will and designate a new beneficiary for insurance policies, pension and retirement plans, and any other assets passed directly to a beneficiary. Existing wills are sometimes but not always voided when a divorce is final.

- Cancel joint equity lines of credit and freeze joint brokerage accounts. Otherwise, you might end up with more debt or fewer investments than you expected. You can call first and send a follow-up letter. If you ask that a notation be made on the account's computer file, you may be able to prevent unauthorized trades.

- Ask your lawyer about changing real property that you own as joint tenants to tenants in common, so you can designate your heirs if you die before the divorce is final. In some states you can do this individually, by filing a record of the deed change where the original deed is registered. In other states, you must both agree to the change, so be sure to check.

- Consider a legal separation to iron out how you'll handle financial responsibilities before the divorce is final.

Agreeing on a custody arrangement may be one of the most difficult decisions you ever make. Joint custody works for many families, but be sure to talk to your advisors about the consequences of any arrangement. Sharing custody may mean smaller child-support payments, which can be a real problem if you're footing most of the expenses. You might try to resolve each parent's financial responsibilities in the divorce agreement.

Financial Settlements

Understanding your rights and responsibilities is crucial.

If you're confident about what you want, rational about why you want it, and realistic about what you can reasonably expect to get, you can use your divorce settlement as the foundation for your future financial security. But if you don't have a clear plan for obtaining and handling your share of the assets, what seems like a fair settlement can leave you and your children short of financial resources.

Once the settlement is final, having a plan in place can also help you avoid potential problems, such as making risky investments, overextending your credit, or tapping into IRAs or other retirement funds to meet daily expenses.

YOURS, MINE, AND OURS

Ownership determines division of property. Generally, but not always, anything you owned in your own name before marriage, and continued to hold separately, is yours to keep, as is anything you inherited or received as a gift.

But money that you and your husband earned during the marriage, along with any investments and property, is divided at divorce. If you can agree on the division without going to court, you save money—sometimes astounding amounts.

In most cases, though, you'll probably benefit from the advice and assistance of an experienced divorce attorney.

DIVIDING RETIREMENT PLANS

In evaluating your marital assets, you may discover that substantial amounts of money are tied up in a pension or other retirement fund. If you both have plans, you may each agree to keep your own. But if you have no plan, or a small one, you can claim a share of your husband's.

To do that, a lawyer must draw up a Qualified Domestic Relations Order (QDRO) as part of the divorce settlement. That's a court order that instructs the administrator of your former husband's plan to divide the pension assets between you. The order must be specific and accurate, so you should consult a specialist in the field. You should also follow up on the paperwork. If your lawyer stalls or forgets to submit the QDRO, you may have trouble collecting your court-ordered share later.

Since the administrator has 18 months to rule on the validity of the QDRO, you can also ask that your share of the assets be set aside, so that they can't be withdrawn or borrowed. The way the pension will be paid out, and the other rights you may have—taking loans, for example—will depend on the plan. So be sure that you understand the provisions clearly.

THE ELEMENTS OF A FAIR DEAL

In agreeing to a divorce settlement, there are more important things than just getting it over with. Chief among them is considering the long-term implications of dividing assets.

Your lawyer or financial advisor can provide advice, but you'll pay less in fees and have a greater advantage if you can give a detailed picture of your assets and your contributions to the marriage. If you can show what you brought into the marriage, what you and your husband have acquired during the marriage, and what

your assets are worth, you'll have a better sense of what your fair share should be.

Obviously, each case is different, but there are several things you should always consider. One is taxes. You owe no taxes when you give or receive property as part of a divorce settlement, although you do owe income taxes on any alimony you receive. But if you later sell the property you received when you divorced, you may owe **capital gains taxes**. For example, if you sell stock to make a down payment on a new home, you may owe tax on any profit. The

GETTING SOCIAL SECURITY

If you were married ten years or longer before your divorce, you're entitled to receive Social Security based on your ex-husband's earnings. He actually isn't involved—it's between you and the Social Security office—and his benefits aren't diminished. But it can be an important resource, especially if your own benefit would be smaller or you wouldn't qualify for Social Security on your own.

INSURANCE PROTECTION

If you or your children are dependent on income from your ex-husband, you'll probably want to make sure he has life insurance to replace that income if he dies or is disabled. You'll want to be sure that the coverage is kept up to date and that you understand how the policy premiums are being paid. You don't want to discover, years after your divorce, that the premiums were paid by loans against

the policy until all the available cash had been used up. In that case, the policy would lapse, creating potential tax problems as well as loss of insurance.

Ask your insurance agent and divorce attorney for advice on the best way to prevent potential problems. One solution may be for you to own the policy as well as be the beneficiary.

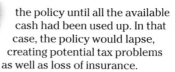

ASSETS & LIABILITIES

WHAT ABOUT ALIMONY?

Whether or not you receive income from your ex-husband after your divorce depends on a number of factors, especially the length of your marriage, your financial situation, your ability to support yourself, and sometimes the tax implications.

Even if the court grants a no-fault divorce, a few states consider fault when deciding alimony and division of property, especially if it's economic fault. An example is a spouse who has depleted property by overspending or waste. And some states won't grant alimony to a spouse who commits adultery. Only about 15% of marriages involve alimony, in most cases paid by the husband to the wife, although wives may also be ordered to pay alimony.

Although each state sets guidelines for child support, alimony awards may vary widely even within the same state.

You should also be aware that while there are strong mechanisms in place to require divorced and separated parents— usually but not always the fathers—to pay child support regularly, it can be more difficult to collect alimony from a former husband.

If you feel strongly that you would rather terminate all ties to—and dependence on—your former husband, you may prefer a one-time payment that you can invest and manage as you choose.

one exception is selling your home, since you can realize up to $250,000 in profit as a single person without owing any tax.

Another consideration is the quality and diversity of the investments that you receive. You don't want a portfolio you can't liquidate, or one that's concentrated in one or two investments. The more you know about what the investments are really worth and how they are likely to perform, the more astute you can be in asking for specific ones as your share of the settlement.

Widowhood

You should be prepared to manage your finances on your own.

Though it's not a welcome thought, women usually outlive their husbands and are much less likely to remarry than widowed men are, especially if they're over 45.

As a woman, that means you must be prepared to make financial decisions by yourself. You may have to choose what to do with an inheritance or find a way to stretch limited dollars. In either case, the best approach is to take your time, plan carefully, and don't allow yourself to be rushed or intimidated.

Make no mistake, your task may be complex. As you navigate the ins and outs of inheritance, probate, and all of your alternatives for investment and income, you may want to develop a relationship with a good, impartial financial advisor who can help you understand your situation, alert you to opportunities, and point out potential pitfalls along the way.

RULES OF INHERITANCE

Each state's inheritance laws are a little different, but unless you have a prenuptial agreement, you are usually entitled to a percentage—often 33% to 50%—of your husband's estate, whether he leaves it to you outright or in trust. And he has the right, in most states, to leave you his entire estate if he chooses.

But if your husband dies without a will, you may get only the percentage of his estate that the law requires, even if he meant to leave you everything.

Property you and your husband owned as joint tenants with rights of survivorship becomes yours at his death, when you transfer the title to your name. For tax purposes, the half that belonged to your husband is **stepped up**, so that its tax basis becomes its current worth. If you were to sell before an increase in value, there would be no capital gains on the half that belonged to him. However, there might be capital gains and potential capital gains tax on your half of the same property. Special provisions may defer or reduce that tax if the property is your primary residence.

Inheritance rules are different if you live in one of the nine **community property states**, since your husband might designate someone other than you to inherit his share. For instance, he could leave his half of the house to a daughter from a previous marriage, even if you're still living in it. Complications like these make it important for couples to discuss their estate plans with an advisor.

STUCK IN THE TRUST

Your husband may leave you assets in a trust that limits your control over the money. For instance, you may be unable to decide how to spend it, invest it, or leave it to your heirs. Although a **marital trust** may be designed to provide you with financial security by paying you income, such trusts are generally designed to pass the bulk of the estate to the next generation. So, you'll want to know ahead of time what kind of estate plan your husband is considering, so you can express your concerns before it is drafted.

FINAL DETAILS

If your husband dies, you can work with the executor of the estate, your financial advisor, and lawyer to take care of the following details promptly:

- Open accounts for the executor to pay his bills from the assets of the estate, including income taxes
- Contact Social Security to report his death and your status as a widow if he was collecting benefits
- Notify his employer, IRA custodians, and insurance agent to request settlement payments
- Change joint bank, mutual fund, and brokerage accounts to your name
- Record your ownership of real estate and other property held jointly with right of survivorship

As you assess your situation, you'll need to think seriously about your life expectancy and goals. A widow in her 50s, for example, may live 30 years or more, and be actively involved in work and play a great part of the time. In contrast, a woman in her 80s is likely to have a shorter time to live, even if she maintains a busy lifestyle.

Likewise, if you're still earning income or collecting a pension, you may want to invest primarily for growth. But if you need more money for living expenses, you'll probably want to shift more of your assets away from growth and into more stable, income-producing investments.

ROLL OVER FOR RETIREMENT

If you're the beneficiary of your husband's 401(k), IRA, or other retirement plan, that money is paid to you directly after his death. Many experts advise you to roll over these funds into your own IRA to invest the money for retirement and postpone paying taxes until you begin withdrawals.

ASSESSING YOUR NEEDS

There are two things you need to know as you evaluate your portfolio: how much you need to live comfortably and how much regular income you receive.

MAKING ESTATE PLANS

If you're the primary beneficiary of your husband's estate, it's your responsibility to plan what will happen to your property after you die. The first thing you should do, if you haven't already, is draw up a will to express your intentions clearly.

It's worth hiring a lawyer to help make sure your will does what you want and to advise you of any estate planning options that might help you. And as your life and assets change, and as estate tax provisions are revised, review your will and your plan to be sure they're still in tune with your wishes.

Marrying Again, Marrying Later

Make sure your money gets along as well as you do.

If you're marrying again, or you marry for the first time later in life, you and your husband may have a more complicated financial situation than a younger couple just starting out. Specifically, each of you probably has personal assets, income, debts, and obligations. One or both of you might have children. And you may have very different financial habits and expectations.

Divorced couples cite money as the number one reason that marriages fail. So, although talking over a pile of tax returns and income statements may not seem romantic, the health and longevity of your marriage may depend on it.

PREMARITAL AGREEMENTS

As you prepare for your wedding, the last thing you probably want to think about is divorce. However, second marriages do fail at a higher rate than first marriages, and in most cases the woman suffers financially. In that context, a premarital agreement might be worth considering. (Perhaps you and your husband-to-be can think of the agreement as a declaration of your good intentions.)

You can use premarital agreements to determine how you'll split responsibilities while you're married, but most couples use them to determine how to divide money and property if they ever divorce and to specify an inheritance for children they had before the new marriage. And if you plan to give up your career to support your husband, you may want a premarital agreement to protect your financial security.

Laws governing these agreements vary by state and can be complicated, so it helps to get professional legal advice. Experts recommend that you each retain your own lawyer, and that you allow plenty of time to review and negotiate the agreement.

PLANNING TOGETHER

If you've been managing your financial lives alone, you may need to make some adjustments to your goals and your time-table for reaching them.

You may also want to examine your investment portfolios for asset allocation and diversification. For example, if you both hold stock in the same company, you may want to rebalance. Your risk tolerance and investing styles may also differ. As you work out your new financial lives, it might help to sit down with a financial advisor to find strategies that work for both of you.

Of course, debt could complicate your plans. If your husband brings debt to the marriage, that debt legally belongs to him alone. However, his debt may affect your shared financial plans, so you may want to discuss his plans for paying it off.

KNOW THY STUFF

Some experts recommend you make a list of the property you bring into a marriage, so in case of a split you'll know what's yours. However, if you put money earned during your marriage into an account you owned before your marriage, that whole account may become marital property. So, if you want to keep your old account separate, it's probably smart to deposit any money you earn while you're married into a new account.

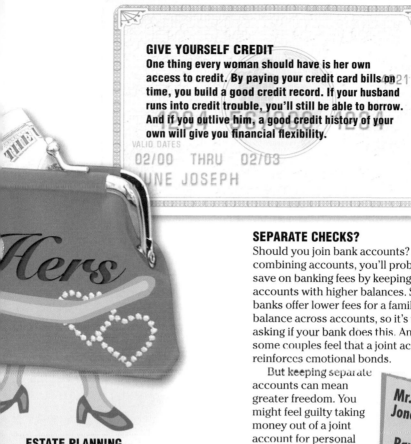

GIVE YOURSELF CREDIT
One thing every woman should have is her own access to credit. By paying your credit card bills on time, you build a good credit record. If your husband runs into credit trouble, you'll still be able to borrow. And if you outlive him, a good credit history of your own will give you financial flexibility.

VALID DATES
02/00 THRU 02/03
UNE JOSEPH

ESTATE PLANNING

Estate planning is vital if you have children from before the marriage. If you leave all your property to your husband to avoid estate taxes, your children might get nothing when he dies. An attorney who specializes in estate planning can help you set up your will and any other necessary legal documents to be sure your estate is divided according to your wishes.

TELL THEM YOUR NAME

If you change your name, the government, your employer, and others will need to know. Start by updating your driver's license and Social Security card. Then be sure to update your name with the following:

- Bank and investment accounts
- Employer
- Credit cards
- Doctors
- IRS
- Lenders
- Memberships
- Passport
- Property titles
- Utility and phone bills
- Vehicle registration and insurance
- Voter and motor vehicle driver registration
- Wills and insurance policies

SEPARATE CHECKS?

Should you join bank accounts? By combining accounts, you'll probably save on banking fees by keeping fewer accounts with higher balances. Some banks offer lower fees for a family's total balance across accounts, so it's worth asking if your bank does this. And some couples feel that a joint account reinforces emotional bonds.

But keeping separate accounts can mean greater freedom. You might feel guilty taking money out of a joint account for personal expenses, especially luxuries, and prefer to use a personal account. If you're older and used to handling finances on your own, separate accounts can lessen the culture shock of marriage. You might also prefer to pay child support and alimony from a separate account if your husband is sensitive about those payments. And if you're taking care of your elderly parents, you may prefer to use your own money.

Some couples use three accounts: his, hers, and theirs. They use a joint account for common expenses and goals such as groceries, mortgage and car payments, insurance, children, retirement, entertainment, and vacations. And each maintains a separate account for personal expenses.

Taking Care of Others

Women are more likely to spend time and resources caring for others.

One of the reasons that women tend to earn less than men over their lifetimes is that women are more likely to take time out of their careers to care for others. Even beyond the demands of mother-hood, women often end up taking on responsibilities for family members who need extra care, such as aging parents and children with special needs.

If you devote your time and resources to care for another, the financial con-sequences may be far-reaching. For instance, if you work fewer hours or switch to a lower-paying job to provide care, your decrease in taxable income will translate to a decrease in Social Security benefits in retirement. You may have less to invest for your own goals and may feel obliged to dip into your own accounts to pay for your loved ones' needs.

While it's difficult to predict whether you'll ever be responsible for someone else's care, you can make sure that the necessary legal documents, financial resources, and insurance policies are in place. You should also keep your own rainy day fund to cover emergency costs—experts recommend enough to cover three to six months of expenses. Otherwise, in a crisis you may have to tap into retirement accounts that could be difficult to replenish.

ELDERCARE

As your parents age, they may need more practical, emotional, and financial support from you. You may find you're exhausting your resources trying to support children and aging parents at the same time.

If this happens, or circumstances make the scenario likely, you might want to sit down with your parents and siblings to discuss how to give your parents the necessary support in a way that works for everyone. Although it may be uncom-fortable to discuss issues like sickness, mortality, and money with your family, it's better to face unpleasant issues now than to be caught off guard in an emergency. If you feel that you need an experienced, impartial mediator or expert advice, you can turn to a geriatric care manager or counselor. You can find one by asking your doctor, hospital, or local **Area Agency on Aging (AAA)**, or by getting in touch with the **US Administration on Aging (AoA)**.

PAYING FOR CARE

Your parents may need custodial care, also known as long-term care: ongoing help with managing everyday life. There's a discussion of the important role long-term care insurance can play in Chapter Five.

MONEY TALK

If your parents lived through the Depression, they may be nervous about spending money. Elders often see an expense like housekeeping services as an extravagance—especially if they can have one of their adult children tidy up for free. However, the cost to you in time and energy may make it worth hiring professional help.

If your parents agree to discuss their finances with you, you can help them find out if they can afford to hire help. You might recommend they discuss their situation with a financial advisor. By thoroughly reviewing what they have and what they need, they may find they can afford to spend more on care than they assumed.

NAME A DECISION-MAKER

If your parents are ever unable to make decisions for themselves, someone will need to manage their affairs for them. Your parents can legally name someone to make decisions for them, by assigning one of the following powers of attorney to a trusted friend or family member.

Durable power of attorney for finances. This document authorizes someone to make the financial decisions that your parent legally makes, such as paying bills, depositing checks, and selling property. It takes effect immediately and continues after your parent is disabled. Your parent can cancel or change the document at any time.

Durable power of attorney for health/ healthcare proxy. This document authorizes someone to make medical decisions for your parent and outline his or her wishes for treatment in case of a serious illness or accident. It too takes effect immediately and continues after your parent is disabled. Your parent can cancel or change this document at any time. You can also suggest he or she draft a **living will**, which details the sort of medical procedures he or she would accept or refuse if terminally ill.

Springing power of attorney. This document covers the same responsibilities as the durable power of attorney for finances. However, it doesn't take effect until your parent is disabled, and once it goes into effect, it can't be changed or revoked.

SPECIAL-NEEDS CHILDREN

Special-needs children often have higher than usual expenses and need financial help for a longer time. While many disabled children achieve great independence in adulthood, it's possible that your child will need assistance throughout his or her life. Therefore, if you have a special-needs child, your life insurance needs, too, may be much greater.

Many disabled people pay for food and shelter with Social Security and Medicaid benefits, and assets in the child's name can reduce the child's eligibility for benefits. However, you can work with an attorney to create a special-needs trust that allows your child to qualify for government assistance while providing supplemental money for things like medical care, education, and transportation. In addition, you may want to provide sufficient money to pay for extras like entertainment and travel.

Many experts recommend life insurance to fund these trusts, since investments like stock and real estate fluctuate in value and may not cover your child's needs when you die. Also, the death benefit is usually free of income taxes and probate fees, though not estate taxes unless the policy is held in a life insurance trust.

Dealing with Fraud

Take steps to protect your identity and your money from thieves and scams.

Fraud takes many forms, whether it's common small-scale pilfering, identity theft, or investment fraud. Vigilance is your best defense. And if you're a victim, you should act quickly to minimize the damage and get your finances on track.

CREDIT CARD STATEMENT

1. GROCERIES	8/23/03	$40.00
2. GASOLINE	6/09/03	$10.00
3. MOON ROCKS	2/11/03	$2000.00

??

I DIDN'T BUY THAT...

You shouldn't throw away your account statements and bills unread, since they may alert you to fraud. If you spot un-authorized charges or withdrawals on your bank statements or phone, utility, or credit card bills, you should contact the company to explain the situation. You may want to ask that your account numbers be changed and any related credit or debit card replaced.

Your liability under federal law for unauthorized credit card charges should be $50, and the company generally erases the charge from your record. With debit cards, you must report your card lost or stolen within two days to limit your liability to $50. After that, your liability can rise to $500. If you wait more than 60 days, you may be liable for all unauthorized debits.

SHRED IT

Your trash may be treasure for thieves. If you toss out sensitive documents, you're handing the keys to your financial identity to anyone with the time to reach into your recycling bin.

You can render documents unreadable by shredding them with a machine that turns them into confetti-sized bits. Remember to shred credit card receipts that carry part or all of your account number, and take the time to shred credit card offers, since thieves could use them to open new accounts.

CLEANING YOUR RECORD

Three credit bureaus keep tabs on your credit history: Equifax, Experian, and TransUnion. You should review your credit reports regularly, once or twice a year. You can correct the ordinary mistakes that creep in, such as when the bureau confuses two people with the same name, and you can look for new, unfamiliar accounts that may have been opened by thieves.

You can call the bureaus or contact them online to order your reports.

Equifax 888-685-1111
www.equifax.com

Experian 888-397-3742
www.experian.com

TransUnion 800-888-4213
www.transunion.com

If you spot irregularities, you should contact the bureau. You may need to fill out a form and contact the creditor to request a correction. The bureaus offer services that allow you to monitor your credit. However, fees for these services are higher than the cost of ordering reports.

IDENTITY THEFT

Identity thieves open new credit cards, phone numbers, or utilities accounts in your name, skip out on the bills, and leave you to deal with tarnished credit and calls from collection agencies. They may use your information to forge checks or government documents. And they could sell your information to other thieves, compounding the danger.

To protect yourself, don't give your personal information to unknown companies or people, even those who claim to work for legitimate organizations such as your bank or the government. In particular, guard your Social Security number, birthdate, mother's maiden name, passwords, and account numbers.

Unfortunately, there's little you can do to prevent identity theft that originates when employees steal sensitive information collected by legitimate organizations, or when family members misuse your information. If you're a victim, you can and should fight to clear your name. In the worst cases, it may take years to undo the damage, but it's

IF YOUR IDENTITY IS STOLEN

- File a police report
- Notify one of the credit reporting agencies, which will place a fraud alert on your account
- Fill out the Federal Trade Commission's ID Theft Affidavit and send copies to all creditors
- Ask creditors about their requirements for reporting fraud
- Consult an attorney, if necessary
- Monitor accounts and credit reports for new instances of fraud

INVESTMENT SCAMS

Investment scams prey on inexperienced or greedy investors who think of the stock market as a lottery where you can get rich quick. If you're a patient, informed investor with a sound strategy, you probably won't fall for these scams. Still, sometimes even experienced investors are tempted to gamble on unknown stock, real estate, or other suspect investments.

You should insist on knowing the risks before you make any investment, and be skeptical of unsolicited recommendations that you don't understand. Many fraudulent recommendations play down risks or hide the nature of the investment, sometimes making complex, risky scams seem simple and safe. Beware the following red flags:

RED FLAG	WHAT IT USUALLY MEANS
Hot tips and rumors	Not backed by facts
Insider information	Either illegal or bogus
Ground floor opportunities	Speculative investment in a company with no track record
Guaranteed profits or high returns	High-risk, no guarantees
Claims of quick profits	Quick profits for the scammer
Pressure to buy quickly	Investment will not stand up to research
Tax-free offshore investments	Higher risk of IRS audit

worth the effort to get your finances back on track. For more information, you might want to check www.consumer.gov/idtheft, maintained by the Federal Trade Commission (FTC).

SEE A PENNY? DON'T PICK IT UP

Penny stocks—low-priced stocks of small companies—are a prime tool for scammers, because small changes in trading volume can cause large fluctuations in price. In the classic scam, a scammer buys shares in an obscure penny stock and spreads false information to pump up the price, often through Internet chat rooms. After investors who have been caught up in the hoax buy shares, the scammer sells at the higher price and disappears, leaving other investors holding worthless stock.

WHAT TO DO

If you believe you're a victim of securities fraud, contact your broker or file a complaint with the SEC by mail, by fax, or online:

SEC Complaint Center
450 Fifth Street, NW
Washington, DC 20549-0213
Phone: 202-942-7040
Fax: 202-942-9634
www.sec.gov

Alternative investment is a financial product that belongs to an asset class other than stocks, bonds, cash, real estate, or the mutual funds and managed accounts that invest in them. Hedge funds and limited partnerships are examples of alternative investments.

Asset allocation is a strategy for offsetting certain risks by investing specific percentages of your principal in different asset classes, including stocks and stock mutual funds, bonds and bond mutual funds, and cash and cash equivalents.

Bank investment representative is a bank employee licensed to sell investments offered through the bank. Bank investment accounts are separate from non-investment bank accounts, are not FDIC-insured, and could lose value.

Benchmark is a standard, such as an index or average, against which investment performance is measured. For example, the S&P 500 index is often used as a benchmark for the performance of individual stocks included in that index and of mutual fund and managed account portfolios investing in those stocks.

Beneficiary is a person or organization whom you designate to receive property or income, often but not always at your death. Life insurance policies, retirement plans, and certain bank and investment accounts ask you to name one or more beneficiaries. If you establish a trust, the beneficiary whom you name may receive assets from the trust.

Brokerage firm is a company registered with the Securities and Exchange Commission (SEC) to buy and sell securities for clients and for their own accounts. Brokerage firm employees may provide additional financial services and investment advice.

Certified family business specialist (CFBS) is a financial advisor who has been trained and certified by the American College to help family-owned businesses create succession plans.

Derivatives are investment products, such as futures and options, whose market value is based on the value of their underlying commodities, securities, indexes, interest rates, currency, or other financial assets.

Diversification is a strategy to help offset risk by investing in a range of companies, markets, and industries to counter the effect that any one investment's drop in price might have on the value of a portfolio.

Face value is the par value of a bond, usually $1,000, which is the amount the bond costs when it is issued and what you're repaid at maturity. The face value of an insurance policy is the dollar amount of the benefit listed on the first page of the policy contract.

Financial planner is someone who evaluates your personal finances to help you define and meet your immediate needs and long-term goals by developing investment, tax, and risk management strategies. Financial planners may or may not have professional designations and certifications, and may or may not be licensed to sell investments.

Growth is an increase in the value of an investment. A growth investment strategy focuses on assets that have the potential to increase in value over time. Most growth investments are not insured and could lose value.

Hedge funds seek to profit in any market environment by using a variety of often risky, speculative strategies, such as selling short, using derivatives, and employing leverage. Individual hedge funds require a high minimum investment—typically $250,000 to $10 million—and are highly illiquid, making them suitable only for experienced high net worth investors. A hedge fund of funds invests in a variety of hedge funds and requires a smaller minimum investment.

Income investments are designed to provide regular payments, such as from stock dividends, mutual fund distributions, bond interest, and annuity payouts. In or near retirement, many people switch their emphasis from growth to income investments.

Insurance agent is a person licensed by the state in which she or he works to sell insurance, covering life, disability, and long-term care, as well as other products. Some insurance agents are further certified or licensed to provide financial advice and sell certain investments.

Leverage is an investment technique that allows you to have control over a large sum of money without putting much of your own cash at stake. Leverage can increase your gain if your assumption about future performance is accurate, but it can also magnify your loss if you are wrong.

Liquid describes assets that can be converted easily to cash with little or no loss of value. For example, you can have the full value of a money market mutual fund transferred to a linked bank account at the end of the business day in which you make the request and be able to withdraw the money the next day.

Managed account is a professionally managed investment portfolio owned by an individual investor and focused on either a particular investment objective or asset class. The portfolio manager buys and sells investments for a group of portfolios on behalf of the account owners, who typically invest through a fee-based brokerage account.

Margin buying enables you to borrow up to 50% of the purchase price of a margin-eligible security from your broker. The margin is the value of the cash and securities you deposit in a margin account as collateral for the loan, and must always be equal to or more than the required minimum value set by the firm. Otherwise, you may receive a margin call, requiring an additional deposit.

Money market account is an FDIC-insured bank savings account that typically pays interest at a rate higher than the rate on regular savings accounts but imposes higher minimum balance requirements and limits the number—though not the amount—of monthly withdrawals.

Money market mutual fund invests in short-term debt securities and typically pays interest at a rate comparable to money market accounts. An investment in a money market fund is neither insured nor guaranteed by the US government. While the fund seeks to maintain a stable net asset value of $1 per share, there can be no assurance that it will be able to do so.

NASD is a self-regulating organization (SRO) of the securities industry formed to protect the interests of individual investors. NASD, formerly known as the National Association of Securities Dealers, sets standards and regulates operations for member firms and individuals.

Preferred stock, which is sometimes considered a hybrid equity and fixed-income investment, pays fixed dividends and promises a greater claim to company assets than that provided to owners of common stock, but usually conveys no voting rights.

Premium is the amount over par or net asset value that you may pay for an investment, or the amount over that value you may receive when you sell. With insurance, a premium is the amount you pay an insurance company to purchase coverage or buy an annuity.

Principal is the amount you invest, on which you have a gain or loss. Principal also refers to the balance of a debt, separate from interest. When used to refer to an individual, a principal is a person for whom a trade is executed or the owner of a privately held business.

Prospectus is a formal written offer to sell stock to the public. It contains information about the issuing company, how it will use the proceeds of the sale, and the risks of making the investment. A mutual fund prospectus explains the fund's objectives, policies, investment strategies, and performance, as well as summarizing any fees and risks associated with investing in the fund.

Registered representative is a person who has passed NASD qualifying exams and is licensed to act on investors' orders to buy and sell securities and to give investment advice.

Risk management is a strategy for helping to protect assets you have accumulated, typically by using a combination of insurance policies to cover your life, property, and healthcare expenses and to ease the financial hardship that could result from a loss of earned income due to a disability.

Rollover IRA is an individual retirement account funded with money you move from a tax-deferred account, such as an employer sponsored retirement plan or another IRA. No taxes are due if you follow the rules for moving your assets.

Securities and Exchange Commission (SEC) is an independent federal agency that oversees and regulates the securities industry in the US and enforces securities laws.

Selling short is a trading technique that lets you take advantage of an anticipated drop in an investment's price. You borrow shares of stock from your broker, sell them, and keep the proceeds until the price drops. Then you repurchase the shares, return them to your broker plus interest, presumably having made a profit. However, if the drop you anticipate takes a long time or stock price goes up, you could lose money.

Stockbroker is an employee of a brokerage firm who is licensed to handle client orders to buy and sell stocks, bonds, commodities, and options in return for a commission or a share of the annual fee in a fee-based account. Brokers may also provide investment advice, and some provide financial planning.

Suitability rules require registered representatives to evaluate an investor's objectives, financial situation, time horizon, and tolerance for risk and consider those factors when recommending investments.

Tax deferral means postponing income or capital gains tax that would otherwise be due on investment earnings or sales until sometime in the future, usually when you retire. Tax-deferred accounts include 401(k) plans, traditional IRAs, cash value life insurance, and annuities.

Tax exempt means that no tax is due, now or in the future. Earnings on some investments, such as municipal bonds, and some designated investment accounts, such as Roth IRAs, Coverdell ESAs, and 529 college savings plans, are exempt from federal income tax and may be exempt from state and local income taxes as well if you follow their rules.

Trust is a legal entity you as grantor create, giving title to the property in the trust to a trustee, who is required by law to administer the trust in the best interests of the beneficiaries you name. There are many types of trusts, each suited to meeting specific financial goals.

Value investments are those whose current market prices appear to be less than they are actually worth. If you are a value investor, you look either for under-priced stocks or mutual funds or managed accounts that invest in them.

Volatility is a measure of the changing value of an individual investment, a portfolio, or an entire market. The more often the value changes and the more quickly the changes occur, the greater the volatility.

401(k) plans 81, **143**-144, 157, 163
403(b) plans.................................... **143**
457 plans **143**
529 plans 121, **134-136**

A

Accountants 12, 86-87, 90-91, 95, 99, 148, 155, 159
Adjustable-rate mortgages 125, 129
Adjusted gross income (AGI)...... 141, 146
Alimony................................159-**161**, 165
Amortization..128
Annually renewable term insurance.. **106**
Annuities.......... **23**, 26, 63, 84, 87, 93, 101, 109, 132, 141, **150-153**, 155
Arbitration 103
Ask yield...52
Asset allocation.............. 10, 43, 55, 68-69, 78, **80-81**, 82, 164
Asset classes 27, 30, 43, 80-81
Asset management accounts...............101
Assets 10, 22, 38-39, **86-87**, 112-113, **155**, **160-161**, 167
Audit, income tax......................... **154-155**

B

Back-end loads 44
Balanced funds.................................41, **43**
Bank accounts 16, 23, 25, 36, 58, 59, 64, 69, 71, 87, 155, 159, 163, **165**, 168
Bank investment representatives 12, 90-91, 101, 150
Bankruptcy 159
Banks............ 17, 38, 62, 101, 123-124, 147
Beneficiaries **23**, 86, 106-107, 109, 112-15, 134-36, 150, 152, 159, 163
Bond mutual funds 26-27, 29, 35, 39, 40-41, 69, 74, 80-81, 145
Bonds 9, 28-29, **34-37**, 65, 87
   Asset allocation **80-81**
   Baccalaureate **137**
   Calling a bond................................36
   Commissions................................36, 63
   Defaults 36, 41, 52, 66, 73-74
   Education investing and................132, 133, 137
   Income investments................ 66-67, 69
   Interest.............................. 27, 34-36, 74
   Interest rates 28, 34-37, 66, 73
   Junk bonds 36, 41, 52, 74
   Laddering 53
   Liquidity of 14
   Maturity 29, 34-35, 37, 52, 74
   Mortgage-backed 35, 40
   Par value 35, 37, 53, 67, 74
   Portfolio diversification....26-**27**, 35, 79
   Principal................. 29, 34, 36, 40-41, 74
   Reinvestment of earnings 53, 65
   Short-term................... 34, 37, 56, 69, 132
   Taxes on 35-37, 39-40

   Types of...35
   Yields..52-53
Brokerage accounts ... 23, 25, 30, 159, 163
Brokerage firms.................. 30, 36, 38, 51, 80, 101, 147
Business continuation plans 115
Business overhead expense insurance..117
Business ownership.............. 10, 104, 113, **115**, 117, **148-149**
Buy and hold **32**, 36, **63**, 123
Buy-sell agreements.......................... **115**

C

Capital gains 61, 66, 127, 160-62
Capital gains tax..................... 1, 33, 38-39, 49, 84-**85**, 133, 136, 141, 144, 160, 162
Capital losses 61, 66, 84
Cash..................... **15**, 26-27, **65**, 79, **80-81**
Cash equivalents...................... 15, 26, 27
Cash flow..56-57
Cash surrender value **107**
Cash value life insurance ...104, **107**, 109, 110, 112-113, 115, 153
Catch-up contributions 143, 147-148
Certificates of deposit (CDs) ... 15, 19, 26, 53, 56, 65, 69, 71, 74, 80-81, 133, 136
Charitable gifts 87, 109, 113
Checking accounts.................. 16, 64, 155, 159, 163, **165**
Children
   College investments......... 133, 136, 139
   Custody and support...............158-159, 161, 165
   Gifts to minors............................... **136**
   Investing with **24-25**
   Life insurance 107, 109, 113
   Special-needs **109**, 166-**167**
Churning 103
Closing costs 124, 128-129
COBRA...157
Collectibles 14, 25, 27
College expenses.............. 54, 86, 108-109, 121, **130-139**
   Education savings accounts....... 39, 85, 109, 121, **132-133**
   Education loans 131, 139
Commissions 30, 36, 44-45, 49, 63, 91-93
Community property states 17, 109, 158, 162
Compound interest.......................53, **130**
Contrarian investing............................**31**
Cost basis...153
Coverdell ESAs 121, **135**-136
Credit bureaus.............................168-169
Credit cards 57, 58-59, 124, 159, 165, 168
Credit counselors...................................59
Credit history 59, 124, 127, 159, 165, 168-169
Creditors 17, 59, 117, 159, 168-169

Credit unions 123-124
Custodial accounts 25, 87, 136
Custodians 17, 87, 113, 147, 149, 163
Cyclicals **75**

D

Death benefits 105-110, 112-115,
119, 150, 167
Debit cards..58, 168
Debt **28-29**, 34, 54, 56, 58-59,
108-109, 129, 154, **159**, 164
Debt investments 28-29, 34
Decreasing term insurance **106**
Default
  Bonds..................... 36, 41, 52, 66, 73-74
  Home equity loans 137
Default risk...**73**
Deferred compensation...................... **115**
Deferred income................................... 142
Dependents............... 54, 104-105, 107-109
Derivatives.......................................52, 132
Direct deposit 44, 57, 59, 64
Direct investment plans **45**
Direct stock purchase (DSP) plans 30
Disability 104-105, 107,
109, 116-117, 154, 167
Disability insurance...............59, 104-105,
116-117
Discretionary accounts 92
Distributions...............................38, 49, 67
Diversification 10-11, 13-15,
20-21, 26-27, 32, 35,
42-43, 46-48, 55, 68-69,
71-72, 77, 82-83, 164
Dividend reinvestment plans
  (DRIPs)...30
Dividends 28, 30, 32, 39, 57, 65,
66, 69, 84-85, 107, 111, 140
Divorce 7, 11, 16-19, 138,
139, 149, 155, **158-161**
Dollar cost averaging..............................47
Dow Jones Industrial Average
  (DJIA) 9, 33, 42
Down payments 123, 127
Durable power of attorney.................. **167**

E

Earning power 6, **10**, 140
Eldercare................10, 118-119, 165-**167**
Elimination period 117-118
Emergency funds 19, 56, 58-59,
156, 166
Employer sponsored retirement
  plans.................. 10, 11, 18-21, 57, 137,
140-141, **142-145**, 146, 156
Equifax 168
Equity **28-29**, 123,
126-127, 129
Equity income funds......................41, 133
Equity investments 27-29, 51, 69,
74-76, 123, 132, 144-145
Estate planning..................... 20-21, **86-87**,
104, 112-115, **163**, **165**

Estates...............**87**, 112-115, 155, 162-163
Estate tax 17, 21, 23, 86-87,
104-105, 107, 112, 154, 167
Exchange traded funds (ETFs) **43**
Expense ratio..49

F

Fee-only advisors 91-92
Fees..................................... 30, 44-46, 49, 64,
90-93, 101, 103, 114, 128,
136, 144, 147, 150-151
Financial advisors   8-9, **12-13**, 18,
20-**21**, 31-32, 42-43, 46-47,
51-52, 55, 60, **62-63**, 72, 81,
83, **88-103**, 136, 140, 147, 150,
155, 157, 159, 162-163, 167
Financial aid........... 131-133, 136, **138-139**
Financial planners........... 12, 62-63, 90-91
Financial planning.....................**54-87**, 88, 164
Financial plans 12, 13, **60-63**, 99, 108
Financial reports 33, 51, 99
Fixed annuities **150**, 151-152
Fixed-income investments 27, 53, 66,
73-74, 81, 93, 144
Fixed-rate mortgages 125, 129
Fraud protection **168 169**
Front-end loads 44-45
Fund managers.......................................39
Futures 27

G

Gender.......6, **10-11**, 12, 105, 118-119, 123
Gifts 22, 57, 86-87, 109, 113,
123, 133, **136**, 139, 160
Gift tax 21, 86-87, 123, 133, 136
Ginnie Mae (GNMA) 35
Global funds..43
GNMA funds...**40**
Goals, financial 8-9, 12-13, 18, 21,
38, 40-41, 44, 46, 54-56,
60-62, 66, 69, 88, 163-164
  Planning for.............................. **120-153**
Government bonds **35**-36, 39-40,
51, 85, 147
Group disability insurance 116
Group life insurance 111
Growth and income funds....................**41**
Growth investments **66-67**, 69-70, 82
Guardian accounts.................................25
Guardians..113

H

Heads of households 18-19
Health insurance...........................59, 111,
118, 154, **157**
High-yield funds **41**
Home equity 123, **126-127**, 129
Home equity loans 15, 127, 136-137
Home ownership............... 15, 23, 54, 106,
109, 121, 122-**129**
Hybrid mortgages 125, 129

INDEX

I

Identity theft **168-69**
Illness 104-105, 107, 111, 167
Income.................. 38, 40-41, 52-54, 60-61,
65-67, 69, 87, 104-105, 108,
115-117, 123, 138-140, 142, 150,
152-153, 155, 157, 159-161, 165
Income investments **66-67**, 69, 83, 145
Income tax 35, 37, 39, 84, 87,
109, 118, 121, 123, 137,
141, 144, 154-155, 159, 160
Index funds 41-**42**
Individual retirement accounts
(IRAs) 11, 18, 21, 23, 25, 61,
81, 87, 132, 137, 141,
143, 145, **146-149**, 155-157
Inflation 15, 30, 34, 37, 55,
69-70, 74, **76-77**, 118,
145, 147-148, 152
Inheritance............... 17, 21, 104, 112-113,
159-160, **162**, 164
Insurance 23, 54, 59, 64, **104-119**,
154, 159, **161**, 165, 167
Insurance agents 90-92, 95, 101,
103, 108, 150, 161, 163
Insurance companies 62, 105,
107, 110-111, 147
Interest 15, 27-28, 34-36,
57-58, 65-66, 69, 74, 85,
121-123, 125, 128-129, 140
Compound.....................................53, **130**
Interest income 15, 28, 34
Interest rate risk...................................**73**
Interest rates 28, 32, 34-37,
40, 51, 53, 66, 69,
73, 124-125, 127-129
International funds 43
Investment accounts 57-58, **64-65**,
121, 141, 154-155, 161, 164
Investment clubs...................... 18, 97, 100
Investment income 52-53, 60-61,
123, 140
Investment plans........................6-7, 9, 13,
121, **134-135**
Investment styles............................. 10, **78**
IRAs. *See Individual retirement accounts*
IRS 139, 149, 154-155, 159, 165
Publications 127, 147, 155
Irrevocable life insurance trusts **114**

J

Joint accounts 16, 159, 163, **165**
Joint and survivor annuities........ 152-153
Joint ownership...................**16-17**, 23, 159
Joint tenants **16**, 23, 162-163
Junk bonds............................ 36, 41, 52, 74

K

Keogh plans **148-149**
Key employee insurance.................... **115**

L

Laddering...53
Lawyers........... 17, 19, 21, 86-87, 90-91, 95
99, 113, 123, 125, 128, 155-156,
158-161, 163-165, 167, 169
Legacies **86-87**
Level loads 44
Level term insurance.......................... **106**
Life annuities 152
Life expectancy 6, **11**, 63, 77,
110-111, 140, 151, 163
Life insurance 59, 63, 84, 87, **104-115**,
119, 147, 150, 154, 159, 167
Life insurance companies 62, 105,
107, 110-111
Limited partnerships...............51, 93, 132
Liquidity.................**14-15**, 39, 56, 122, 132
Living wills 167
Loads 44-45, 49, 92
Loans 15, 19, 59, 61, 123,
127, 131, 136-137,
139, 154-155, 165
Loan to value ratio (LTV) 126
Long-term care (LTC) insurance........104,
105, **118-119**, 166

M

Managed accounts............................78, 85
Management fees 30, 144
Management risk.....................................73
Margin 43, 103
Marital property...................... 16-17, 155,
158-161, 164
Market capitalization........................30, 51
Market cycles 48
Market risk..**73**
Married women 6, 7, 16-17,
86-87, 89, 105, 107,
109, 112, 146, 157
Annuity payout.................................153
Investments **20-21**
Recordkeeping........................ **154-155**
Remarriage **164-165**
Spousal IRAs 11, **148**
Matching contributions **143,** 145
Maturity 15, 29, 34-35, 37, 52, 74
Maximum offering price (MOP)............49
Medicaid 109, 118, 167
Medicare 118-119, 157
Money management 8, **11**, 24-25
Money managers.....................................92
Money market funds..... 15, 19, **41**, 56, 69,
80, 81, 132, 144, 147
Mortgage-backed bonds 35, 40
Mortgage banks 124
Mortgage brokers 123-124
Mortgages 15, 23, 106, 109, **122-129**
Municipal bond funds...............39-**40**, 147
Municipal bonds (munis)................**35**-36,
40, 85, 147
Mutual funds.................. **26, 29, 38-49**, 65,
78-79, 83, 87, 101,
123, 144, 150, 163

INDEX

12b-1 fees 45, 49, 92
Indexes 51
Liquidity 15, 39
Loads 44-45, 49, 92
Mutual fund companies 38-39, 42, 44-45, 48, 51, 147
Prospectuses ... 26, 40, 45-46, 49, 63, 92
Reinvestments 38-39, 46, 65, 69
Return calculation 50-51
Types of **40-41**

N

National Association of Investors
   Corporation (NAIC) 100
NASD 92, 95
National Foundation for Credit
   Counseling (NFCC) 59
Net asset value (NAV) 43, 46, 49
No-load funds 44-45, 49

O

Online brokerage accounts 30
Online records 154
Online trading **100**
Options 27
Over-the-counter (OTC) stocks 30
Over-the-counter bonds 36
Ownership **16-17**, 22, **112-113**, 114, 158-60, 163

P

Par value 35, 37, 53, 67, 74
Penny stocks **169**
Pensions 11, 23, 77, 81-83, 140, 146, **148-149**, 151, 154-155, 157, 159, 160
Percentage return 48, 50
Permanent life insurance **107**, 111, 115
Planning **120-169**
   Expectations and goals **120-153**
   Unexpected expenses **154-169**
Points (prepaid interest) 128-129
Portfolios 6, 10-11, 14, 19-21, 26-27, 35, 39, 42-43, **46-47**, 51, 67-77, **78-83**, 135, 164
Powers of attorney **167**
Premiums, insurance 105-107, 109-110, 113-114, 117-119, 157, 161
Prenuptial agreement 155, 162, **164**
Prepaid tuition plans **135**
Prepayment penalties 128
Preservation of principal 71
Price/earnings (P/E) ratio **33**
Principal 27, 29, 34, 36, 40-41, 71, 74, 126, 153
Principal protected funds **41**
Property 16-17, 87, 109, 117, 155, 158-162, 164
Property rights 22
Property taxes 15
Prospectuses 26, 40, 45-46, 49, 63, 92

Q

Qualified Domestic Relations Order
   (QDRO) 160

R

Real estate 14-16, 26, 51, 66, 81, 85, 87, 122-123, 129, 132, 159, 163
Real estate taxes 15, 85, 121-123, 129
Realized gains 51, 67
Real return 30, 71, 74, 76
Recession risk **73**
Recordkeeping 88, **154-155**
Refinancing **128-129**
Registered advisors 12, 95
Reinvestment of earnings 8, 34, 38-39, 46, 53, 57, 65, 69, 132, 140
Remarriage **164-165**
Renewable term insurance **106**
Retirement, early 155, **157**
Retirement planning 11, 13, 18, 21, 23, 25, 34, 54, 61, 77, 81, 87, 99, 132, 135, 137, **140-152**
Retirement plans
   Annuities .. **23**, 84, 87, 93, 141, **150-153**
   Divorce settlements **160**
   Employer sponsored 10-11, 18-19, 21, 57, 137, 140-141, **142-145**, 146, 156
   Payouts 151-153, 155
   Pensions 11, 23, 77, 81-83, 140, 146, **148-149**, 151, 154, 155, 157, 159-160
   Portability 145
   Retirement accounts 11, 18, 21, 23, 25, 39, 61, 81, 84-85, 87, 121, 132, 137, 140-149, 155-157
   Social Security 11, 18, 77, 140, 161, 166
Return **27**, 29-30, **50-51**, 64, 68-69, 71-72, 74, 76
Reverse mortgages **129**
Riders, insurance policy **107**, 119
Risk 10, 14, 26-30, 41-42, 44, 46, 50-52, 55, 67-69, **70-75**, 82, 88, **110-111**
Risk tolerance 72, 78, 80
Rollover IRAs 145, **149**, 156-157
Roth IRAs 25, **141**, 146-**147**, 149

S

Salary reduction plans 142-146
Sales charges 44-46, 49
Savings accounts 14-16, 19, 64, 132, 145, 147, 155, 159, 163, **165**
Savings bonds 121, 133, **135**
Scams **12**, **169**
Secondary bond market 37
Second-to-die life insurance 107
Sector funds **41**
Securities and Exchange
   Commission (SEC) 95, 169
   SEC Public Reference Branch 95

Securities fraud 169
Self-employment 117, 148-149
Seminars 9, 18, 62, 97
Separation............................. 138, 159, 161
Short selling..43
Short-term bonds 34, 37, 56, 69, 132
SIMPLE plans **143**
Simplified Employee Pensions
  (SEPs)...................................... **148-149**
Single women.......................7, **18-19**, 104,
  123, 146-147, 153
Socially responsible funds **41**
Social Security 11, 18, 77, 108-109,
  117, 140, 161, 163, 165-167
Special-needs children **109**, 166-**167**
Special-needs trusts 109, 167
Split-dollar life insurance **113**
Spousal IRAs 11, **148**
Standard & Poor's 500-stock Index
  (S&P 500) 33, 42, 51
Stepped-up tax basis 162
Stockbrokers 12, 90-91, 95, 101
Stock indexes...........................**9**, 33, 42, 51
Stock markets 14, 32, 49, 74
Stock mutual funds 26, 29, 39-41, 66,
  69-70, 80-81, 132-133, 145
Stocks **30-33**, 87, 123
  Asset allocation **80-81**
  Balanced funds **43**
  Buy and hold strategy **32, 63**
  Buying of 30-32, 92
  Capital gains and losses....................61,
    66, 133, 160
  Child's ownership of 25
  Dividends 28, 30, 32
  Education investing and...........132-133
  Equity investments.................. 27, 28-29
  Growth investments........... 66-67, 69-70
  Liquidity of 14
  Penny stocks **169**
  Portfolio diversification....26-**27**, 32, 79
  Price/earnings ratio **33**
  Reinvestment of earnings ... 65, 69, 132
  Return......................................50-51
  Selling of................................. 32-33, 92
  Volatility of **74-75**
Stop orders 75
Straight life insurance **107**
Surrender fees 151
Survivorship life insurance............... **107**

T

Taxable equivalent yield **85**
Tax advisors 17, 84, 118, 147-148, 155
Tax-deferred investing............9, 57, **84-85**
  Annuities 26, 84, 93, 141, **150-151**
  Mutual funds...39
  Retirement accounts 18, 23, 39,
    84, 121, 140-149
Taxes 15, 19, 23, 25, 35-37, 39-40,
  49, 57, 67, **84-85**, 113, 115,
  117, 121-23, 127, 129, 133-137,
  139-149, 151, 153, 155, 162
Tax-exempt accounts......................57, 85

Tax-exempt municipal bonds 36, 40,
  85, 147
Tax-exempt zero-coupon bonds... 36, 137
Tax-free gifts 22, 86-87, 123, 133
Tax-free retirement accounts 18, 39,
  85, 121, **141**, 147
T-bills. *See US Treasury bills*
Tenants by the entirety **17**
Tenants in common **17**, 23, 159
Term life insurance **106**
Titles............................... 16, 155, 162, 165
Total return........................... 45, 48, 50, 52
Totten Trusts **23**
Trustees 16, 23, 114
Trusts 16-17, **23**, 86-87, 93, 109,
  112-15, 132, 139, **162**, 167
Turnover rate 39, **49**

U

UGMA/UTMA custodial
  accounts 87, 136
Underwriting
  Bonds...36
  Life insurance 110-111
Unemployment............................. **156-157**
Uniform Gift to Minors Act
  (UGMA) 136
Uniform Transfer to Minors Act
  (UTMA) 136
Unit investment trusts..................93, 132
Universal life insurance..................... **107**
Unmarried partners................. **22-23**, 89,
  112, 153-55, 157
US savings bonds 121, 133, **135**
US Treasury bills, bonds, notes..... 15, 19,
  35-36, 52, 56, 69, 71, 80-81, 133

V

Value funds **40**
Value stocks..**31**
Variable annuities **150**, 151-152
Variable life insurance **107**
Variable universal life insurance....... **107**
Vesting................................. 145, 156-157
Volatility 28, 68-69, **74-75**

W

Whole life insurance **107**
Widows... 11, **18-19**, 78, 149, 154, **162-163**
Wills 16-17, 22, 86, 113, 154,
  159, 162-163, 165
Withdrawal penalties...... 15, 84, 137, 141,
  144, 147, 149, 151, 156
Withholding 57, 84

Y, Z

Yield................................ 52-53, 68-69, **85**
Zero-coupon bonds 36-**37**, 51, 133, 137